UNCORKED!
The Diary of a Cricket Year

DOMINIC CORK
WITH DAVID NORRIE

RICHARD COHEN BOOKS · London

British Library Cataloguing in Publication Data:
A catalogue record for this book is available from the British Library

Copyright © 1996 by Dominic Cork

ISBN 1 86066 059 2

First published in Great Britain in 1996 by
Richard Cohen Books
7 Manchester Square
London W1M 5RE

1 3 5 7 9 8 6 4 2

Design by Roger Walker Studio

Typeset in Sabon by Rowland Phototypesetting Ltd,
Bury St Edmunds, Suffolk

Printed in Great Britain by
Butler & Tanner Ltd,
Frome and London

Contents

Prologue   1

April 1995   Derbyshire's Record-breaking Start   6
May 1995   Derby Despair – but Texaco Triumph   13
June 1995   My Lord's Prayers Answered   30
July 1995   'You bowled like a pillock!'   56
August 1995   Lara Runs – but Athers Defiant   80
September 1995   A First Winter with the Big Boys   103
October 1995   Mandela Greets the Destroyer   109
November 1995   Hanging Around and Splashing About   117
December 1995   Stalemate – with Glory   138
January 1996   Cape Town Catastrophe   163
February 1996   World Cup Hopes and South
                  African Hangovers   179
March 1996   Sri Lanka Conquer the World   192

Postscript   205
Index   209

List of Players
Names and Nicknames

ATHERS   Michael Atherton, Lancashire & England captain
BOMBER   Colin Wells, Derbyshire
CHALKY   Craig White, Yorkshire & England
CREEPY   John Crawley, Lancashire & England
DAFFY   Philip DeFreitas, Derbyshire & England
DAZZLER   Darren Gough, Yorkshire & England
DEV   Devon Malcolm, Derbyshire & England
DIGGER   Peter Martin, Lancashire & England
DINOSAUR   Wayne Dessaur, Derbyshire
DOC HOLIDAY   Dr Philip Bell
EDIE   John Edrich, England batting coach
GALLEY   Jason Gallian, Lancashire & England
GRIZZLY   Chris Adams, Derbyshire
GUSSIE   Angus Fraser, Middlesex & England
HARRY   Richard Illingworth, Worcestershire & England
HARVEY   Neil Fairbrother, Lancashire & England
HICKIE   Graeme Hick, Worcestershire & England
ILLY   Raymond Illingworth, England chairman of Selectors
JACK   Jack Russell, Gloucestershire & England
JACK   Allan Warner, Derbyshire
JUDGEY   Robin Smith, Hampshire & England
KRIKK   Karl Krikken, Derbyshire
LUGGSIE   Wayne Morton, England physiotherapist
NORMAN   Tim O'Gorman, Derbyshire
PLANK   Peter Lever, England bowling coach
RAMBLE   Mark Ilott, Essex & England
RAMPS   Mark Ramprakash, Middlesex & England
ROLLY   Adrian Rollins, Derbyshire
SMUDGER   Neil Smith, Warwickshire & England
STEWIE   Alec Stewart, Surrey & England
THORPEY   Graham Thorpe, Surrey & England

TROUT   John Barclay, England Tour Manager
TUFFERS   Philip Tufnell, Middlesex & England
WINKER   Mike Watkinson, Lancashire & England
WORM   Dermot Reeve, Warwickshire & England

Illustration Credits

Prologue

Attempting to keep a diary is a new experience for me. I'm not one for living in the past or reflecting too long on what I no longer have control over. Actions have always spoken louder than words for me, although my critics will claim that words have never been thin on the ground when Dominic Cork is around. So why the urge to put pen to paper? The simple reason is that I have reached 'crunch time' in my chosen profession – I believe this is going to be the most important summer of my cricketing life, for a variety of reasons. If we reach the end of August and I have not played Test cricket for England, or if I am not selected to go to the World Cup in India, Pakistan and Sri Lanka when the winter parties are announced a few weeks after that, then I will have some serious soul-searching to do. I will also probably be in a state of total despair. As much as I love cricket, I cannot see myself existing for ever solely as a county competitor. I've got to play for England, big-time.

It's not just wishful thinking. I know I can do it. I just need the chance. I've loved my taste of international action in my five Texaco appearances for England against Pakistan, Australia and South Africa at home. And I've been on four – yes, *four* – A tours. I was very disappointed to miss out on the senior trip last year. An Ashes tour is something I've always dreamed about. My big mate Darren Gough made it, and I felt slightly consoled when I was put on the standby list. That's not a bad place to be given the recent injury record on England tours. Yet what happened when Craig White suffered his side strain? Nothing, as far as D. Cork was concerned. They had decided they didn't want an all-rounder. Well, they did really, because they called up one Chris Lewis, who was playing grade cricket in Victoria. Before you could blink, Lewis was in the side for the Adelaide Test, and England won on a spectacular last day. I

1

should have been there. I should have been part of a winning England side. Instead, I was languishing with the A team in India. The subcontinent can get to you, so at that point I really felt I'd been singled out for exclusion. By that stage, England had flown in replacements from all over the world. What about me? What was wrong with Dominic Cork, who was less than half a day away by plane? I felt very hacked off. The conspiracy theory and persecution complex soon rolled into one. My only conclusion was that someone out in Australia didn't want me. I was pleased for Philip DeFreitas and Devon Malcolm, my two Derbyshire colleagues, in that winning England side. But, inside, I was gutted. Chris Lewis is a talented cricketer but he'd had his chance, as far as I was concerned. His chance – his many chances, you mean.

I felt helpless. I still do. That's why it's make-or-break time for me. I'm still only 23, but I've been knocking on the tour door for quite a while. I think four A tours testify to that. Is there someone in power who doesn't like me? Have I earned a black mark somewhere, somehow that's going to count against me for ever? I've always been something of an extrovert on the field. I love competition and I love competing. The word is out that England wants fighters, characters, winners, blokes with bottle. That sounds like me. I'm sure I can provide most, if not all, of those qualities.

All I've ever wanted to do is play cricket. I remember my dad, Gerald, being slightly mortified when he learned I'd written to Warwickshire at the age of 15, asking for a trial. Like my two older brothers, Simon and Jonathan, I'd started my cricket career with Betley, where my mum, Mary, still makes the tea. Dad had played in the North Staffordshire League and faced the likes of Sobers, Hall, Tyson, Ramadhin and Valentine. Cricket was in the blood. After my trial at Edgbaston, Alan Oakman asked me to come back for 12 weeks' coaching. I did. But I ended up at Derbyshire when Alan Hill approached me and the club offered me a job in the youth training scheme. It meant leaving school early, but I can assure you that no place of further education was deprived of my presence because of that. My studies were going nowhere and I'm not sure whether I would have added to my one history O-level.

I've been at Derbyshire ever since. I did play for Staffordshire in 1989 and 1990 while I waited my chance. That came five years ago, against the touring New Zealanders, and I took a wicket in my first over. Later that season, I hit a century as a nightwatchman for the England under-19s against Pakistan. In 1991, I celebrated my 20th birthday by taking eight Essex wickets before lunch at Derby, and I

Right: the men of Cork – brothers Simon and Johnathan, my Dad Gerald and me.

Below: Mum, who still makes the teas at Betley.

BETLEY CRICKET CLUB 1988
Champions. N.s.S.c. League Division 1 section ´B´

J. CORK	S.J. BASE PROFESS.IONAL	N. HARRISON	S. BASKERVILLE	I. COWAP	M. JERVIS
S. JERVIS	S. CORK	D. SNAPE CAPTAIN	D. CORK	S. OWEN	I. ELLIS II-6-88

was picked for my first A tour at the end of the summer. My England one-day debut came in the final match of the 1992 Texaco series against Pakistan. That was a fantastic day. Playing for England was special, but being in the same England side as my hero, Ian Botham, was all my dreams come true at once. I can't tell you how many times the lethal bowling attack of Cork and Botham had destroyed the best batting line-ups in the world – but only in my mind.

I played twice against the Aussies in the 1993 Texacos without taking a wicket. That July I took the Gold Award in a Lord's final with an undefeated 92 as Derbyshire beat Lancashire to lift the Benson & Hedges Trophy. In '94 an operation on my left knee hindered my start, but I returned for the two-match Texaco series against South Africa, taking 3/49 in the second game at Old Trafford. The A tours appeared like clockwork but, despite many entries in Probable and Possible England XIs in the not-always-well-informed newspapers, that final step to the Test side eludes me.

At times my exuberance has got me in trouble. At my junior school, fighting meant a week in the girls' class. Some punishment! At St Joseph's College in Stoke-on-Trent, the Christian Brothers channelled my energies on to the rugby field, where I broke my nose three times by charging in recklessly off the side of the scrum. I still struggle to breathe sometimes, and my sense of smell is almost nil. By and large, the skipper Kim Barnett has kept me under control at Derbyshire. We're from similar backgrounds. I admire and respect him. But I am an aggressive bowler. I was once ordered out of our attack after supposedly running down the pitch against Lancashire. And I've been told off in Tasmania and Bombay on A tours for my incessant and vigorous appealing. You can blame Ian Botham for that. I've tried to copy everything he did, and that includes those wholehearted shouts and heart-felt pleas. I've got one of Jack Russell's prints on my mantelpiece, showing Beefy giving it his all to an umpire. I don't see how the umpire could possibly have refused. I was accused of sledging on that A tour to India, too.

I've always had a fair bit to say for myself on the field, but then I don't remember taking any vows of silence. I might have gained a reputation for being a loud-mouth and big-head. But I've heard less of that sort of criticism the more wickets I've taken. That's fair enough. You can't live on hot air for ever.

I had a long chat with Mark Ramprakash during last winter's A tour. He warned me that once you are labelled a rebel or bad boy, it's very difficult to lose the tag. He's suffered from that. I suppose that I did have too much to say for myself on the field earlier in my career. That was particularly true on my first two A tours. The sub-continent makes for a hard tour, mentally and physically, and I let it get to me. There was one game in Calcutta when I had two batsmen plumb LBW. They weren't given and it affected my bowling. The next stop was Chandigarh and I kept going over the incident in my mind. I realised that I had to channel my energies and aggression properly.

I believe I've quietened down since my marriage to Jane in 1993 and the birth of our son Gregory last September. Jane is from Leeds and we met at Scarborough when Derbyshire were playing Yorkshire in July 1991. She was working in the club's gift shop. I asked her the price of a scarf with white Yorkshire roses on it. She knew I wasn't being serious, but she asked me whether I wanted to buy it for my wife or my girlfriend. I should have guessed then that I'd met my match. I popped in a couple of times more during the game, then left my number and told her to give me a call if she ever fancied watching Derbyshire. She rang. Two years later, we were married. And that's been great for me, especially since the arrival of Gregory. My family is the most important thing in my life, but it hasn't dampened my burning desire to play Test cricket. If anything, it's increased it. Now it's not just myself I'm playing for.

So I'm going to keep a diary of this summer to record all the highs (hopefully) and lows. The England side had a poor Ashes tour and I keep reading that I'm next in line. I've heard that before. I've got to start well for Derbyshire. You can't just set your sights on England and forget about your county. They pay my wages, after all. Derbyshire is a team that regularly under-performs, and I've been told to get myself to a more fashionable county. But this is home for me. I don't believe that being at Derbyshire has cost me a Test spot. I don't know what has. Maybe I'll feel differently at the end of the summer if I'm still kicking my heels. I'm more concerned that I'm considered a one-day specialist by the selectors. That can be a difficult spell to break. But I'm not really worried. I genuinely believe that my cricket destiny is in my own hands. If I take loads of wickets and score a few runs, the England selectors won't be able to ignore me this summer. As a life-long supporter of Stoke City, I know that every season must start with your aspirations and dreams sky-high.

Dominic Cork, Derby, March 1995

April 1995

Derbyshire's Record-breaking Start

MONDAY 3 APRIL   DERBY

Derbyshire are off to Malaga tomorrow for eight days. It's going to be tough. The county has imposed a new code of fitness and I understand that it will be enforced severely over the next week. We can't deny that there is considerable room for improvement. Last season was described by our skipper Kim Barnett as 'a disgrace for a squad of our ability'. None of the players argued with that.

There should certainly be a better atmosphere this season, as Peter Bowler has left for Somerset. By the end of last year relations between him and Kim were very strained. Basically, Bowler thought it was time Kim stepped down and allowed someone else to take over as captain. And the man he believed should be the next skipper was Peter Bowler. I've always been a great supporter of Kim and have made no secret of that fact. We both come from Stoke and are similar people. We both speak our minds. Kim's not one to make excuses and neither am I. Any attempts to invite to me to participate in Kim's demise have always been rejected. He's a great captain for a bowler. He'll give you everything you want until it's time to step in. It's important for a captain to have faith in his bowlers. Anyway, Kim's right. We should do better, especially with a bowling attack that includes Devon Malcolm and Daffy (Philip DeFreitas). Daffy arrived last year via Leicestershire and Lancashire. I'd heard stories that he was a fair-weather player who tended to duck out when the going got tough. I've seen no evidence of this. He tried really hard last year and set a good example to the younger players. I don't think that includes me, even though I'm still in my early twenties.

MONDAY 10 APRIL   MALAGA

Our last day tomorrow. The trip has been hard, especially the training. We've been running on the beach at seven-fifteen every morning.
If you are not there, the squad leaves without you. That is not too
painful until you realise that unless you've caught up with the others
by the far end of the beach, a severe fine is imposed – £15, to be
exact. And on a county cricketer's wage, you can't afford to be late
very often. On top of that, there have been plenty of press-ups,
sit-ups and the obligatory 'bleep' tests, popularly known as 'creeping
paralysis'. We don't all have to reach the same levels. Your age and
fitness are taken into consideration. Most people passed. There were
fines for failing here, too, and these could be even larger because the
level was determined by how far off the target you were. We've been
practising on an artificial wicket, the same we used with the A squad
before touring India and Bangladesh last winter.

There's a certain amount of socialising on these trips. It's a new
season, another campaign. There's been a mood of optimism out
here this week, helped by our recent departures. I'm not blaming
anyone, but when there are divisions in the dressing room the chances
of suddenly becoming a team when you take to the field are slim.
For all parties concerned, a change of scenery was essential. There's
a general feeling here that we can win something this summer, if we
all pull together and perform anywhere near our potential. England's
new supremo, Ray Illingworth joined us from his holiday hide-away
for our end-of-trip dinner. He was full of encouragement, suggesting
that I might have been given my chance last summer but for that
knee operation. What about this summer, Illy? Wait and see, lad!

SUNDAY 16 APRIL   TRENT BRIDGE

A warm-up game against Nottingham at Trent Bridge, which I sat
out with the England A game coming up. We welcomed our newest
recruit, our South African overseas player, Darryl Cullinan. I played
against him in the Texaco Trophy last year. He seemed a nice chap.
Kim talked to me about him. Our fast bowler Simon Base told Kim
that Cullinan has committed himself to doing well. Derbyshire have
had a succession of good cricketers from overseas. In my time, they
have been the West Indies fast bowler Ian Bishop and India's captain
Mohammad Azharuddin. Both are quiet blokes. 'Bish' is great to
talk to about fast bowling and great to have bowling at the other
end. I'm sure his presence there helped me pick up wickets I might

not have got. Even when a back injury threatened his career, he was very much the team man. 'Azza' is always busy helping players, spotting when they need some assistance. Being a captain, he knows the signs of a player in trouble. So – much is expected of our new overseas man, even though Cullinan is a much less experienced player than those two.

TUESDAY 18 APRIL   EDGBASTON, BIRMINGHAM

Tetley Bitter Challenge   *Warwickshire 240   England A 6/0*

The first chance of the summer to impress England's new supremo, Ray Illingworth. And a typical start to an English season. The umpires were walking out when they were bombarded by an incredible hailstorm, which delayed the start by an hour and a half. Everyone is keen to see how Warwickshire are going to perform without the great Brian Lara. He's on West Indies duty this summer. I don't think they'll do that badly. I never regarded them as a one-man band last season and I have a lot of respect for the man who is going to replace Lara – the South African Allan Donald. Not a bad start for me with the A team – I ended up with 3/56, although I had to wait for a bowl behind Mark Ilott and Glen Chapple. My first wicket of summer 1995 was Roger Twose. Most of the credit must go to Mark Ramprakash, though. He took a brilliant diving catch to his right at backward point. That's the sort of catch that can make a hell of a difference to your figures and, ultimately, your international prospects. Stempie (Richard Stemp) did his chances no harm with three wickets.

FRIDAY 19 APRIL   EDGBASTON

England A 390/7

A less active day than I'd hoped. We've already got a lead of 150 runs, but my contribution was a miserable nine. Our A skipper Alan Wells seems intent on forcing his way into the Test side. Alan hit a tremendous 178, with all but 40 of the runs coming in boundaries. He and Ramps (Mark Ramprakash) put on 152 for the third wicket. It's great being with the A boys again. Sometimes you can't recapture a tour spirit in a one-off occasion, but this is like a continuation of our successful winter trip to India. Much of the dressing-room talk concerns the full England side, though. There has been a lot of speculation about the England captaincy. I can't see beyond Atherton but, according to press reports, Illy (Ray Illingworth) has put the names of Alec Stewart and Alan Wells in the frame. The word today is that there will be no announcement for another fortnight. That surprises me. Maybe Illy really is thinking about a change.

THURSDAY 20 APRIL   EDGBASTON

England A 503   Warwickshire 205/9

We should have had a day off tomorrow, but we couldn't quite finish off the county champions. Our chairman didn't make it today. I gather Illy spent the day at home in bed with a virus. I hope he gets good reports of my bowling as I picked up another four wickets. The dull and overcast conditions have certainly favoured the men with the ball. I'm rather sad that the chairman missed my spectacular catch at long leg. Keith Piper top-edged a sweep off Min Patel and in the end I had to make a desperate dive forward to reach it. Both Min and Mark Ilott hit career-bests earlier in the day as they put on 124 runs for the eighth wicket. I'm very well aware that I'm not the only person around Edgbaston trying to impress the Test selectors.

SATURDAY 21 APRIL   EDGBASTON

Warwickshire 205   England A won by an innings and 58 runs

Almost a day off. The contest lasted for only six deliveries before Donald lobbed a simple caught and bowled back to Stempie. Our victory celebrations were muted after the news that one of the game's senior statesmen, Bob Wyatt, who had been the oldest surviving England captain, has died aged 90. He was born in the year Queen Victoria died, 1901, and first led England in 1930, at the Oval against Australia. That was the match, apparently, when Douglas Jardine first noticed that Bradman wasn't too happy with Harold Larwood's short deliveries into his body. Wyatt was vice-captain on the 'Body-line' tour and took over from Jardine. He led England to their only victory over Australia at Lord's this century.

MONDAY 23 APRIL   COUNTY GROUND, DERBY

Benson & Hedges Trophy
Northamptonshire 179   Derbyshire 180/2
Derbyshire won by 8 wickets   Gold Award: Chris Adams

A perfect start to what I expect to be a much better season for
Derbyshire. Northants are strong favourites to knock Warwickshire
off their perch and claim at least one of the four domestic trophies,
but that certainly didn't look likely today. Devon Malcolm was the
pick of our wicket-takers with 4/50, with the rest – me apart –
keeping it tight. We did well to restrict them to under 200. Several
of their attacking batsmen, like Allan Lamb, Rob Bailey, David Capel
and Kevin Curran (my only wicket) all got starts, but failed to go
on. Lambie top scored with 41. I was able to put my feet up as our
skipper Kim Barnett played the anchor and Chris Adams smashed
94 at almost a run a ball. The extent of our superiority can be judged
by the fact that we won with more than 15 overs to spare.

TUESDAY 25 APRIL   TITWOOD, GLASGOW

Benson & Hedges Trophy
Derbyshire 220/6 (55 overs)   Scotland 174
Derbyshire won by 46 runs   Gold Award: Darryl Cullinan

Two out of two, although this was a lot closer than the scores suggest.
Our new overseas star Cullinan apart, our batsmen couldn't get
going. We might have been in real trouble if extra cover hadn't
dropped him off that well-known Scot, Malcolm Marshall, when he
had made only 13. The West Indies maestro is still world class.
What Malcolm has lost in speed in recent years, he's more than
compensated for with guile and cunning. I would have said that even
if he hadn't got me out! Cullinan fully deserved his century, showing
real class on a difficult wicket in difficult conditions. It was Marshall
and the former Yorkshire batsman Jimmy Love who threatened us
at 113/4, but another four wickets from Devon – our sixth-choice
bowler – saw us home. I will be disappointed if we don't make the
Benson & Hedges quarter-finals now.
  The West Indies squad has been announced for the summer tour.
There's no place for Desmond Haynes. He's been left out of the
current series against the Aussies after missing the start of the Red
Stripe trophy for Barbados. I gather Dessie is suing the West Indies

Board. They claim that the court action had no bearing on his exclusion and that he was available for selection. I can't believe it – it seems like cutting off your nose to spite your face to me. Haynes is still one of the best openers in the world and the Windies aren't exactly spoilt for riches in that department. I'm pleased – purely from a fellow fast-bowler's and county colleague's point of view – to see Ian Bishop's return after his recent back troubles. He's a quality performer and he's been a great asset to the Derbyshire dressing room in his days as our overseas player. As ever, it looks a very strong squad. I hope I get the chance to find out just how powerful they are.

THURSDAY 27 APRIL   DERBY

Britannic Championship   Sussex 111   Derbyshire 263/1

The dream start continues. However well you do in the limited-overs matches, it's much more pleasing to perform to a high standard in the first-class game. And membership figures published in the morning papers today emphasise why Derbyshire must improve. The Derbyshire total went up from 2,100 in 1993 to 2,216 last year. But we are still at the bottom of the pile, with Northants just above. How much easier life must be for Lancashire and Glamorgan, who each have over 13,000 members. Our treasurer would love that sort of guaranteed income.

You are always slightly worried when you roll a team over for around 100 as we did today, because questions are inevitably asked about the wicket. Fortunately, any queries were answered by a marvellous batting display by our skipper. Kim's undefeated 153 was majestic. When he is in this sort of form, his four Test appearances seem a ridiculous return for someone of his ability. Maybe without the cares and worries of leading Derbyshire for all these years, he might have made a greater impression at international level.

Sussex were bowled out in less than 40 overs, with Devon doing most of the damage. His 6/61 means he's taken 14 wickets in his first three days for Derbyshire this summer. I'm pretty happy with 2/12 in nine overs, especially as the two wickets were Bill Athey and Alan Wells.

FRIDAY 28 APRIL   DERBY

Derbyshire 603/6 declared   Sussex 68/4

A day of Derbyshire records. The most significant is that we reached 600 for only the second time in our history, although that's still some way short of the 645 we scored against Hampshire at Derby in 1898. Our first-innings lead of 492 is the biggest ever. How do I know all this? I'd like to say that I'm a great student of Derbyshire facts and figures. I would like to, but I can't – it's just that a new statistical book about the club has come out. Sadly, much of it is already out of date after today's batting. Kim only added 11 to his overnight score, but Grizzly (Chris Adams) and Darryl also scored centuries. I might have made it four, but Kim declared me on 84 not out. I'm not complaining. It was the right decision because we've already removed four front-line Sussex batsmen.

SATURDAY 29 APRIL   DERBY

Sussex 113
Derbyshire won by an innings and 379 runs

More records. Our biggest-ever victory. And Philip 'Daffy' DeFreitas took 6/35, his best bowling figures for his third county. Daffy needed no help from any of us – four LBW and two bowled. It was all over in 80 minutes. It's been a great first week for us. Three good wins and the side is certainly performing much more as a unit than last year. But we've had a few false dawns at Derby before. A buoyant April will count for nothing in September if standards are not maintained.

MAY 1995

Derbyshire Despair – but Texaco Triumph

Britannic Championship
Nottinghamshire 244   Derbyshire 43/0

Our impressive start continues. We've had a few days off as it was our turn to miss out on Tuesday's zonal round of Benson & Hedges matches. Our matches against Notts have always had more than a touch of healthy local rivalry about them. With our pace attack, it was no surprise to be confronted by a wicket that looks as if it will suit the spinners. Notts won the toss and decided to bat. At least that meant an early-season work-out for our under-used and under-estimated leg-spinner, one K. J. Barnett, who deserved more than a solitary wicket in a 20-over spell between lunch and tea. Devon had taken a couple of early wickets, but Notts looked well set at 163/2. We managed to drag it back, with Devon and me finishing up with four wickets apiece. I felt pretty good. I got rid of both Paul Johnson and Wayne Noon LBW with balls that cut back sharply, while Chris Cairns was picked up at first slip by Darryl. Kim (Barnett) and Adrian Rollins made sure there were no setbacks late in the day. Now we are in a strong position. A satisfactory day considering that Johnny Owen, Tom Harrison and Andrew Cottam were making their debuts.

Friday 5 May   Trent Bridge

Derbyshire 312   Nottinghamshire 31/0

We've struck gold with Darryl Cullinan. With everyone scratching and struggling around him, our new overseas signing scored a magnificent century, his third in four innings for us. He's yet to be dismissed for less than a hundred. The day started badly with Cairns removing both our openers in his first two overs. Darryl apart, we all struggled and looked in real trouble at 196/7 before Karl Krikken joined our South African for a stand of 74. Our final lead was 68, valuable runs on this sort of wicket. Darryl has always been regarded as a player of talent, but his temperament has been questioned. It's early days yet, but he looks a top performer to me.

Saturday 6 May   Trent Bridge

Nottinghamshire 302   Derbyshire 24/1

My best bowling day of the summer so far. Notts were again threatening at 260/4 when I took three quick wickets with the second new ball. I was on a hat-trick, as was Dev as he cleaned up the tail, leaving us needing 235 for victory. That is no formality, but a total we must make if we have any aspirations to challenge and beat the best and have any pretensions that things have really changed at the County Ground. The day didn't start well when we learned that our wicket-keeper Karl Krikken had chicken-pox. He was sent home and Adrian Rollins was handed the gloves. He took a couple of catches off me and Devon, but it wasn't an easy day for him, especially with Kim's leg-spin thrown in.

Today makes it eight wickets in the match for me on the ground where the First Texaco game is to be played on the 24th. The England squad is to be announced next Friday and already the papers are beginning to speculate on the likely players. Most of the pundits have me in. I just hope these championship performances are beginning to persuade the England selectors that I've got more to offer the national side than just limited-overs ability.

SUNDAY 7 MAY   TRENT BRIDGE

AXA Equity & Law   Derbyshire 219   Nottinghamshire 198
Derbyshire (4 pts) won by 21 runs

Our unbeaten run continues as Notts let us off the hook again. Our
score looked short of the mark when the home side reached 158/3,
but four run-outs contributed to their downfall as the final seven
Notts batsmen all failed to make double figures. Not that I made
much impression with the bat. Fortunately, Kim and Darryl got stuck
in again, Darryl hitting three sixes and six fours in his 64. The one
relief for both sides is that the Sunday League has reverted to 40
overs. I'm giving no secrets away when I say that it's the least popular
of all the domestic competitions, not least because it intervenes three-
quarters of the way through a county match. I'm not sure that it is
the proper environment for young quality bowlers trying to learn
the trade. On Sunday matches, the emphasis shifts towards not giving
runs away rather than taking wickets. There's no great incentive to
charge in and find the edge when the only close catcher is the man
behind the stumps with the gloves on. But cricket is taking a back
seat this weekend with the sacking of England's rugby captain, Will
Carling, causing complete uproar. Cricket's bosses have taken their
fair share of stick over the years, but even they have never created
a fuss like this. From the outside, it appears ludicrous that the most
successful rugby captain England has ever had is kicked out for a
remark about '57 old farts'.

MONDAY 8 MAY   TRENT BRIDGE

Derbyshire 120
Derbyshire (7pts) lost to Nottinghamshire by 114 runs

The bubble has burst. And how! What a shambles. Our season's
100 per cent record in all competitions was shattered half an hour
after lunch. I'm afraid it was a return to the bad old days – Derbyshire
capitulation in spectacular fashion. The two spinners, Andy Afford
and Jimmy Hindson, did the damage with four wickets apiece, but
this was self-destruction on a mammoth scale. Not too many deliveries turned. I hope it's just a one-off, but all the familiar faults were
there. Darryl had his first failure for us – a duck – but you can't
criticise him after the runs he's been piling up. He was unlucky,
anyway, as the ball came off the bottom of his bat and rolled back

on to the stumps. And it didn't help that we were a batsman light with Krikken still at home in bed. But, if we are as good a team as we would like to think we are, those are obstacles we should be able to overcome – not go arse over tit at the first hurdle. The batsman who lasted longest was our nightwatchman, Andy Cottam. Only he, Kim and Daffy DeFreitas (11 not out) reached double figures. I made just two before I was deceived by Hindson's quicker ball. The mood in the dressing room was sombre, not least because we've seen it all before. But it's not disastrous – only a couple of counties (Warwickshire and Glamorgan, who are top) out of 14 have won their opening two matches. We would have been level with Glamorgan if we had picked up 16 points today. The only benefit of the early finish was that it allowed me a leisurely drive over to Worcester for our B&H match.

TUESDAY 9 MAY   WORCESTER

Benson & Hedges Trophy *Worcestershire 267/7   Derbyshire 135 Derbyshire lost by 132 runs*

Another fine mess. There was some excuse for Worcestershire's big total because Graeme Hick had one of those days. But there was no excuse for our response. At 34/5 the tie was over. Now we need to win our final zonal game to give us a chance of making the quarter-finals. I'm disappointed that our early season promise is vanishing so rapidly. At least England will be pleased that Hickie is in such great nick. He came home early from the Ashes tour with back trouble, but there were no signs today of any restriction in his movements. Nobody argued with his Gold Award for 127 in 124 balls, although the less familiar Worcestershire name of Gavin Haynes did the bowling damage by removing Kim, Grizzly Adams and Tim O'Gorman. Daffy, Tim Harrison and myself offered a bit of token resistance, but it was little more than a gesture. What a Jekyll and Hyde side we are. One day we can look a million dollars; the next you wouldn't give tuppence for our prospects of winning a single trophy. Six days of cricket against Yorkshire will be a good guide as to whether we've made any real progress or not.

Illy has announced his batting and bowling coaches for the summer. Geoff Boycott had been expected to be half of the team, but the word is Lord's couldn't afford him. John Edrich has been given the job instead, with Peter Lever there to help the bowlers. I just hope that I'll be one of those seeking his advice.

THURSDAY 11 MAY   QUEEN'S PARK, CHESTERFIELD

Britannic Championship   *Yorkshire 177   Derbyshire 122/7*

There's no way this is going to last four days. It's freezing cold, the ball's jagging about, 17 wickets have fallen and both sides had a key batsman in the X-ray department of the Chesterfield Royal Hospital with broken bones in their hands. Martyn Moxon, not for the first time in his career, has a broken right thumb, and Darryl has a cracked right index finger. The early prognosis is that he'll be out for a fortnight. We didn't bat well again, although this time there was some excuse. There was always the danger of getting smacked on the hand or worse. At the start of the day, I didn't mind that too much as I was bowling and it was a great opportunity to impress the watching Raymond Illingworth. The Yorkies found themselves facing a wicket-keeper with a familiar name – Bairstow. Because of Karl's chicken-pox, we have registered Andrew Bairstow, the 19-year-old son of David, who took over 1,000 victims behind the stumps for the White Rose. In the past couple of weeks, Andrew has played for the Derbyshire and Lancashire second XI. Now he's got his big chance.

Looking at the wicket, Kim had little hesitation in asking Yorkshire to bat. Moxon tried to bat on after Devon hit him on the hand, but couldn't. I got rid of Mike Vaughan and the Yorkshire overseas newcomer, Michael Bevan. Richard Blakey and Craig White steadied the innings, but Daffy and Devon turned 136/3 to 177 all out. Not that our dressing room was champing at the bit to try our luck with the bat. It wouldn't have been so bad if we hadn't been so cold. It's no fun getting hit on the hand at the best of times, but when it is freezing cold as well, it's agony. There was hardly a sweater left in our dressing room when we were in the field. I found myself batting with Daffy with the score 36/3. It was five actually because, as well as Darryl being pinned by Darren Gough, Adrian Rollins has pulled a hamstring. I didn't see any point in trying to get my head down because it might have been knocked off. I thought the best policy was to chance my arm and go for my shots. I felt there weren't going to be too many blinding catches taken in these conditions. Unfortunately, my careless waft outside the off-stump went straight through to the only person wearing padded gloves. Malcolm Mar-shall has been signed up to have a couple of days with the Derbyshire bowlers. As well as working with us in the nets, he's chatted with me in the pavilion. He's one of the modern legends of fast bowling and I'll do well to be half as good as Maco's been.

FRIDAY 12 MAY   QUEEN'S PARK

Derbyshire 140   Yorkshire 90/8

Another Arctic day, this time with freezing rain. It might have been
all over if the wet weather hadn't intervened and wiped out more
than half the play. Normally it's not much fun hanging round the
dressing room and pavilion, but anything was better than being
outside today. Again, batting wasn't easy, but I felt we bowled pretty
well. The Yorkshire lead is 127 at the moment and I wouldn't fancy
chasing much more than 150 on this wicket. Moxon appreciates the
need for runs. He was padded up, despite that damaged hand, next
man in when the rain came.

SATURDAY 13 MAY   QUEEN'S PARK

Yorkshire 104   Derbyshire 134
Derbyshire (4pts) lost to Yorkshire by 7 runs

Our third defeat in six days. It could have gone either way, but a
career best 9/41 from Peter Hartley won the day. Pete took a hat-
trick, with me as the final victim, in a spell of five wickets in nine
deliveries. At 76/2 with another 66 runs needed to win, we weren't
exactly cruising, but the finishing line was in sight. Unfortunately,
the scoreline read 77/7 a few minutes later. We were still 48 runs
short with only tail-enders Allan 'Jack' Warner and Devon and our
new No. 11, the injured Darryl. Dev hit Goughie for a huge six, but
was out with us 22 runs short. Darryl was only able to hold the bat
with his left hand, but the pair kept edging closer. I thought we were
going to do it when the ball unluckily ran from Jack's gloves on to
the stumps.

SUNDAY 14 MAY   QUEEN'S PARK

AXA Equity & Law   Yorkshire 167/7   Derbyshire 108
Derbyshire (0 pts) lost to Yorkshire by 59 runs

We saved the poorest performance of a miserable week for last. This
time last week, we were riding high, full of hope and belief that we
had developed the backbone necessary to mount a serious challenge
in the four domestic competitions. Now I don't know. Of course,

there are always going to be bad days along the way, but I worry that this is more than just a brief hiccup.

This fourth defeat was again down to poor batting. We have some great stroke-makers who murder any attack when things are going our way. But our weakness is exposed when the going gets tough. Too many of us don't get going, we get out. It's no good. The top sides have line-ups that score runs when they're needed, when they're under pressure. It's no good everyone piling in just because conditions suit. In a week, we have put together scores of 120, 135, 140, 134 and 109 – a grand total of 638 runs at an average of 12.76 per visit to the crease. Hardly title-chasing stuff. Just over two weeks ago, we scored more than 600 in an innings against Sussex. We could have done with those runs today. Yorkshire's total was nothing special, but we never looked like mounting a serious challenge. Only two batsmen got into double figures, we suffered three run-outs and lost with more than seven overs to spare. Already the jokes are starting about Derbyshire holding their end-of-season dinner before the start of June, as usual. That upsets me because Derbyshire are a much better side than we've shown this week.

WEDNESDAY 16 MAY   QUEEN'S PARK

Benson & Hedges Trophy   *Derbyshire v Yorkshire*
Match abandoned   Derbyshire 1pt   Yorkshire 1pt
Derbyshire (5pts) 3rd in Group B – Yorkshire (7pts) &
Worcestershire (6pts) qualify

Well, that's our Benson & Hedges ambitions over for another season. The rain ensured that we bowed out in anonymous style. We arrived at Queen's Park exactly a week ago. It seems like a lifetime. Nothing went right for us there. I drove down to Leicester earlier this evening.

FRIDAY 18 MAY   GRACE ROAD, LEICESTER

Britannic Championship   *Derbyshire 256   Leicestershire 73/3*

The Derbyshire roller-coaster continues with another up and down day. We reached 70 for the loss of just Kim, but then the wickets began tumbling. Soon it was 81/4 and there looked no way back at 166/8. Even my presence at No. 5 did little for the stability of the middle order. But we were saved from a poor total by an exciting and unorthodox last-wicket stand of 58 between our fast bowlers,

Jack and Devon. The great thing about those two is that they give the ball some real 'tap' – whatever the situation. Both hit big sixes today. Dev's was a monster blow off Alan Mullally. We knew it might be coming after Mullally bounced the ball off Dev's helmet. For a bloke who's recognised worldwide as one of the genuine No. 11s in the game, Dev has been involved in more than his fair share of controversial incidents during his time as a batsman. He was at the receiving end when Aqib Javed had his flare up with Roy Palmer during the 1992 Manchester Test. Palmer no-balled the Pakistan bowler for running through the crease and then all hell broke loose. And it was Dev who was given a fearful working over by Courtney Walsh in Jamaica last year, when many felt that the umpire should have stepped in and protected him from what was thought to have been intimidatory bowling. I've never known why frustrated bowlers want to bounce and blitz Devon out. The slow yorker has always appeared the best way of bamboozling him. He's so keen to launch himself into the shot that he's normally completed his follow-through before the ball has even reached him. But if the ball is bowled in the slot and Dev connects, it really does fly. Without a doubt, he has played some of the most powerful cricket shots I have ever seen. Today Devon helped us get to what was about a par total for the wicket. And we would have settled for those three wickets by the close, especially as I got rid of Nigel Briers, who has a nasty habit of sticking around, off the last ball of the day.

FRIDAY 19 MAY   GRACE ROAD

Leicestershire 357   Derbyshire 121/2

A good day for me – a five-wicket haul and a place in England's Texaco squad. The two events are not related, as the selectors had already made their decision. I don't seem to have a problem convincing Illy's panel of my one-day capabilities. David Graveney is the new selector this season. He's just finished a 20-odd-year playing career and is well respected throughout the game, so at least the players can't complain about *this* selector being out of touch with the modern game. The after-effects of the poor Ashes tour are evident in the Texaco squad. Graham Gooch and Mike Gatting have retired. There's no place for Craig White, John Crawley or Steven Rhodes. Devon is missing, but he has never really been part of England's one-day thinking. Alan Wells gets his chance at 33, while Peter Martin is the surprise bowling choice. It's strange. When you're waiting for your chance, looking at the bowlers already in the side, wondering which one you can come in for, you tend to forget that others can come from behind, overtake you in the pecking order and win a Test place before you. It almost seems that if you are on the verge of getting in the side for too long, the selectors take you for granted and start looking elsewhere. I hope I'm not reaching that stage. I've just got to keep trying to put in the performances.

Another five-for won't do any harm, although once again James Whitaker showed his fancy for the Derbyshire bowlers. I checked his record afterwards, and apparently today was his 28th first-class century. How many have been against us? Six! Over a fifth. We are obviously being singled out by this talented batsman who played just one Test for England – on Gatt's all-conquering Ashes tour nine years ago. A great future was predicted for him then, but he has hardly even been mentioned since. Some may call him a 'one-cap wonder' – but it's still one more than I have played. Whitaker's knock, especially in his partnership with Phil Witticase, was the main reason for Leicestershire's 101 run lead. We manage to wipe out that advantage by the close. With Kim and Colin Wells going strong, we're still in with a good shout.

The South African captain Hansie Cronje is Leicestershire's overseas player this season. He's got a reputation for not being that keen on quick bowling. Naturally, I thought it was advisable to test that theory, and I must admit that I think there's something in it. Cronje has an impressive record at Test level, but he doesn't give the impression of being that comfortable when the ball is dropped short and starts whistling around his upper body. There's a lot of psychology when you're discussing a batsman's weakness. If a batsman has a real weakness that is not apparent and can be corrected, then no bowler is going to go around telling the rest of the world about it. You try to exploit it for as long as you can. Sometimes it's not a weakness at all – you're just trying to wind the batsman up, get him wondering about a shot that he executes perfectly well. Most batsmen, after all, are at their most vulnerable when being aggressive and going for shots. I want batsmen to take me on, have a go. I'm more than happy for the batsman to be thinking 'That Cork is all talk. Just wait, I'll show him' when I run in to bowl. If he's concentrating on the bowler, then he's not as focused on the delivery. That makes my job easier. Anyone who believes that cricket is about ability and effort doesn't know the half of it. It's near the top of the mind-games league. Anyone who can't cope with that side of it shouldn't really be out there. And there are quite a few.

Saturday 20 May Grace Road

Derbyshire 173   Leicestershire 73/1
Derbyshire (6pts) lost to Leicestershire by 9 wickets

Another big problem in county cricket is fair-weather performers, and we have more than our fair share at Derbyshire. Today was an unmitigated disaster. I wrote last night that we were still in with a shout. The only shout that was appropriate today was 'help'. In less than two hours our final eight wickets went for 39 runs, leaving Leicestershire's winning target a formality. Before today, they had won just one match in all competitions. We made them work hard for the runs and bowled over 30 overs, but the result was never in doubt. That's our third successive championship defeat. It's hard to argue that nothing has really changed at Derbyshire. We have some inexperienced youngsters in the side, but that doesn't excuse these collapses. This diary is beginning to sound repetitive and the season's only a month old. It's going to be pretty boring reading if the script doesn't change soon.

Sunday 21 May Grace Road

AXA Equity & Law *Leicestershire 217   Derbyshire 194*
Derbyshire (0 pts) lost by 23 runs

Another disaster. We needed fewer than 100 runs to win with nine wickets left when Tim O'Gorman and I were at the wicket. But off-spinner Adrian Pierson claimed the pair of us in successive balls and the rot set in. He proved Leicestershire's match-winner with a Sunday League career best of 5/36. There's little more to say other than that it was another sub-standard performance, with Derbyshire's batsmen folding under the slightest sign of pressure.

The Sunday papers brought little relief. It's always interesting to read the thoughts of cricket correspondents after the England squad has been chosen – not least to see if it's going to match their views after the game. Once again Peter Roebuck of the *Sunday Times* raised the question of that final step when he described me as 'perhaps neither quite a Test bowler or a Test batsman'. Until I get my chance, I can't prove him wrong. Much as I love Derbyshire and the County Ground, I'm quite looking forward to getting away from the environment for a week after our recent run – especially as I'll be with England for the Texaco match. As for the lads, they've got the next

Right: Bowling flat out for England 'A' versus Warwickshire in April, in a bid to impress England's new supremo Ray Illingworth.

Below: Hansie Cronje, the South African captain, whose weaknesses against pace I carefully studied.

championship round off and we're not involved in the Benson &
Hedges quarter-finals.

WEDNESDAY 24 MAY   TRENT BRIDGE

Texaco Trophy   England 199/9   West Indies 76/1
Match carried over to reserve day

Rain and bad light means we're back at Trent Bridge tomorrow. It
looks like a formality. I'm no quitter, but it's going to take a miracle
to pull this match out of the bag. And to be honest, we didn't display
any signs today that we're likely to produce one. Our batting was
below par, despite a rather under-the-weather Curtly Ambrose.
Stewie (Alec Stewart) had the top score with 87. I ran down the
wicket to Keith Arthurton with three overs to go, planning to smash
him back over his head. I missed. Then the rain held up play between
innings.

Our total was all the more disappointing because there had been
such a good atmosphere in the nets over the past couple of days.
This was the first England get-together since the services of team
manager Keith Fletcher were dispensed with. Athers and Stewie ran
the fielding, with Illy looking after the nets. Despite the disappointments of the winter, everyone seems confident of giving the West
Indies a good run for their money. First victory of the summer went
to Richie Richardson and we were inserted. The two newcomers to
our squad were left on the sidelines. A combination of accurate
bowling and a slowish pitch made finding the boundary difficult. We
only managed a dozen fours, 11 going to Stewie and the other to
Ramps. The West Indies have already matched that total. I needed
to make amends after a first over that cost 12 runs. I repaired some
of the damage when I got rid of Carl Hooper with an absolute beauty.
A perfect length, it pitched on middle and took off. Unplayable! Well,
I'd have been disappointed if he'd got anything on it. That might
just quieten those who claim I only get wickets with bad balls. Not
that I'm too worried about gaining that reputation. It didn't seem
to do Ian Botham much harm.

The Windies finished up at 76/1 off 19.5 overs before they came
off for the last time for bad light. We found that rather strange.
They are one delivery short of the requirement to make the match
valid. So, if there's no more play tomorrow, the match will be
declared abandoned. If Brian Lara had faced one more ball tonight
and we get no further tomorrow, then the West Indies would have

won on a faster scoring rate. Obviously, someone wasn't thinking clearly – but that often happens in the hurly-burly atmosphere of one-day cricket. It's a terrible anti-climax when one-day matches don't live up to their name, leaving players and umpires to come back the next morning. The biggest problem is that the crowds do not. One-day internationals are invariably sold out (Trent Bridge today was no exception), and there's no better feeling than running out in front of a full house. The great tragedy is that 24 hours later you repeat the experience in front of the faithful few, with the crowd *and* the atmosphere gone.

THURSDAY 25 MAY   TRENT BRIDGE

West Indies 201/5 (52.4 overs)
England lost by 5 wickets

No miracle. The West Indies won with 14 deliveries to spare, but it was never as close as that might sound. It's the first one-day international the West Indies have won in England for 11 years. More importantly, we're one down with two to play. Campbell and Lara took the West Indies to 180/1 and the contest was over for us and the 1,200-odd spectators. We took four wickets for 14 runs, but the result was never in doubt. We were just trying to score a few points for the forthcoming Test series – hopefully. Darren Gough got Lara with his famous leg break, then continued Richie Richardson's recent poor run. I chipped in when I trapped Jimmy Adams LBW. That pleased me because he's fast gaining a reputation as one of the most difficult batsmen in the world to dislodge. England certainly had problems in that department in the Caribbean last year. After the match, I drove to London on my own and checked in at the Conrad Hotel in Chelsea Harbour. It's a top spot. The lads have no complaints about staying here.

FRIDAY 26 MAY   THE OVAL, LONDON

England 306/5 (55 overs)   West Indies 281
England won by 25 runs   Man of the Match: Peter Martin

A great win in what was, apparently, the 1,000th one-day international. And I've played in seven of them! Now we're all square after a much better all-round performance that gives us real hope of taking the series. Our 305/6 was a record score against the West

Indies and it sounds like an awful lot of runs. But not at the Oval. All the England bowlers were well aware that it was a more than attainable target for the West Indies, especially if a Hooper or Lara or Richardson got cracking. We were surprised when the West Indies captain asked us to bat again. An overcast Lord's or Trent Bridge, yes. But a bright, bouncy Oval and I'd take first crack with the bat every time. One-day cricket is a much more fashionable commodity than Test cricket, and I'm not just referring to the coloured clothing. There was a time when most teams felt they were better off chasing; that they were in much more control of their destiny knowing exactly what the task was. Not any more. The current trend is to bat first; get the runs on the board. Sides seem to be less pressured at the end-of-innings slog when they are setting the target. One thing hasn't changed, though. Wickets in hand is the key to a big total. Athers and Hickie put on 144 for the second wicket today to give us the platform. But the reason we got past 300 was the acceleration of runs provided when Neil Fairbrother – known as 'Harvey' – appeared. Watching Harvey play like he did today – splaying some of the best bowlers in the world with such precision and timing to all parts of the ground that some of the best fielders in the world found themselves stranded – left me wondering yet again why he hasn't made his mark in Test cricket. His huge talent and ability was on show at the Oval for all to see. Yet these days, he's exclusively labelled a one-day performer.

I wonder all the more because that's a tag that's beginning to drift in my direction. I seem to be good enough to represent my country one day at a time, but not for the full five days. A good one-day reputation is a double-edged sword. The plus side is that it keeps you in the frame, in the selectors' thoughts and on the national stage. And the chaos of the one-day contest also gives the selectors a good idea of how you might handle the pressure of the Test arena. That could get you the nod ahead of someone they are considering picking 'blind' from the county game. The downside is that you can start to feel locked in that one-day compartment. The longer you wait for the Test call, the more inclined the selectors are to throw away the key and leave you where they know you can perform. Then there are those who appear from nowhere and grab the chance in dramatic fashion. Step forward Peter Martin, who had come in for Angus Fraser. The Lancashire fast bowler had a dream debut today. It didn't take him long to find his feet. Peter was the fifth bowler we used. But with only his fifth ball at international level, Sherwin Campbell skied the ball to Graham Thorpe at mid-wicket. Jimmy Adams was trapped LBW in the next and, finally, the prize catch, Lara's off-stump, took a direct hit in the fourth. The West Indies looked out of it at 114/5 when I took a return catch off the touring skipper. But Junior Murray kept us on our toes. The West Indies needed 46 runs off the final five overs and Murray was more than capable of getting them home. But they ran out of wickets, with Murray the last to go.

My figures were 1/56. Not great, but not too bad considering I bowled three overs at the death. I like bowling then. They say that one-day cricket is all about the final ten overs, so it's great to be involved then, whether batting or bowling. I'm often asked what's the perfect ball to deliver. Simple. The one that doesn't go for runs. You can do little more than try to keep it right up in the block hole. Because you are so pumped up and trying so hard, that delivery can easily become a full toss. The real crime is to give the batsman width. Even if he doesn't smash it, there's always the danger of the umpire signalling a wide and there's another ball to bowl. Anyway, it was a great day's cricket. There's no better feeling than turning it on against a team like the West Indies in front of your home crowd. The bottom line is that we're back on level terms. And deservedly so. This was a good all-round team performance. I'm sure the bars around the Oval were crowded late into the evening. Everyone expects the champagne corks to be popping at the team hotel, but I can assure you there's no more exhausting day's cricket than a limited-over international. And we've got the decider on Sunday.

SUNDAY 28 MAY   LORD'S, LONDON

England 276/7   West Indies 203
England won by 73 runs

A great day for our skipper. After his problems in Australia, Atherton showed all his resilience, determination and ability by treating the Lord's crowd to one of the best one-day innings ever seen at the home of cricket. It also enabled us to take the match and the series. We were really up for the decider. It was a big help that we didn't have to get into our cars and head for another city after the Oval win. Motorway travel is one of the big bugbears of the modern England cricketer. Touring teams, like the Windies, just sit on a luxury coach with refreshments and videos. Even traffic jams aren't too stressful when you're not the man behind the wheel. We have to make our own way from match to match.

Yesterday, we netted at Lord's and then headed for 'Shoeless Joe's' – the England rugby star Victor Ubogu's place in the King's Road – to watch the England rugby team struggle to beat Argentina. But the rugby was forgotten this morning. It's difficult to imagine any better sporting venue than a packed Lord's. There's a mystique about the place even when it's empty, but when it's full and brimming with anticipation it's magical. You can't help but be overcome by the history of it all – imagining the likes of W.G., Hobbs and Bradman in the same surroundings – but that feeling doesn't intimidate. Instead it inspires. Lord's is not a place that lives in the past.

Today must have been a special moment for Alan Wells. At 33, he's waited longer than most for his England opportunity. He was the skipper on my final two A tours and is someone else who has probably suffered from playing with an unfashionable county. Alan's got a good reputation against quick bowling, so he must have a chance of selection this summer. Richie asked us to bat again. It was a more marginal decision than at the Oval, but Athers certainly made him pay. The skipper was rather slow out of the blocks, getting his first run off his 27th delivery. But Athers then proceeded to play one of the great one-day knocks at Lord's. I find it incredible that he didn't play for England's one-day side for nearly three years after taking the Man of the Series award against the West Indies in 1991. Injury kept him out of the World Cup the year after and he couldn't find a way back until he was skipper. Part of the problem was that Goochie was doing the job that Athers does now and the side didn't need two anchors at the top of the innings. I'm sure Athers put paid to any lingering doubts that his style is not equipped to accelerate in the one-day contest. Our skipper is technically correct, but had no problem improvising today as he played shots that were worthy of I. V. A. Richards in his heyday. His standing ovation was well deserved. Sadly, I wasn't able to contribute to England's total. I came in with two balls to go. I jumped across to Kenny Benjamin and attempted to flick the ball over short fine leg, as I'd done in the Benson & Hedges final a couple of years ago. This time I missed and the umpire had no hesitation in sending me on my way. Peter Martin did rather better, driving the ball to the boundary off his only delivery. I love walking out with a couple of balls left – unless you need six to win! When you're batting first, you've got a licence to go out and have an almighty swing. Nobody gives you stick if it doesn't come off.

I was much more confident that we had set a winning total than I was at the Oval. The ball tends to swing more at Lord's, especially with the slope, and the outfield's not as quick. I had a great start, dismissing the three batsmen at the top of the West Indies order. That might look very impressive on the scorecard, but it goes to show how misleading figures can be. Stuart Williams went to a horrible half volley that he walloped straight to Athers in front of square leg. Lara was caught behind. If he'd left it, the chances are it would have been signalled a wide. After that, I knew it was going to be one of my lucky days. Hooper was next. He tried to pull one that wasn't short enough and the catch dollied straight to Goughie at mid-on. So I finished with 3/27. With figures like that everyone assumes you're in the groove. In fact, I've felt a bit scratchy in the series, although I feel I've contributed something in every game – the leg-cutter that saw off Hooper at Trent Bridge, a tight spell at the death at the Oval and now the best England figures at Lord's. But I could have bowled a lot better. Still, I've taken wickets and England has taken the Texaco series.

The day's work doesn't finish with the presentation ceremony. While the fans celebrated, I headed back for home. The biggest drawback about Lord's is that it takes me an hour to get to the bottom of the M1. The motorway brought little relief; I simply joined the tight convoy of Sunday drivers for the 120-mile trip up to Derby, trying to make sure I reacted quickly enough to the brake lights that regularly flashed in front of me.

June 1995

My Lord's Prayers Answered

Britannic Championship *Derbyshire 258/6 v Middlesex*

Back to Lord's. Unlike most cricket grounds, it's still a very special place even when attended by the proverbial two men and a dog. The only difference from the Texaco match is that I've moved to the other end of the pavilion and the visitors' dressing room. We are staying in our usual London spot, the Post House in Hampstead. I drove down with Allan Warner, Derbyshire's beneficiary this season. He's one of my favourite and regular room-mates. The biggest attraction? I'm a light sleeper and Jack doesn't snore.

Kim won the toss and chose to bat. It looked a reasonable track and we didn't want to face Phil Tufnell and John Emburey in the fourth innings. Paul Alfred came in for his debut when Grizzly failed a fitness test on his knee ligaments. John Carr led Middlesex with Gatt injured and they left out Richard Johnson who took ten wickets against us last season.

The day was only memorable for the announcement that Roy and Ken Palmer were the first brothers to umpire at Lord's. Our best knock by far came from Colin Wells with 81 in just over two hours. It was totally out of keeping with the rest of the day's dawdling. I didn't win too many friends among the sparse crowd with a grafting and boring 28. I plan to accelerate tomorrow.

FRIDAY 2 JUNE   LORD'S

Derbyshire 267 & 83/1   Middlesex 174

Quite a good day, but it should have been better. So much for my good intentions! I slapped Gussie Fraser's long hop straight to Ramps at backward point in the first over of the day and out last four wickets crumbled in 20 minutes. We should have made Middlesex follow-on, but Jason Pooley, who carried his bat for 85 (almost half the Middlesex score), was dropped off my bowling when he'd made 13. There was some consolation when I got Ramps out. He's been in good nick and it took a good delivery, which he edged to our keeper. That was Adrian Rollins, who'd taken over from Karl Krikken who – having recovered from chicken-pox – was suffering from a migraine. We extended our first innings of 93 runs to 176 by the close, but I have this nagging feeling that we haven't made the most of our chances. Kim wasn't too happy at his dismissal. Gussie was charging in when the loudspeaker boomed out some unimportant announcement and he pulled up. When Kim edged the next ball to the keeper it was apparent that he felt the hold-up had disturbed his concentration.

SATURDAY 3 JUNE   LORD'S

No play – rain

This wash-out has probably saved Middlesex and emphasised our failure yesterday. But my day was dominated by an off-the-field confrontation with our new South African player, Darryl Cullinan. Cricketers are like everyone else; they behave like big kids when they're bored. And there is nothing more boring than days spent hanging around a wet cricket ground, twiddling your thumbs. It's not so bad when you're playing at home. At least there are other things to do and it's only a few minutes' drive home when the day's play is finally called off. Away is a different story. You're only swapping a dressing room for a hotel room.

It wasn't long before the mischief-makers got to work. My kit went missing, a common enough prank. There was no need to call Sherlock Holmes. Eventually, I tracked it down to the home dressing room. My spies told me the culprit was Cullinan, who by this time had settled down to watch one of the rugby World Cup matches being played in his home country. I tried to come up with a clever and suitable response. With the rain pouring down, what better revenge than to drive his car to the far end of the ground? Not the most subtle of gestures, but I felt pretty pleased with my efforts when I slipped the keys back in his blazer pocket and headed back to the Post House. Unfortunately, we've discovered that Cullinan doesn't have an enormous sense of humour – or even a middle-sized one. Our overseas player appeared back at the hotel, shooting out of the back of a taxi with steam coming out of his ears. He was pretty sure the culprit was either Karl Krikken or myself. That field was quickly narrowed to one. I was astonished by his reaction. 'Don't mess with me. Don't touch my personal things. If you mess with my car, you're messing with me. I'm a South African. Watch out.' It was pathetic. Cullinan is happy enough dishing it out, but it's clear that taking it is a different matter. I could have understood it if the car was his pride and joy, but it's a sponsored vehicle. I wasn't going to argue the toss with him. I got his car keys off him and drove down to Lord's with Daffy. Mick Hunt, the groundsman, had to open the ground up so I could drive the car out. When I got back to the hotel, I just put his car keys in an envelope along with a fiver to cover his taxi fare from Lord's. I hope that's an end to it. All the lads went out tonight, but Cullinan wasn't around. I, for one, wasn't too unhappy about that.

SUNDAY 4 JUNE   LORD'S

AXA Equity & Law   *Derbyshire 152/9   Middlesex 128*
Derbyshire won by 24 runs

I've failed to make the England squad for the first Test. Derbyshire's bowling is well represented by Daffy and Devon, though. I'm trying to be philosophical, but it gets harder to take every time I hear or see my name missing. Most of the Saturday and Sunday papers predicted I'd be in. I tried not to take too much notice, and just as well. I clicked on Ceefax and the name Cork was conspicuous by its absence. I've been in numerous newspaper sides over the past couple of years, but this time I really thought I was going to make it. Initially, I just felt empty. Then I began wondering what I've done wrong. Peter Martin has come from nowhere to make the side. I don't feel any jealous, just envy, I suppose. He bowled really well in the one-dayers and I'm pleased for him. I would love to know how he's feeling right now.

It was raining when I got to Lord's and I had lunch at mid-day.

Cullinan offered me condolences and tried to make a joke of what happened yesterday. But I know he meant it. I don't think this matter is finished. The rain relented and we started a 31-over match. Despite Gussie taking a Sunday League best 5/32, we won comfortably. But the England selection has dulled my day. I'm still just another aspiring Test player, waiting for his day to come.

MONDAY 5 JUNE   LORD'S

Derbyshire 209/3   Middlesex 130/4   Draw

No win. Adrian Rollins, with sixes off Gussie and John Emburey, and Wayne Dessaur accelerated well in the morning, setting Middlesex a target of 303 in 71 overs. Unfortunately, it was a difficult pitch for batsmen and bowlers to make things happen. We got some early wickets, but Ramps batted well to deny us. It was a good opportunity for Paul Aldred to bowl. Another journey back from London in the rush hour. Nightmare. I'm sure I wouldn't have found it such a hassle if I'd been heading home to prepare for the first Test at Headingley.

THURSDAY 8 JUNE   DERBY

Britannic Championship   *Derbyshire 113 & 59/3*
Northamptonshire 120

What an incredible day. After we were bowled out in less than 40 overs, I almost took all ten Northants wickets. I'm not complaining. I got a career best of 9/43, beating the 8/53 I took against Essex on my 20th birthday in 1991. Ironically, we were playing on the same strip today. Not that these latest figures impressed everyone up at the first Test at Headingley. I was walking round the ground as we batted again when someone called me over to listen to *Test Match Special* on the radio. I was the topic under discussion and Jonathan Agnew suggested my performance would give the England selectors something to think about. I expected confirmation of this from the other commentator, but I was sadly disappointed. David Lloyd's view was rather different. 'You only have to put the ball on the right spot at Derby.' What a cheek! I was angry at first; then I felt sad and hurt that a cricketer with his reputation and experience should demean my achievement, from another part of the country. How do you equate taking nine wickets, whatever the state of the pitch? It must be like a batsman scoring 150 or a double century. However easy-paced the wicket, you'd still give a batsman credit for scoring that many runs. Obviously nine wickets don't come into the same category. What made it worse was that Lloyd was commenting on something he hadn't even seen. I'm trying to make it into England's Test team and here he was disregarding my career best.

Although 23 wickets fell in the day, it wasn't the fault of the pitch. I bowled 22 overs on the trot and didn't want to come off. It was one of those occasions when the batsmen nicked everything and the ball flew to the fielders, who kept catching it. Well, almost. I'd taken the first nine when Russell Warren, who'd batted throughout, snicked one to Colin Wells at first slip. He couldn't hold on to it. That was it. Paul Aldred yorked Paul Taylor for his first championship wicket for Derbyshire, so I had to be content with nine. I had no complaints about the drop – it was a difficult chance. Of course, I would have loved to take all ten. I might never get that close again.

We were 52 ahead by the close. If one of our batsmen can get a 60 or 70 tomorrow, we can win this game. It certainly wasn't a day for openers. All four on show got ducks. Our skipper Kim Barnett got two. So, I wasn't the only one to make to reach an individual milestone today. After 17 seasons in the game, Kim wasn't too happy to record his first pair.

When I came off, I was told it was the best Derbyshire bowling performance for 20 years. But the lads will have to wait for that career-best drink. I was absolutely whacked and headed for home – fortunately not too far from the County Ground. For once, Gregory was still up, although I'm not sure I had his undivided attention when I took him through the day's bowling performance – though what can you expect from a 9-month-old? I did celebrate with my favourite meal – pork chops, new potatoes, broccoli and cabbage. Jane didn't have to prepare it specially. It's what I eat nearly every night. That may sound unadventurous and boring. Guilty! But I like it and see no reason to change. My pudding choice hardly ever varies, either. It's tiramisu, the Italian dessert – sponge, cream and a little bit of chocolate. All washed down with the odd glass of Tyrrell's Aussie chardonnay.

Devon Malcolm in action for Derbyshire against Felton of Northamptonshire in the Benson and Hedges semi-final.

A career best against Northants – 9 for 43. I was sad to hear later that day that I had failed to impress David Lloyd, commentating on *Test Match Special* from Headingley.

FRIDAY 9 JUNE   DERBY

Derbyshire 139   Northants 135/6
Derbyshire lost by 4 wickets

The best match figures of my career – 13/93. Not much to celebrate, though. We lost before tea on the second day. Winning close games like these is the key to having a good season. The match was never going to reach a third day; Northants even checked out of their hotel this morning. We needed to set them a target approaching 200, but we never got close. For the fifth time in 11 matches this season, we were bowled out for under 150, setting Northants 133 for victory in something over 16 hours! It wasn't a formality and Northants wobbled at 92/5, but a couple of dropped catches made it easier than it might have been.

SUNDAY 11 JUNE   DERBY

AXA Equity & Law   *Northants 200/6   Derbyshire 200/9   Tie*

We should have won easily. The day actually produced just seven runs less than the total for the 40 wickets of the championship match. After being 161/3, the last pair were at the wicket needing 14 to win off the last over. Paul Taylor was bowling to Paul Aldred, who hit a six, four and two from the first five deliveries, but he could only scramble a bye off the final delivery.

   Not a great day for England teams at home. The West Indies won easily at Headingley and Brazil were too good at Wembley. But the day was dominated by England's rugby World Cup quarter-final victory over Australia, thanks to Rob Andrew's late dropped goal. Much as I hate seeing England's Test team losing, there are more likely to be changes now they've made a bad start to the series – which could be good news for me. My career best has helped put me at the top of the bowling averages with my 43 wickets costing 14.0.

THURSDAY 15 JUNE   DERBY

Britannic Championship   *Derbyshire 376 v Somerset*

The long-awaited return of Peter Bowler to Derby. Peter came to Derbyshire from Leicestershire in 1988 and quickly made his mark. There was even talk of an England call-up. Peter scored over 2,000 runs in 1992 and he was voted Derbyshire's Player of the Year. But he was also ambitious and it became increasingly obvious that that was going to cause problems at the club. The crunch came at Cambridge in 1993 when he and John Morris went to 'Jack' Warner and told him there were plans afoot to get rid of Kim Barnett as captain. Jack came to me and asked what he should do. We both told Kim. He approached Peter and John, who denied the whole thing. The pair's regular moan was that the wickets at Derbyshire were too much in favour of the bowlers, but that was hardly Kim's fault. He was a batter after all. Kim was annoyed, not only because they'd been plotting, but because they didn't have the guts to own up when he confronted them. John left the club at the end of 1993 for Durham, despite being offered a big five-year contract. Peter Bowler headed for Somerset at the end of the following year. Had Peter and John won the power struggle, I would certainly have reconsidered my future at Derbyshire. When Peter left, he and Kim had something of a slanging match in the national papers. So with Mr Bowler back in town, the local papers were not slow in opening up wounds that had had little time to heal.

This match is going to be played on a pretty flat track. After the previous game, that's the word that came from Lord's, although the Northants pitch provoked no criticism in the umpires' report. Mushtaq did turn it on the first day. Kim went for his third duck in the row. I know some batsmen who would be suicidal after something like that, but not Kim. He doesn't go around with the cares of the world on his shoulders and never seems to lose his pleasant disposition. Cullinan batted well and showed what a world-class talent he has with 30 boundaries in his 161 runs. Somerset struggled. They didn't have a great seam attack. I didn't make much of an impression, though. I'd scored three when I tried to hit Mushtaq over the top. My swishing bat made contact with nothing but fresh air as I became one of the Pakistan leg-spinner's five wickets.

FRIDAY 16 JUNE   DERBY

Somerset 189 & 123/2 following-on

Poetic justice. Peter Bowler went first ball, caught by Colin Wells off Devon. As we went up, it was obvious he wasn't happy with the shout and thought it came off his arm guard rather than his glove. We made it crystal clear that on this special occasion, we weren't expecting him to be given the benefit of the doubt. Somerset finished up 181 in arrears. I took four of the last five wickets to follow. Our advantage might have been more if I hadn't dropped Keith Parsons' first ball at second slip. He had the top score with 43. As Somerset's eighth and ninth wickets departed, Kim discussed the rights and wrongs of making them follow-on. If we batted again, it would take Mushtaq out of the game. But the bowlers felt fresh and we thought we could get much of the job done in the second part of the day. Wrong! After Somerset slumped to 20/2, Peter Bowler and Richard Harden were still there after putting on a stand of over a century. Often we struggle at Derbyshire because we haven't got a spinner to tie up one end or rip a couple out. But two early wickets tomorrow should see the job done. I was the subject of Simon Hughes' Cricket Profile in today's *Daily Telegraph*. As usual, it was pretty complimentary and predicted that I would get my Test chance soon. It finished up with: 'There is a suspicion that his bowling is a tad too innocuous to be really devastating in Test cricket, his batting a shade too fragile. Now is the time to find out if he has the talent to match his enthusiasm.' I have to agree with that final sentiment.

SATURDAY 17 JUNE   DERBY

Somerset 434   Derbyshire 28/4

Disaster. Peter Bowler was magnificent, pulling and hooking Devon. He looked very determined to show everyone what a good batsman he is. I might not like his attitude to people and cricket, or the way he played at Derbyshire, but I could never say he isn't a good player. Peter scored 138, but the real damage was an undefeated century by Rob Turner. And that was a real problem for our South African player. South Africa played their World Cup semi-final against France today in Durban. When Cullinan went to hang up his clothes, he was greeted by a couple of Tricolour flags, tastefully drawn near his pegs by two of our resident jokers. That was the start. Much of the pre-play dressing-room banter was conducted in a French accent. I kept out of it because I've basically decided to have nothing to do with him. He's even been complaining about Daffy's ghetto-blaster in the dressing room. On the field, Turner's defiant knock really seemed to wind him up. From mid-on, Cullinan started having a go. Eventually, the umpire Nigel Plews told him to get off the park and cool down. Not that the rest of us were happy with proceedings. A ninth-wicket stand of 83 and then their skipper Andy Hayhurst returning after being smashed on the finger by Devon, enabling

Turner to reach his century, left us chasing a winning target of 248. You could say that we have not made the best of starts. We need something very special on Monday, especially with our batting.

SUNDAY 18 JUNE   DERBY

AXA Equity & Law   Somerset 212/7   Derbyshire 193/6
Derbyshire lost by 19 runs

I've made the England Test squad at last! I still can't quite believe it. I was driving Jane down to the garage this morning to pick up her new car, and I switched on Radio Five. Although I knew I must be close, deep down I didn't think I'd make it this time after the disappointment of a fortnight ago. Then suddenly my name was read out. Jesus, they've picked me! My first reaction was relief. Whatever happens from now on, at least they thought I was good enough to make a Test squad. Devon was left out and Bumpy (Steven Rhodes) came in with a strong suggestion that he was going to take over the gloves from Stewie.

Yet there is a huge cloud on my Test horizon that may cost me my England debut at Lord's. When I came off the field late yesterday, I could hardly breathe. It was as if someone had stuck a knife in my side. I'd felt something there after the Northants game, but I'd put it down to bowling so many overs on the trot. Last night I could hardly sleep I was so uncomfortable. My big fear is that it is an inter-costal injury, the curse of fast bowlers because it takes for ever to clear up. In a weird way, I was almost hoping my name would be missing from the England squad. Imagine being picked and then having to drop out. Jane was ecstatic when my name came over the radio, but I was thinking, 'Why has this injury cropped up now? Haven't I suffered enough?' My side still feels stiff tonight. It was difficult to concentrate on the Sunday League match, more because of the injury than the England selection. I bowled a gentle eight overs before Kim and I put on 63 for the first wicket as we fell 19 runs short.

Everyone's congratulating me on the news, but I can't escape the feeling that I'm not going to make it. After a chat with our physio, I've decided to see a specialist before going to Lord's. I've not told anyone in the England camp about my problem, but I won't be travelling to London if I'm not fit. That wouldn't be right, however desperate I am for that first cap. Breaking down in those circum-stances would be unforgivable and totally unprofessional. I couldn't live with letting my team-mates down. My mum and dad phoned up to congratulate me, and I told them not to be disappointed if I have to pull out. At this precise moment, I'm not sure where I'd put my money.

MONDAY 19 JUNE   DERBY

Derbyshire 168
Derbyshire lost to Somerset by 79 runs

My side is much improved and I'm pretty sure I'm going to make it. I headed off down the M1 to Nottingham for an eight-fifteen appointment, fearing the worst. Fortunately, after hearing my symptoms and examining me the specialist Jonathan Webb is sure it's not an inter-costal. He thinks it's either a tissue injury or inflamed fibres. He gave me an anti-inflammatory injection, and I knew immediately he'd hit the exact spot. I felt sick afterwards. He told me not to bowl for 24 hours, but said he was sure I'd be fit to play at Lord's, adding that if I still felt a sharp pain, I shouldn't play. His final words were: 'It's your body, it's your decision.' I didn't get back to the County Ground until ten o'clock. I can't have looked great because quite a few people asked me if was feeling all right.

The game went from bad to worse, although Colin Wells, who was awarded his county cap before the start, batted well. It was finished in the third over after lunch, with Peter Bowler taking the catch to end proceedings. Then, as acting Somerset captain, he shook hands with the not-out batsman – Kim. A poignant moment indeed. Apparently, this was Derbyshire's first defeat after enforcing the follow-on for 113 years. Yet another Derbyshire season has faltered far too early.

Our chairman had a word with Kim after the game and the cricket committee are meeting on Wednesday to discuss playing standards after losing five championship matches out of six. I don't blame them. We've too many good players not to be challenging for trophies. Kim's position is not under threat. He has already announced that this is his last season as captain after 13 seasons in charge. Of course, I'm not happy with my county's performances, but I'm trying to focus on England at the moment. You've got to be selfish at times and forget what's going on outside your direct line of vision. The injury is certainly much easier tonight and I'm looking forward to a better night's sleep.

WEDNESDAY 21 JUNE   LONDON

I've made it. On Tuesday the chairman told me I was playing and on Wednesday I knew that my injury worries were completely over. Daffy and I travelled down to London yesterday in his car as the club has booked us flights up to Durham on Thursday morning if we're not required by England, and there'd be no point in both of us leaving cars in London. Most of the papers predict Daffy and I will be contesting the final bowling spot. Even driving into Lord's two days before the Test was special. Athers and Illy both congratulated me when I got to the dressing room. Everyone made me feel at home. It was as though this day, which I have often thought would never come, was inevitable.

If I was quieter than usual it wasn't because I was overawed. The injury was nagging at the back of my mind. I still had not told anyone in the England party. Was I doing the right thing? Could I blot my copybook with England for ever? I wasn't trying to con anyone. Nor would I contemplate playing if I wasn't 100 per cent. I had already decided that if I had a serious problem in the nets on Tuesday afternoon, I would pull out there and then. And I wouldn't have got even that far if the specialist had not been optimistic about me playing. The media were keen to talk to me as the new boy. On the way over to the nets, Illy told me I'd be playing. That gave me a great boost. He said, 'Go out and do the things you do for Derby.' My side was a bit sore and stiff when I bowled, but there was no longer that jagged pain and it was certainly improving – the anti-inflammatory tablets I was taking were doing their job. I slept well on Tuesday and woke confident that the crisis had passed and I was ready for a full work-out in the nets. I didn't hold back and charged in at full pace. After that I knew I would not break down because of my side problem.

Athers had a word with me, confirming the chairman's view that he didn't want me to change anything. 'Stick it up the tail-enders like you do at county level. Don't be in awe of anyone out there. You're as good as them.' However confident you are, it's a great help to get that sort of assurance from the England captain. I've waited a long, long time for this game, and Athers knows I'm nervous.

This afternoon was spent winding down. I went for a massage in the leisure complex in our hotel, the Marriott at Swiss Cottage, and the masseuse gave me a real going over for an hour. My side didn't feel tender at all. It's the first time I've ever had a massage and if this match goes well for me, I might make it a regular part of my preparation. We had a team meeting, then the team meal. Because I'm the new boy, I was put next to the chairman, who – as usual – was full of sound advice. I didn't hang around for long after the meal. It's just after nine o'clock and I'm about to put the light out.

THURSDAY 22 JUNE   LORD'S

Second Cornhill Test   England 255/8 v West Indies

I'm a fully fledged England cricketer at last. I slept like a top and woke up feeling really fresh. I was convinced that this was going to be a fielding day. The selectors changed their minds about fielding a specialist wicket-keeper and Bumpy Rhodes headed off last night to Southampton, where Worcestershire are playing. Daffy was omitted this morning, so he caught the flight to Durham and left me his car. I was at Lord's early – about eight-thirty. There were only groundstaff and workers around, but I could still feel the atmosphere. My side wasn't troubling me in any way. If I had pulled out prematurely because of it, I would have been pig sick this morning.

Atherton won the toss, with a new two-pound coin given to him by the chairman. I presume it's on loan. The morning papers were full of stories of strife between the captain and the chairman, suggesting Athers is about to resign. It was my first day in the England Test dressing room, so I'm no expert, but I didn't see or sense any signs of disharmony or tension. Athers decided to bat. I was a bit sad that I didn't walk out with the team on my first morning as a Test player, but it was the right decision. There were quite a few telegrams and faxes for me in the dressing room, some from friends I haven't seen for ages. Normally, I'm not a great cricket watcher, but I spent the first hour on the balcony. There was so much to soak up. I just wanted to be part of it all. I hadn't really expected – or wanted – to be batting today. But after a fourth-wicket stand 111 from the Judge (Robin Smith) and Thorpey, I found myself walking out with us precariously placed at 187/5. Thorpey and Goughie didn't last long, so the West Indies were in the ascendancy with us 205/7, with about 15 overs left in the day. I had gone out with the intention of being there at the close. I did not face a baptism of fire because, as luck would have it, Carl Hooper was bowling. He was certainly much higher up my list of preferences as the man to deliver my first ball in Test cricket than Curtly Ambrose, Courtney Walsh or Ian Bishop. Even better, that first ball was short outside the off-stump. I was able to cut it to the boundary to join an exclusive band, which includes David Gower, who've hit their first ball for four. A bad ball is a bad ball in any form of cricket and I've played that shot a thousand times. But I was pretty pumped up and it was a great relief when I saw it heading in the right direction.

I found a more than willing ally in Peter 'Digger' Martin. In the past the England tail has rarely wagged with anything other than token defiance. I think the Windies thought they would roll us over quickly, but Digger and I started pushing the ball around and they got frustrated. Walsh and Ambrose bowled too many bouncers. I have faced most of the West Indies bowlers in county cricket, but there's one big difference between then and now. Unless you're exceptionally unlucky, there's only one of them in county cricket. Facing this sustained onslaught was a very different proposition, and rather uncomfortable. One of their great strengths is the ball that lifts from nowhere. Digger and I had put on 50 before I was bowled in the final over of the day. I was very disappointed, not least because I never even saw the ball. Courtney was bowling from the Nursery End. He'd bowled one a couple of overs earlier which I'd lost in the trees and it hit the top of my bat handle. This time I never saw it leave his hand and the next thing I knew was the clatter of my stumps. I'd been yorked. That was the end of the day's proceedings and we came off at 255/8. I had been within three balls of safety. I felt I'd done a useful job in helping us push towards 300, but I would dearly love to be going out to bat tomorrow. The whole day has wiped me out. I had a quiet meal at an Italian restaurant in Hampstead with Stewie, Thorpey and Hickie, and we discussed how the day had gone. Certainly, we would like to get past the 300 mark. Anything less will make it hard for us bowlers.

FRIDAY 23 JUNE   LORD'S

England 283   West Indies 209/6

Even-Steven. We might just have our noses slightly in front. I drove in with Thorpey this morning. I think I felt more nervous today because I knew I could be bowling. We batted for another 40 minutes, helped by two dropped catches by Junior Murray. With less than 300 on the board, Athers emphasised that we could not afford the wayward bowling that contributed to the Headingley defeat. It was a tremendous feeling walking through the Long Room and out on to Lord's with the England team. Gough and Gussie opened the bowling, but I got my chance from the Pavilion End before lunch. Athers had asked me if I had a preference. I have always bowled well from that end for Derbyshire. I felt very nervous, very aware that this was my first bowl in Test cricket. My opening delivery in all three Texaco matches had gone for four, so I was looking for some sort of an improvement. This time I managed a dot ball to Hooper, who had given me my first runs in Test cricket. The Windies went in to lunch at 28/2. The ball wasn't swinging, so I concentrated on my line, trying to make the batsmen work for their runs.

It wasn't my bowling, but my catching which let me down in the afternoon session. I dropped Richie Richardson off Peter Martin. I was at backward cover point and it was such an easy chance. I couldn't believe it when the ball ballooned out of my hands. I still can't. It's a chance I would take nine times out of ten. I could hear the groans round the ground and just wanted to dig a big hole and lie in it. Dropping catches is annoying at the best of times, but when you've given a life to one of the best attacking batsmen in the world at Lord's in a Test match, you can't help thinking how calamitous the consequences might be. What happens if he gets a hundred now? Or a double century? Or more? For the sake of your sanity and peace of mind, you've got to try to forget it as quickly as possible. Anyway, I was bowling at the other end, so I didn't need any distractions. There's not much you can say to the bowler, either. Nobody drops them on purpose. I just said 'sorry' to Digger at the end of the over.

One or two other catches went down and the Windies reached 166/3, but then Gussie removed Richie (thank goodness – he got an extra pat from me) for 49 and Jimmy Adams for 54. By the close the Windies were 209/6. Unfortunately, I'm still waiting for my first Test wicket, although I felt I bowled reasonably well. My 13 overs have cost 43 runs. I had a reasonable shout for LBW when Keith Arthurton played inside the ball near the close, but the umpire's finger remained where it was. I felt much more relaxed tonight, having bowled for my country. Some of us headed for Planet Hollywood. We were way down the list of celebrities there tonight, with Andre Agassi, Paul Ince, Ian Wright and Gaby Roslin just some of the famous faces I saw, but didn't talk to.

SATURDAY 24 JUNE   LORD'S

West Indies 324   England 155/3

Another tense day, with the Windies edging ahead. We'd been looking to get a first-innings lead, but Arthurton led a late charge and the tourists got 41 runs in front. I bowled the first over of the day. That was a special moment for me. Because of school, it was always the Saturday of the Lord's Test that I watched when I was growing up, and I especially remember the England bowlers, like Willis, Dilley and Foster, who started the day. Now I've joined them. It was freezing today and the Windies kept us out in the field for much longer than expected. But I did get my first Test wicket in mid-afternoon. I'd just bowled a bumper to Ian Bishop and we had a little stare at each other. I angled the next one in and it removed his middle stump. I had a feeling of great relief. I've got a Test wicket and they can never it away from me. The Windies innings closed with Goughie taking a great diving catch when Arthurton hooked Gussie. It was a top effort, but that didn't stop us taking the mick out of Goughie for making a meal of it.

Thankfully I was a spectator for the rest of the day. Our lead was only ten runs by the time both our openers had gone. Then we lost Thorpey, hit by a Courtney Walsh beamer. Courtney was attempting a low yorker, like the one that did for me on Friday, but this time the ball slipped out of his hand. Thorpey lost sight of it, ducked and the ball smashed full on into his helmet. You could tell it was an accident, and Courtney held his hands up in apology straight away. But the bottom line was that one of our mainline batsmen was out of action. After being treated in the pavilion, he was whisked away in an ambulance and I gather he's being kept in hospital overnight. So, effectively, we were three down and could easily have lost the game in that final session. But Hickie and Smith got their heads down to save the situation. Hickie was out in deteriorating light and the players came off a few minutes later. Our lead is now 114, but we need to get past 250 tomorrow to give ourselves a real chance.

SUNDAY 25 JUNE   LORD'S

England 336   West Indies 68/1

This is turning into one hell of a Test match. The Judge was today's hero. He fell ten runs short of a century – no one has ever deserved one more. Jane came down yesterday, leaving Gregory with my mum and dad, but our quiet night in was disrupted when the fire alarm bell went off late. It was a false alarm.

England's day started badly when we lost Ramps in the first over, so he has bagged a 'pair' of ducks on his home patch. It's painful seeing him struggle like this. We've been friends since we played together for the England under-19s. He's so talented, but that final breakthrough keeps eluding him. I thought he had finally made it when he flew out from the A tour to join the Ashes tour as a replacement and scored 72 and 42 at Perth. But he's now had four failures against the West Indies and the questions will start all over again. I don't know what the answer is. Thorpey joined Judge, showing no ill-effects from his experience on Saturday. He told me he'd encountered the same problem as I had, losing sight of the ball in the trees at the Nursery End. The blow has obviously only hardened Thorpey's resolve for the fight. The pair were still together at lunch with England 232/4.

I went out to join the Judge shortly after the break. My sole intention was to hold my end up and give him all the support he needed. We always felt we needed to set the Windies a target of 250 to give ourselves a real chance. We'd put on 50 before I chased a wide ball from Bishop and was caught behind. I'd have settled for that score when I walked out, but I was still very annoyed with myself for giving it away. Goughie joined the Judge and they took the score to 320/6. Judgey was the next to go to the new ball just after tea. He'd batted for over six hours and the knock was all the more remarkable because he was fighting for his Test life. He'd been dropped mid-way through summer 1994 and wasn't selected for the Ashes tour. He returned to open without success at Headingley and the chairman made a public pronouncement before this Test that now was the time for Smith to stand up and be counted. The consequences of him failing to do so were clear. But the arguments have been settled now. Today's innings was one of class, character and guts. I can't believe there were some who thought his England days were over.

The new ball accounted for our final four wickets for 16 runs, always likely against a fired-up Curtly. We were all out for 336, leaving the Windies needing 296 for a 2–0 lead in the series. There have been reports in the papers that the West Indies coach Andy Roberts is far from happy with the Lord's wicket. I gather he was summoned before the International Cricket Council (ICC) referee. I must admit that I don't think it has been that bad. There has not been a lot of inconsistency in the bounce. Some have kept low. It just seems a typical Lord's wicket to me – flattish, with a little bit of uneven bounce now and again. Goughie got Hooper out tonight, but Lara is still there, looking menacing, and is the key to winning this Test. Still, I feel confident and wouldn't swap our position for theirs. No lavish dinner for Jane tonight. Just KFC in the hotel room. Aren't I the romantic one?

MONDAY 26 JUNE LORD'S

West Indies 223
England won by 73 runs Man of the Match: Dominic Cork

The most incredible day of my life. We won a great victory and I was named Man of the Match. But I'm absolutely wiped out. I've just driven to March for Derbyshire's first round NatWest game against Cambridgeshire. The report of the day's events will have to wait until tomorrow night. I'm not sure I would be able to make too much sense of them now if I tried.

TUESDAY 27 JUNE MARCH, CAMBS

NatWest first round Derbyshire 289/3 Cambridgeshire 132
Derbyshire won by 167 runs

Has the world gone mad, or what? I've been hounded from morning to night and even after. The phone started ringing at just after six this morning and didn't let up. I was late for the game and even had to come off when we were fielding. Fortunately it wasn't a hard contest, because I don't think I would have been much use to the boys today. One thing is certain. I cannot let my life be turned upside down like this. It won't take long for my cricket to suffer and I'll end up a one-test wonder. I've waited too long to let that happen.

It all started yesterday morning when we walked out at Lord's. The final morning, with everything to play for. The West Indies needed 228 runs to win. We needed nine wickets. Lara could win the game single-handed, but I was confident we'd do it. I was pleased that my first Test was such an enthralling match. I must confess to being disappointed by the relatively small crowd when play started, but that didn't matter when Goughie got the wicket we wanted, thanks to a superb one-handed diving catch by Stewie. He took it low down in front of Athers' left hand at first slip. None of us was counting his chickens, but we knew only too well that if Lara had still been firing at lunch, we would be in trouble.

I didn't bowl for an hour. I'm used to opening the bowling, so I was rather champing at the bit. After taking just one wicket in the first innings, I felt I owed the lads a few more. This time I went to the Nursery End. The ball hadn't swung from the Pavilion End, so Athers and I felt there was little to lose by trying something new. The gamble paid off. From ball number one, it swung. The slope at Lord's helped, too. I picked up two wickets before lunch. Jimmy Adams was batting. Left-handers aren't a problem for me. I know some bowlers have trouble with their line and length, but I bowl close to the stumps and get a lot of LBWs with the ball that swings in. Adams went when he edged one to Hickie at second slip. It was almost a half volley, but Adams didn't get out for the drive. Richie was next in. I'd seen the way Peter Martin had got him out LBW in the Headingley Test, so we decided to forgo the short leg and put in a man at short mid-wicket. Richie sometimes shuffles across early on as he tries to play through the on-side. I kept nagging at him and he took a chance. He played across the line and was LBW. The Windies were 130/4 at lunch. Definitely our morning.

Just after lunch, I got rid of Arthurton, who was caught by our bat-pad substitute, Middlesex's Paul Weekes. I really felt good. The Nursery End was obviously the place for me to bowl. Now that the trio of West Indies left-handers had gone, I felt I had a real chance against the rest. Weekes was on as a substitute for Thorpey. He was off all day, still feeling groggy after his knock on the head and suffering from a touch of flu. David 'Shep' Shepherd was the umpire who gave Arthurton out. It was bat-pad catch. Shep told me that if he hadn't nicked it, he would have been plumb LBW. There was a real buzz around the place now that the West Indies were struggling at 138/5. But Sherwin Campbell was batting really well and he began dominating the strike. He slapped me a couple of times in front of cover. He's dangerous because you don't worry about him in the way you do about Lara, Adams and the other big names. Then you look at the board and he's got 70-odd. Weekes took an even better catch to get rid of Murray. The Windies were 177/6. Both Goughie and I had taken three wickets each. A five-for haul wasn't in my mind. I just knew we were going to win this Test now. We deserved to. I just wanted to keep bowling.

I got Ottis Gibson when he wandered in front of his stumps and the next over I got rid of Campbell for 93 when he edged it to Stewie. Five wickets in my first Test. Wow! Campbell didn't want to go, but

That stance again. I had just got my first Test wicket – Ian Bishop clean bowled. So why am I bothering to appeal? Richie Richardson at the non-striker's end seems uncertain.

Seven wickets later, I am Man of the Match and England have beaten the West Indies on my debut, so levelling the series. Ranged behind me are Messrs Hick, Smith, Martin, Stewart, Illingworth, Fraser and Atherton.

his disappointment was more to do with realising that the Windies' last chance had gone, rather than with Shep's decision. We went into tea needing just two wickets. Athers said, 'Well bowled. Do you feel OK?' I felt great. Just try taking the ball away now! The crowd had been building up all day and there were probably about 10,000 spectators in now. The atmosphere in the old place really was extraordinary.

I tried to get Curtly out after tea. I probably tried too hard. A few went down the leg-side as I attempted to put a bit extra in. I also bumped him a couple of times – just to let him know I was around. I'm not a tail-ender. They let me have enough, so I'm happy to dish it out. I got the feeling that Athers was about to take me off. I'd bowled 20 overs on the trot and was nearing the end of my spell, then Curtly hit a fairly average ball straight down extra-cover's throat. A bonus. Now it was one wicket for victory. Courtney had given me such a working over that I decided it was pay-off time. I bumped him first ball and he did his usual jumping-about act. The next ball was chest high and he managed to hit it off the face of the bat into the hands of our keeper. Victory! In my first Test. Then it suddenly dawned on me I had taken seven wickets. Seven wickets!

I looked around trying to take it all in. The most vivid memory is of Athers jumping up and down. That made me realise how important this was to him. I had never suffered at the West Indies' hands. He had. This might be a dream moment for me, but you could see how much it meant to him. I ran back to collect a stump then raced off as the crowd invaded the ground. The pavilion was full of members clapping as I went through the long room and up the stairs. Next thing I knew I was on the balcony being presented with the Man of the Match award. After that I was plonked in front of the press: TV cameras, microphones, lights and Uncle Tom Cobbleigh, with everyone asking me how I felt. Overwhelmed was the best description. It wasn't the seven wickets that were so important. It was being part of a superb England performance and win. That was what I had waited years and sweated blood for. I felt so proud. I don't believe that anything will ever compare to this win. The game could have gone either way for most of the four days and we came through when the pressure was on.

Bob Taylor from Derbyshire, who also works for Cornhill, was in the dressing room and congratulated me. I rang my mum at home. She was looking after Gregory, and apparently, she bounced him up and down on her knee every time I got a wicket. I told the press corps that he'd probably been sick. They lapped up all that human interest stuff. I went up to Judgey after the Man of the Match and said, 'You deserved this.' I was pretty emotional at the time, but even 24 hours later I think the same way. Without his runs, my wickets would not have happened. I enjoyed the press conference. It was all smiles, but I could see the faces of those who'd said that I wasn't good enough. That I had too much to say for myself. That I would never make it.

I couldn't believe how many cricket pressmen were crammed into the room at the top of the pavilion. Now they wanted to be part of my life. We will have to see about that. At least the press boys only wanted one interview. The radio lads all wanted an exclusive piece. Tricky, that, when they all ask the same questions. By the time I got back to the changing room, quite a few of the team had gone. Me and Stewie were the last to leave. Embers and Gatt, those Middlesex and England veterans, came in and offered their congratulations. Like Gussie, they were heading off to Cornwall for the first round of the NatWest. That was the great sadness for me; that we couldn't celebrate this day as a team. We were all expected to travel all over the country that same night for county matches.

The faxes were beginning to gather in the dressing room. *The Big Breakfast* and TV-am were both after me. They could wait. Jane was still there, and it seemed my press duties hadn't finished as the snappers wanted a picture of me and the wife. Jane was happy to oblige. So was I. It was a rare chance for her to be near me. Then we headed for the Cornhill hospitality area in the MCC Indoor School before I dropped her off at Euston Station.

I was in Daffy's car in heavy traffic as I headed for the M11. I was being recognised. Some people shouted 'brilliant' and tooted their horns. I didn't have the radio on. I listened instead to one of Daffy's CDs by a soul group called Brownstone – I think I might buy it. I needed to wind down. It was about this time that the seven wickets began to sink in. I kept thinking 'Yes, Yes!' I also began to feel very tired. I came off at the Cambridge exit and stopped at a petrol station to find out where March was. I didn't have a clue. It was another hour before I finally got here, and I couldn't believe my eyes. The lads were all waiting for me when I arrived just after nine o'clock. I could have done with going straight to bed, but everyone was buying champagne, so I didn't make it until after midnight. Then I caught the end of the BBC Highlights of the Day. That apart, I hadn't watched TV or listened to the radio, so I wasn't really aware of the impact of England's win and my seven wickets for 43 runs. I now gather it was the best performance by an Englishman on his

Test debut this century, beating John Lever's 7/46 in Delhi in 1976. It was also England's first win over the West Indies at Lord's in ten attempts and 38 years.

Daffy's my room-mate and he wasn't too happy when the phone started ringing first thing this morning. *The Big Breakfast* called and I was chatting to Gaby Roslin. I gave her a bit of a hard time, pointing out that she didn't exactly rush over to make my acquaintance at Planet Hollywood the other evening.

I didn't have time for breakfast or even to read the papers. Everyone had gone to the ground by the time I left. I was totally unprepared for the media scrum that greeted me there. I can't believe many of them had even heard of March before last night. Now there were TV crews, journalists and radio commentators all wanting the exclusive story of Dominic Cork. It was only at the ground that I saw the morning papers. I'd expected to be all over the back, but not the front as well. I was staggered. I was relieved when Kim won the toss and we batted first. I was also grateful it wasn't a big game. I felt exhausted, physically and mentally. We got a big total and I wasn't required to bat. I thought I'd feel better once I started bowling, but after five overs I had to go off. Kim could see I was in distress. I could hardly stand. I sat in the dressing room for an hour, just sipping water, trying to get my thoughts together. I needed to have some time to myself. I couldn't cope with much more of this hassling. The trouble was that coming off created more problems as now all the press wanted to know what was wrong.

I drove home with Daffy, who had taken 5/28. I know I have to sort out this side of my cricket life pretty quickly, and that means getting someone looking after my affairs. When I got home I told Jane I can't have another day like this. I've got to be able to concentrate on my cricket. She was only too well aware of what was going on – the phone hadn't stopped ringing at home. Then I found out that there were four cameras outside my mum and dad's house. One afternoon looks like changing my life for ever.

WEDNESDAY 28 JUNE   DERBY

I may have found the man to help me. TV-am's Nick Owen is a Derbyshire supporter and a regular visitor to the County Ground. In the past he has mentioned Jon Holmes, the man who looks after the affairs of Gary Lineker, Will Carling, David Gower and Mike Atherton. In the murky world of agents, Jon is one of the few with a good reputation. I haven't met him, though I spoke to him on the phone about a year ago. At that time I didn't think I needed an agent, and that was fine with him. He just said that when I did or if I needed help at any time, to give him a call.

I rang his office after a bit of a lie-in. I was still shattered. Our answering machine is on permanently at the moment and we only pick up the phone when we want to. Jon was out of his office, but I got him on his mobile. I told him about all the hassle I was getting, and he told me what I wanted to hear. 'Whoever rings up, give them my number and tell them to phone me.' A great weight lifted off my shoulders. There was no commitment beyond that. But for the moment I had a buffer between me and the outside world.

The papers are still full of it today. I'm amazed. They've got pictures of me as a kid and loads of stuff about my childhood. I can't believe it. My whole life has been thoroughly investigated by the newspapers in the space of a day. I cut the grass and did a bit of gardening to try and relax. But I still can't escape that final day. Sky have kindly given me a video of my wickets. It might sound terrible, but I've been watching them all day, maybe because even now I can't quite believe that it happened. It was great just watching the reaction of the others, like Athers, when we won. Maybe I've set myself standards that are going to be impossible to keep. I'm not going to worry about that at the moment. I'm still just a proud England cricketer.

THURSDAY 29 JUNE   DERBY

Britannic Championship   *Derbyshire v Hampshire*

Kim told me to go home this morning. I turned up for the game against Hampshire and wanted to play, but Kim said no. He told me, 'I think you're tired. It's hot. It's a flat wicket. Get yourself right. After all that hassle at Cambridge. Go home and rest.' Kim has always been thoughtful like that. Some of the members were apparently upset that I pulled out. I heard rumours of a cold, of a sore shoulder. I didn't go straight home; instead I phoned Jon Holmes again and he's coming up tomorrow to discuss things. I've asked our chairman Mike Horton if he will sit in and give me his thoughts afterwards. Jon had no objection to this.

Bill Day was there from the *Mail on Sunday*. Of all my critics, he's been the most hostile over the years, especially on A tours. First I wasn't ready for England, in his opinion. Then it was my temperament that might let me down at Test level. It was all negative stuff. What really annoyed me was that he would say one thing to

me, then write another. After South Africa last winter, he told me
I'd had a great tour. When I got home I read in his tour report that
I wasn't good enough. It's a bit childish, but I decided that it was
pay-back time. Keep him waiting. See how he feels. I got the message
that he was offering to lay on a chauffeur-driven car so that I could
go back to Betley CC, near Crewe, where I'd played from the ages
of 12 to 17 with my two brothers and where my mum, Mary, is still
the tea lady.

I had a chat with the Judge and said that I could do with a good
manager. He asked if I had anyone in mind, and I mentioned Jon.
He said, 'You don't need to ask me, then. You've got the right
person.' That was reassuring. Judge added that Jon is very professional in what he does and projects the right image. I tried to give
Ian Botham a ring for advice. He's always been my cricket hero, my
idol. I felt a little bit scared about ringing him, even though I had
made my England one-day debut in the same side as him. Ian has
always given me a good press: 'Dominic Cork has a lot of talent.
It's time England gave him a go.' It was an unbelievable day when
I was in the same England dressing room and team as the Great
Man. He wasn't in, so I left a message. Then I set about working
out what I wanted to ask Jon. I've heard a lot about certain agents.
I'm sure the only thing worse than not having an agent or manager
is having a bad one.

FRIDAY 30 JUNE   DERBY

I haven't given Jon the final nod, but I think he's the one for me. I
slept in late again. I don't think I appreciated how much Lord's had
taken out of me. The weekly family shopping trip to Sainsbury's was
different too – a lot more people recognised me. There were no
special items on the list, though. As usual, I was at the meat counter,
requesting boneless pork chops. I don't mind food shopping, but I
hate wandering round shops aimlessly. I go in to buy something.

I got down to the County Ground for my three o'clock meeting
with Jon Holmes. Bill Day was still there. So were the cameras. I've
been pleasantly surprised by the fact that although there have been
cameras outside my parents' house, there have been none outside
ours. I'd seen what happened to Goughie when he came home from
the Ashes tour. I felt sorry for his wife Anna then. I don't want Jane
to go through the same. I'm determined to make sure my success
doesn't disrupt or intrude on my family life.

Jon was much as I'd expected. I told him what I wanted – a long relationship and someone to look after me properly. I plan a long career in cricket and I want someone to take care of all my off-the-field activities. The bottom line is my cricket; that must not suffer for the sake of commercial gain. Chasing money is short-sighted and short-term in my view. Jon explained his business, and I was impressed. He knew what I wanted. The chairman asked him questions, too. It felt right – I think I can go a long way with this bloke. I was also impressed that he didn't want a decision there and then. 'Have a think about it. Come down and see the offices in Nottingham.' He also talked about finances, having an adviser and accountant and looking after my money properly. In the past I've not been that careful with money. My attitude has very much been 'enjoy it while you can'. But now I've got a family. I want to give Gregory a good education, and the sort of start in life that both Jane and I had.

Jon and I were together for about an hour and a half, watching the cricket while we chatted. One thing I did make clear to him was that I don't want him to get involved with my cricket contract at Derbyshire. I've no desire to get someone in to try to screw the club down to the ground because I've become a Test player. I've always had a good relationship with the club and I intend to continue to negotiate with the chairman myself. Anyway, my current contract doesn't run out until 1998.

I have thought about the whole thing tonight and talked it over with Jane. I'm 90 per cent sure about Jon, but am I jumping in too fast? What if Lord's was a one-off? That's not my way, though. I'm decisive. When I see something, I go for it. Like my first house. I saw it, I bought it. The Derbyshire office has been flooded with calls and faxes about me over the past few days, and they're struggling to cope. I feel I have to make a decision pretty quickly.

JULY 1995

'You bowled like a pillock!'

SUNDAY 2 JULY   DERBY

AXA Equity & Law   Hampshire 154/8   Derbyshire 159/5
Derbyshire (4pts) beat Hampshire by 5 wickets

For the first time since I began to have international aspirations, I'm
not sweating on the announcement of the England Test team. The
Sunday papers are full of me. After the initial media avalanche, it
had begun to lie down by Thursday. But that was the daily papers.
I'd forgotten about the Sundays! There was another new name sharing the sports pages – Jonathan Edwards. His massive triple jump
in the European Cup in Lille was the first time anyone had ever
cleared 60 feet in the event, although it was wind-assisted. I'm sure
his week has just been as hectic as mine! Bill Day has done a piece
in the *Mail on Sunday* looking at my early beginnings in club cricket.
When I popped in to the ground yesterday, Bill was still hanging
around. I actually began to feel sorry for him. I got the secretary to
tell him that I wasn't speaking to anyone, so he wasn't missing a
story that anyone else was getting. After that Bill dropped me a note,
expressing his disappointment at my lack of co-operation and adding
that he hoped there was no bad feeling between us. After lunch
yesterday, I went for a walk with Jane and Gregory. It was about
the first time I felt back on an even keel and as if my life was my
own again. I told Kim that I need to get back playing. After all,
today was my only chance before the Edgbaston Test.

It was good to return to the cricket field this morning. I understood
Kim's reasons for giving me a rest – I really needed it – but I do
miss playing cricket. Also, the press had begun speculating that I
might not be fit for the third Test because I had dropped out of the
championship match. No way. Certainly, I needed the work-out with

56

the ball. It was swinging all over the place and I had a lot of trouble trying to put it in the right place. I sprayed it everywhere, bowling half of the 20 wides we conceded. In fact, extras ended up as Hampshire's top scorer with 32. We won comfortably with 15 balls to spare. I opened and hit 57, so I am reasonably pleased with the day's efforts.

The England selectors have decided to dispense with Ramps for the time being. I feel sorry for him, especially as he followed up that Lord's pair with a double hundred for Middlesex. It can't have been easy for the selectors. So much talent. With a six-Test summer and our Lord's victory, I thought they might have given him one more go. There are two new names in the England XII, both from Lancashire – Jason Gallian and Mike Watkinson. Athers has been given the nod for the rest of the summer. What a surprise!

WEDNESDAY 5 JULY   BIRMINGHAM

My spell as the new boy on the block is well and truly over. The final confirmation came at the team dinner tonight when Jason Gallian had the privilege of sitting next to our chairman. The lads are really bubbling after Lord's and there's a great feeling that we can build from here and win this series. That feeling has been boosted because the Windies have had a few problems of their own since Lord's. First, Winston Benjamin was sent home, apparently for not pulling his weight. Then they went down in one of their heaviest defeats, losing by an innings and 121 runs to Sussex at Hove. It's the first time these tourists have lost to a county side in five visits. The press reports have more than hinted that the tourists are in disarray, but most of the England side are treating that judgement with extreme caution. It's actually been the wicket at Edgbaston which has been focus of the pre-Test reporting. It certainly looks a bit strange with its bare ends. I know it's bouncy because I have taken the precaution of testing it with a ball. I don't think that Bishop, Ambrose and Walsh will be unhappy with a quick, bouncy pitch. Neither am I. Just as long as the bounce is even. Uneven bounce makes a mockery of any contest. It's not just players who get nervous before their first Test. It's the groundsman Steve Rouse's first Test pitch. I first came across him when I was 16 and had gone to Warwickshire for a trial. He was one of the coaches and I've always had a soft spot for him as he picked me out in that session.

I've certainly felt much more part of this build-up – not only because of all that happened at Lord's, but because I've finally sorted myself out outside cricket. I said 'yes' to Jon Holmes on Monday. Jane and I put Gregory in a crèche, and drove down to Nottingham to see Jon and his offices. He showed us around and I met his associates. If truth be known, I'd already made up my mind. You can analyse and weigh up the pros and cons until the cows come home, but the bottom line for me was that I felt in safe hands. There was no contract to sign. That may appear strange in this day and age, but it is Jon's way and it certainly suits me. I didn't want to sign any bit of paper that would tie my hands and allow someone else to act on my behalf for the next three years. I basically want a relationship, a partnership. If it works out, great. And my gut feeling tells me that there will be no serious problems with Jon. But, if the unexpected happens and it doesn't work, then we will just part, amicably I hope. Jane was happy and comfortable with Jon and my decision, too. That was important. On the way back home, I popped into the club to pick up my mail. I got more letters last week than I've had in the rest of my career.

THURSDAY 7 JULY   EDGBASTON

Third Cornhill Test   England 147   West Indies 104/1

What a day! What a pitch! Lord's has become a distant memory. I think it faded away after the very first ball of the morning, bowled by one Curtly Ambrose. I don't know what was more alarming – the way the ball flew up just short of a length and shot over the keeper's head to the boundary or the devilishly widening grin that spread over Curtly's face as he realised the West Indies bowlers were going to have a field day. He knew that delivery wasn't a one-off. My own day started with a chat with Chris Evans live on Radio One. He didn't believe me when I told him I'd been tucked up in bed last night without a drink or hitting the night spots. I don't know who he's been listening to.

Athers won the toss and batted. Looking at the scoreboard now, that decision will be questioned, but it seemed the right thing to do at the time. It only took that one delivery to spread doubt and a wave of panic throughout the England dressing room. Athers went in the first over and we never really recovered. Thorpey was about the only one who coped before he got a brute of a ball. Getting Thorpey out was the last we saw of Curtly today. He limped in before lunch and looked very unhappy when he passed me in the pavilion. It was the sort of wicket that he'd be happy to bowl on all day. Jason Gallian's big day was not a happy one, either. Batting at No. 6 he only managed seven before he had the middle finger of his right hand broken. It was that sort of wicket – getting in line could be costly. I tried to be brave against Courtney Walsh, but I was beaten for pace as the ball nipped back and thumped into my pads. We were all out in just over three and half hours for a total that left everyone saying we'd been 'snookered'. Very funny! Yet even then, I didn't think we were out of it. It's the same pitch for both sides.

Unfortunately, we weren't up to the calibre of the West Indies strike bowlers on this occasion. However hard we tried, we couldn't get the same steepness of bounce. The length we bowled just didn't react in the same way. On top of that we bowled too many 'four balls'. Our minimum requirement was three down by the close. Instead, the Windies are past the 100 mark and Lara is threatening. Small wonder Ladbrokes are giving match odds of 9/1 on the tourists. I got Hooper caught down the leg-side but, after a day like this, it's a small consolation. It's as bad a day as I've experienced on a cricket field. It's very disappointing to go from such high hopes to the depths like this. I am seriously hacked off. No one's throwing the towel in and we're going to keep fighting, but the England dressing room is seriously unhappy about facing one of the greatest fast-bowling attacks in the world on a pitch like this. We really feel it's an unfair contest.

FRIDAY 8 JULY   EDGBASTON

West Indies 300   England 59/3

Not a great day, and a pretty upsetting evening. Robin Smith was abused and then threatened in a pub tonight. A bloke – and a pretty big one, I have to confess – was getting stuck in about our perform-ance and followed Robin into the toilets where he decided verbal abuse was not enough. At this point, he pulled out his front teeth, mentioned something about practising martial arts for ten years, told Robin, 'You're a disgrace – all of you' and suggested that if the Judge wanted to shut him up, now was the time to try. You'd have to be taking your life in your hands to challenge the Judge – he's one of the hardest and strongest blokes I've ever come across. But the day didn't need an 'England cricketer in pub brawl' finish, so Robin bit his lip and walked back out into the saloon bar. After a bad day in the field, some people think you should lock yourself away in shame.

Often that's what I do. But other times you need to go out, have a few drinks and try to put the bad experience behind you. Dwelling on the situation can be counter-productive. Players don't need this sort of abuse. I tend to think that anyone who has a go at me is jealous. I just say, 'I'm sorry you feel like that.' It's their problem, not mine. The Judge was fairly tense when he came back to the bar, concerned that turning the other cheek might be construed as a sign of weakness. The man has a lot of pride. I knew the best strategy was to leave the pub before the eye-balling got too intense. I was worried when the Judge said he wanted a final word with the bloke, but he kept himself in check just long enough to tell him, 'I think you've got the wrong attitude,' before we left. Of all the blokes to have a go at about commitment and courage, the Judge is the last person who deserves it. The bloke's a hero and he's proved it time and time again – no one has stood up more bravely against the fierce West Indies' fast bowling. Another reason that the Judge should have been spared this attack is that he's just about our last hope of extending the tourists in this Test.

We slowly grafted our way back into the match, but the Windies grabbed three quick wickets to put us back on the ropes. The Edgbaston wicket was certainly the centre of attention of this morning's papers, with a good old-fashioned row brewing between our chairman and the groundsman. I'm not party to the instructions given to groundsmen about what sort of Test wickets to prepare, but I can't believe one that suits the West Indies as much as this does was the order. Steve Rouse reckons Illy got what he ordered.

We needed quick wickets and got off to a great start when I had Lara LBW to the third ball of the morning as he tried to flick a straight one to leg. I got rid of Adams and Campbell before Gussie dismissed Arthurton. At that stage the Windies were only 24 in front, but Richie Richardson played a great captain's innings by curbing his attacking instinct to take the tourists to exactly 300. He was the last man out, although Athers had given him a life at slip off me during his seventh-wicket partnership with Bishop. That left us with 17 overs to bat and with this sort of wicket and the West Indies' fast bowlers, most people's minds went back to Trinidad when England had to survive 15 overs. That time England finished the day in tatters on 40/8. There was one big difference this time. Curtly Ambrose is out of action for the rest of the Test with his groin strain. But the Windies had already proved in the first innings that they didn't particularly need him on this track. And so it proved. Walsh and Bishop had us 26/3 with Athers, Hick and Thorpe gone. It's even more serious than it sounds because two of our three remaining specialist batsmen – Stewie and Jason – have broken fingers. Judgey is 33 not out and his partner at the wicket is me. I never thought I'd come in at No. 5 for England. With me holding the fort, you can judge how serious the injury crisis and situation is for England.

For some reason I was the man hauled in to meet the press afterwards. It was a totally different audience from my moment of glory at Lord's. I've already decided that I am never going to go into a press conference with a negative attitude. Maybe declaring, 'We will win' was rather going over the top. Most of the questions hinged on 'when' England are going to lose, rather than 'if'. I suppose that's fair enough. The main thrust was – can we prevent England losing in three days in a home Test for the first time since 1966? Of course the situation looks absolutely hopeless. But that doesn't mean you throw your hands up and surrender. Sport, and especially cricket, is littered with remarkable escapes. But that said, I'd much rather be in the West Indies' position than ours. It was because Judge and I were batting together that we decided to continue our partnership into the evening. Another reason for going out was that I didn't fancy sitting down. Bishop hit me on the backside and it hurts like hell. I won't be sleeping on my back tonight.

SATURDAY 8 JULY   EDGBASTON

England 89
England lost by an innings and 64 runs
Man of the Match: Sherwin Campbell

What a turnaround from Lord's! The crowd would have crowned us that day. This lunch-time I thought we were going to get lynched. I've never seen a cricket crowd so hostile. I knew not every Test match was going to be like Lord's, but I didn't expect to crash to the bottom so quickly. I've seen pictures round the world of home fans taking it out on their side over the years, but I never thought it would happen in England. At least all the ill-feeling and hostility was only translated into harsh words and chanting – there was no damage to players or property, although I gather the chairman did require a couple of security guards as he walked from the pavilion to the press conference. We weren't sure who he was protecting himself from – the mass or the media. I understand the disappointment of the fans. After the emotion of Lord's – not only winning, but getting back into the series – there was a great buzz around

Edgbaston on Thursday morning. With just one delivery, all that disappeared. The players knew sooner than anyone that we shouldn't be playing the Windies on this sort of track.

This morning wasn't great. We lasted just 78 minutes. I set things off by edging the ball to third slip in Walsh's first over. Both Peter Martin and Jason went for ducks and 61/3 became 63/6. Goughie gave some support to Judgey, but 88/6 became 89/9. That was it, because Stewie wasn't able to bat. The dressing room resembled a battlefield. Richard Illingworth, Stewie and Jason will probably miss the next Test with their broken hands, while the Judge was black and blue. I would have liked the loud-mouth from last night to have spent a couple of minutes in the dressing room with the Judge today. Whether the Windies' bowling had been intimidatory, I don't know. It was difficult to be anything else on this pitch. Certainly, many of the deliveries appeared to be aimed at the Judge's body. The sight through the window was just as incredible. The field was littered with thousands of spectators having their lunch. You might have thought it was a throwback to the days of the Eton–Harrow match at Lord's if it weren't for the hostile mood emanating from the outfield. I expect more from the true England supporter. Both Athers and the chairman attacked the wicket, and I can't add anything to their criticism. It was not the sort of pitch to play the West Indies on. We played into their hands.

The one compensation of a three-day defeat is normally a couple of days off. Not in England! We hadn't got back to the pavilion before the phones started ringing. Suddenly, England's cricketers were heading off round the country to play in Sunday League matches. To be fair, it was me who rang Kim and said I'd like to play at Maidstone. I haven't had much of a bowl since Lord's. Others had less choice as once again the counties called the tune. It took me three hours to drive to Kent and I went straight to the ground. The Derbyshire lads held a barbecue outside the pavilion after play, and I had a chat with Peter Willey, now one of our top umpires. 'That was an interesting wicket to play your second Test on!' I couldn't argue with that.

SUNDAY 9 JULY   MOTE PARK, MAIDSTONE

AXA Equity & Law   Kent 253/7   *Derbyshire 249/7*
Derbyshire (0 pts) lost by 4 runs

The Sunday papers made great reading this morning. While some of our complaints about the pitch have been accepted, England's performance has been generally registered as a fairly gutless one. I

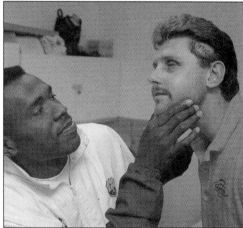

Batting was certainly no fun on the
pitch from hell at Edgbaston.
Amazingly, having survived the
attentions of Ian Bishop (*left*) during
the Third Test, Robin (the Judge)
Smith (*top and above*) had his cheek
fractured in the Fourth. It required an
operation and ended his participation
in the series.

must admit to being slightly confused by it all. My biggest quandary is how a whole nation can be behind us on Thursday morning and three days later we're being hung out to dry. I'll just have to get used to it, I suppose. No relief today as I found myself on the receiving end of the fastest-ever Sunday League century. Mark Ealham came to the wicket with Kent 105/5 and only 14 overs left. It took him just 44 balls, including nine fours and nine sixes, to reach his ton. Everyone's figures took a battering, mine included. Chris Adams wasn't happy either. He dropped Ealham three times around the 50-mark. My drive south looked even more of a waste of petrol when I top-edged Martin McGague to third man where Graham Cowdrey took a great catch right at the start of our reply. But my opening partner Grizzly made amends for his three drops with an even-timed 79. We kept in the hunt to the very end, needing six off the last ball, but Karl Krikken could only scramble a single. On yet another Sunday-driver long trek home, I reflected on what tomorrow will bring. In my case, it's presenting a cheque for around £21 million to the latest winner of the National Lottery. One thing is certain. He's had a much better weekend than me!

TUESDAY 12 JULY   HOVE, SUSSEX

NatWest Trophy Second Round   Sussex 222/8   *Derbyshire 225/2*
Derbyshire won by 8 wickets   Man of the Match: Chris Adams

Back on the winning trail – Derbyshire and me. Such has been our decline that an early exit from the NatWest was the last thing we needed. It's our final chance to scramble something out of the season. In the end it was a comfortable win.

It's funny how you miss out on some grounds on the county circuit. This was only my second game at Hove; the other was a second-team match five years ago. The wicket was well-worn and far better suited to the spinner. We dragged it back in the middle of the Sussex innings. Jamie Hall batted 50 overs for his 70 and the Sussex total looked a good 30 or 40 runs short of the mark. I bowled a lot of rubbish early on and couldn't get it right, but finished with 4/50, still the most expensive of the Derbyshire bowlers. That was the end of my efforts for the day and I put my feet up as Grizzly steered us home with an unbeaten century and over six overs to spare. I didn't hang around and was back in Derby just after nine o'clock. It was my fourth long drive in four days – from Birmingham to Maidstone,

Maidstone to Derby, Derby to Brighton on Monday (that was a nightmare because there had been an accident on the M1, so we went down the M40) and now Brighton to Derby. I could have gone from Maidstone to Hove on Monday, but that would have meant missing out on seeing Jane and Gregory for another two days. Now I'll be at home for about a fortnight, thank goodness.

SUNDAY 16 JULY   DERBY

AXA Equity & Law   *Sussex 198   Derbyshire 1/2*
Match abandoned. Derbyshire 2pts

A typical Derby day – overcast conditions followed by a downpour. I look around the County Ground some days in bad weather. There's nothing special about the facilities or the dressing room. It can be freezing out there when the wind blows. Yet I just love the atmosphere of the place. I really enjoy playing there. It's home for me and I can't imagine ever playing anywhere else.

I'm sure Ed Giddins isn't thinking too fondly of the place tonight. He was all set for a hat-trick when the heavens opened. The first ball of our reply was a wide, the next bowled me off my pads and Ed's third trapped Adrian Rollins LBW. But Darryl Cullinan never made it out of the pavilion as the storm started and we knew almost immediately that was the end of the day's entertainment.

The fuss of about the Edgbaston pitch shows no signs of abating. It always amazes me how many thousands of words are written about cricket matters. You'd assume there must come a time when the talking stops. Not in cricket. The arguments rage on about Bodyline and, if we follow that rule of thumb, ball-tampering will be an issue until about the year 2050. Another cricket issue has been in the papers this week and it involves two of my bowling mates at Derby. Devon and Daffy have decided to sue over an article in *Wisden Cricket Monthly*, 'Is it in the blood?' I didn't take too much notice of it, but I gather it claimed black and Asian players could never be fully committed to England. I think our boys have got a case. No England team this weekend. With the Benson & Hedges final, there's an extra week between the third and fourth Tests. Reports suggest that none of our Edgbaston broken-bone merchants is going to be fit for Old Trafford.

WEDNESDAY 19 JULY   CHESTERFIELD

Tour Match   Derbyshire 191   Young Australians 171/7

THURSDAY 20 JULY   CHESTERFIELD

Young Australians 234   Derbyshire 290/8

FRIDAY 21 JULY   CHESTERFIELD

Derbyshire 316/8 declared   Young Australians 276/6
Derbyshire lost by 4 wickets

A taste of things to come, perhaps. I've been captain for the past
three days. This was a planned move, as Kim wants to give me
captaincy experience. It's certainly a job I want to do full-time in
the future, but not at the moment. I've too many other things to
concentrate on as I try to establish myself at the top. I was captain
of Staffordshire under-19s and I've led the second team on a few
occasions. Kim's been great. He talks to me, asks my advice and has
let me have my head when he's had to go off.

The Derbyshire team is a long way off full-strength with only three
capped players, and the Aussies have a top line-up with batters like
Ricky Pointing, Stuart Law and Matthew Hayden. I chose to bat on
a flat wicket, but we were soon in trouble at 16/3. Johnny Owen
rescued us with a career-best 65. We bowled well and had the Aussies
in trouble at 107/7, but we couldn't finish them off on the first night.
The Aussies finished with a lead of 48. Tim Tweats batted well. I
like him. He gets stuck in and it was a gutsy knock of 58. He's
unusual in that he doesn't worry about not scoring. Most youngsters
get frustrated if they get bogged down and feel they have to go for
the big shot to make up for lost time. I came in at No. 8 in the
second innings. The youngsters need the experience – not me. They're
not going to learn much if you don't give them a chance. Today, I
set the Aussies 274 to win in 51 overs. That gave both sides a chance.
I didn't mind losing because it gave us an opportunity to see some
of our younger talent under pressure in the field. Martin Love's
century off 99 balls saw the tourists home with five balls to spare
by four wickets. But it was a good contest for most of the day and
I'm sure our lads have learned a lot. We didn't bowl too many four
balls and, although we missed a run-out and a few catches, we put
on a competitive display. I was very pleased with and for them –

especially as they all came into the dressing room disappointed at losing. So was I.

THURSDAY 27 JULY   OLD TRAFFORD, MANCHESTER

Fourth Cornhill Test   *West Indies 216   England 65/2*

I think you can say we've put Edgbaston behind us. The West Indies have been bowled out on a goodish track and we've already made serious inroads into their total. It's no more than a start, but we could not have afforded to stumble today. Actually, not too many of us remain from the Birmingham catastrophe. Our three broken-bones casualties have been joined on the sidelines by Peter Martin and Darren Gough, who both picked up injuries in those Sunday League games they rushed to. Goughie was picked in the squad, but the selectors decided to leave him out. He's got a problem with his foot and, although he was passed fit, the selectors must have thought it was too much of a risk as we're only going in with two seamers. Hickie was the sixth change from the third Test when he was omitted this morning, giving John Crawley another chance. Mike Watkinson made his debut and his spinning partner is one of the old school. John Emburey has been recalled at the age of 42.

Despite the changes and what happened at Edgbaston, the atmosphere has been very positive since we assembled. The feeling is that Birmingham was a one-off and the best way to prove that is to give the Windies a hard time here. Athers told me that he'd bat if he won the toss. I wouldn't have minded that because our selection means I'll be taking the new ball for the first time for my country. That's a great honour, though hardly surprising as we only have two quick bowlers in the side, with Craig White as the all-rounder. At Lord's I was second change, at Edgbaston first change. Now I had the new ball. Opening the bowling hasn't always been my preference, but I've felt more able to take on that responsibility over the past two years. My four A tours certainly helped. Although I was young, I became one of the more experienced bowlers at that level and, as such, had to show the way. Anyway, what's wrong with the new ball – it's harder, it swings and the batsman hasn't yet settled. It's the perfect opportunity to attack straight away.

Gussie and I both ended up with four wickets, but he bowled much better than me, delivering far fewer 'four' balls. I bowled far too short, especially to Lara, who scored 87. Gussie's 4/45 was a top performance against some of the best attacking batsmen in the world on a good wicket. He frustrated them. They don't like to be tied down. It's the best ways of encouraging the West Indies batsmen to take chances.

My first wicket was Carl Hooper. As soon as I let it go, I knew it wasn't a very good ball – short and outside the off-stump. Hooper went for the pull. I thought it was going to clear the leg-side field, but Creepy (John Crawley) made a lot of ground and took a great catch. Creepy received a fair amount of stick for his fitness and fielding during the Ashes tour, but he has worked hard to lose weight and improve, and that catch was the proof of the pudding. The Windies were 94/4 at lunch, with Gussie getting the other three wickets, the final two coming in his last two overs before the break. That turned the contest firmly in our favour. Whenever the opposition decides to bat, more than two wickets in the opening session is a bonus. Gussie would have got his fourth soon after the resumption, but I managed to drop my second catch in Test cricket. Drop isn't really the right word because I never got my hands to the ball. I was fielding in the gully. Arthurton slashed at one and I never picked it up. There was a thud into my chest, quickly followed by an agonising groan from the Old Trafford crowd. It's a noise I'm getting used to. Mike Watkinson came on for his first bowl in Test cricket at the other end and my dismay increased when Arthurton hit him for six. Still, Mike claimed his first Test wicket in his third over and, wonders may never cease, one Dominic Cork was the catcher. My first Test catch. I was fielding at extra cover and I had Arthurton's drive covered all the way, which meant I had enough time to think about dropping it. But I was determined that this one was not going to hit the deck. I felt relief more than anything. That turned to joy when I got Lara out – LBW for 87. It was plumb – it must have been. Dickie Bird was the umpire and always – correctly – comes down on the batsman's side if there's any doubt at all. Lara almost walked. Dickie was in top form today, especially when the sun started reflecting off some nearby greenhouses. Eventually, he took us off for an early tea and no doubt the story of how he came off for 'bright light' in a Test match will join his massive repertoire of anecdotes.

Lara's exit left the Windies 166/6, with all their specialist batsmen gone. I took my total to four with the wickets of Bishop (again) and Kenny Benjamin. Bishop snicked it and it flew to Nick Knight at second slip. The ball bounced up and there was little ceremony as Jack Russell (back for his first Test for 15 months) barged Thorpey out of the way to grab the rebound. I was wondering why our wicket-keeper had been so determined when the loudspeaker announced that it was Jack's 100th dismissal in Test cricket. I didn't realise how hard he'd hit Thorpey until I saw the highlights tonight. Thorpey was knocked off his feet!

The West Indies tail wagged a bit to take them past 200, but we'd done well to bowl them out in 60 overs on a pitch like this. Once again our batsmen were going to face some torrid overs late in the day. They stuck to the task well, although it was bitter disappointment to lose John Crawley in the final over. Nick Knight did well in his first Test knock. His tally of 16 runs might not look much, but he batted with a lot of guts through 17 overs and was unlucky to drag a ball from Walsh on to his stumps. Creepy was not playing a shot when the same bowler rattled his stumps in the final over. Those dismissals always look bad. The popular cry is, 'How can he not have known the ball was going to hit his stumps?' Well, let's give us bowlers a bit of credit here. Maybe you come in from a bit wider. Maybe you change the angle of delivery. Maybe you get the ball to swing in instead of out. And, at that pace and in that environment, there's minimal margin for error. But Creepy's misfortune did not spoil a solid, professional performance, especially taken in the context of Edgbaston. No one was thinking that the job was even a quarter done. We all know the first session tomorrow is now the crucial one. We've got to make the Windies work hard for every single wicket. After play, I went to raise a glass of champagne to toast our sponsors, Cornhill. This is the 100th England Test match they have sponsored going back to 1978.

If you're wondering why I've written so much about the day's play, it's because of the heat. The hotel is like a sweat box and sleeping is almost impossible, even with the windows wide open. That means the diary is likely to get a comprehensive report of this fourth Cornhill Test.

FRIDAY 28 JULY   OLD TRAFFORD
England 347/7

A great batting day for England. Hopefully, there's even more to come. We'd love a lead approaching 200. I can't claim too much of the credit as all I've done today is face two balls from Arthurton before we came off for bad light. Old Trafford, like Hove, is not a ground that I've played on much. I played for the England under-19s against New Zealand here in 1988. Yet, although I've appeared in the odd Texaco and Sunday League game, this Test is my first first-class game on this ground.

With only two wickets down, it was unlikely I'd be required for duty before lunch. But, with the Windies desperately charging in to retrieve the situation, you keep a careful eye on the first few overs. Once there are no early mishaps, you can relax a bit and that's what happened today. I watched a bit from the balcony, read the papers and lay on the physio's couch. Like most grounds, Old Trafford has a gym, but I never work out seriously during a match. The serious fitness work should be done beforehand. Anyway, the press would have a field day if you picked up an injury or strain in the pavilion.

The first session went England's way. Athers was the only casualty. He'd already been dropped by Lara at slip before a ball from Ambrose brushed his glove. Walsh, as he'd done in Jamaica last year, gave Athers a real working-over. But our skipper loves challenges like that. One ball thudded in just above his heart. It must have hurt. I felt it on the balcony. But one of Athers' strengths is that he doesn't allow outside factors, even his own well-being, to affect his batting judgement. The next ball was played purely on merit, a clear indication to Walsh and the whole of Old Trafford that he was not going to win this particular battle of wills. England's lunch-time score was 168/3. You've got to be pleased any time more than 100 runs are scored in a session against that pace of attack for the loss of only one wicket. That's how you've got to play the West Indies – a session at a time. Time and time again, they've been outplayed and struggling for eight or nine sessions, then exploded in the next session and turned the game their way. That's happened to England quite a few times. Even with Curtly injured, the Windies have such a good attack that you can never relax, never switch off until you've taken the 20th wicket. Those fears are always at the back of my mind. They should be every game, but it seems to more relevant with the West Indies.

We repeated our morning's achievement after lunch. Another 100 runs in the afternoon session for the loss of just one more wicket – Robin Smith. There was a difference this time. Now we were in front – by over 50 runs with just four wickets down. It was an opportunity we couldn't miss out on. Robin was actually a bit unlucky, as the players came off for bad light the next ball. I don't know why, but umpires always seem to start an over when there's a problem with light. Then, as sure as Christmas, the batting side either loses a wicket or the team comes off after a couple of deliveries. Whenever that happens, the batsman who's been dismissed inevitably feels short-changed. There was great excitement in the dressing room when Thorpey hit four fours in an over from Benjamin. The first was a cracking cover drive, followed by a pull, then a straight drive and finally a mid-wicket flick. Runs are precious against these boys – 16 (all boundaries) in an over is a feast. Thorpey was denied his century when Bishop angled one across him and he was caught behind for 94. Thorpey was the star performer today, but everyone chipped in. It was a great team effort. By the close we'd scored nearly 300 runs in the day for the loss of five wickets. It was a great grafting day, with Thorpey's knock the highlight. We didn't need flashy 50s. We needed to bat all day and frustrate the tourists. And that's exactly what we did.

Jane turned up this evening. My mum and dad were here for the first two days. Jane left Gregory with them when they went back to Stoke. I had planned to take her out tonight, but as I'm batting tomorrow that will have to wait. Instead, it was room service in our personal sauna. We're just not geared for the heat in this country. It's impossible to get cool.

SATURDAY 29 JULY   OLD TRAFFORD
England 437   West Indies 159/3

My first Test 50. And a controversial one at that. Trust me! I'm involved in a stump-tampering incident that shows I'm riding my luck at the moment. How did it happen? I hit an all-run four in the first over of the morning. I kept a careful eye on Bishop as he stopped the ball just inside the ropes. There's nothing worse than being run out through carelessness. But I had time to jog the final run, especially as he was throwing to the nearer bowler's end. The Windies keeper Junior Murray, who'd come up to the stumps, had turned and was walking back to his spot. That was when I noticed something odd. There was a bail on the ground. I assumed Junior had accidentally knocked it off when he'd rushed up while we were running. I walked round the wicket, picked the bail up and put it back. Umpire Cyril Mitchley came over to make sure I'd put it back straight. That was the beginning and end of it as far as I was concerned. It was only when everyone was back in their positions and getting ready for the next delivery that Richie shouted 'Howzat'. Dickie looked at Cyril, who said 'Not out'. I thought the West Indies were trying to pull a fast one. I just laughed it off and I believe Cyril said something about the wind. At the time, he, like me, simply didn't know how the bail came off. During the next over, when I was standing at the non-striker's end, Cyril asked me, 'You didn't tread on your stumps, did you?' I told him 'no', although I was beginning to wonder. I went back over the shot. No. I couldn't have.

About four overs later, Cyril and I had another chat. 'You did, you know,' he told me after hearing the news on his two-way radio with the third umpire. 'I'm sorry. I genuinely didn't know,' I told him. I was gutted. I wasn't trying to stuff anyone and didn't want to earn that sort of reputation so early on in my Test career. Cyril kindly added, 'It's my fault. I should have called for the third umpire.' He was relieved afterwards to discover even that would not have resolved the situation. I would still have been given 'not out'. The BBC pictures which the third umpire, Chris Balderstone, was watching did not show the incident, though there was a noise of the wickets being broken. The Sky TV cameras, who were not broadcasting live, did capture my carelessness. Had Balderstone seen those, he had the authority to communicate that news to Cyril. As usual, it was those out in the middle of the action – the players – who were the last to know. They found out when one of the West Indies fielders went off and came back with the news.

The Windies, desperate for wickets, weren't happy. Their coach Andy Roberts had a word with the ICC referee John Reid. During the morning session I also apologised to Dickie Bird. It was a genuine error. But I got no stick from the West Indies' fielders, even when the word was out. It was a bit of luck and I had to ride it for all it was worth. I tried to forget it and concentrate on my job, although on occasions like that you tend to think it's going to be one of your good days. And I've had a few of those recently. I'm fast coming to the conclusion that, if this is going to be my year, I'm going to make as much impact as possible. There are bound to be hard times in the years ahead, so I'm going to take my chances while they're here. I certainly felt confident batting today, not just because it wasn't the Edgbaston strip. I had time to duck bouncers, dig out the yorkers and punish the bad balls. Batting's such a pleasure on days like this. I was also determined not to go the way of Lord's and Edgbaston, where I gave my wicket away with rash shots. My 50 came up when Bishop bowled me one outside the off-stump and I steered it to third man for the single. I don't think it was a favour to a former Derbyshire colleague. I felt great as I ran for the single. All the lads were on the balcony standing and clapping as I took off my helmet and raised my bat to the heavens. I can't believe it. It seems that something special happens to me every day at the moment. Yet it was only just over a month ago that I was beginning to despair of ever playing Test cricket.

We went beyond lunch, eventually finishing up with a lead of 221. I was undefeated on 56 and it was another special moment coming off with all the members in the Old Trafford pavilion on their feet. They used to say about Ian Botham, 'Who writes your scripts?' That magic pen seems to be dictating my career at the moment. But England have enjoyed healthy leads against the West Indies before only to be struck down by whirlwind Caribbean batting or bowling – sometimes both. This match is a long way from over. We've got three out and the Windies are still 62 runs behind. We would probably have settled for that at the start. But Richie and Lara are at the crease. Lara, especially, looks in awesome form. I must admit I'm rather disappointed he's still there because I thought I had him caught behind. Cyril didn't. It's always a blow when you think you've got a batsman of his standing and class out, although I could hardly complain after the way my luck's been going. Hooper has a busted finger, so Arthurton opened with Campbell. Their batting has looked much more positive and determined second time around. There was one moment of madness when Arthurton was run out – a complete waste. Then Mike Watkinson dismissed Campbell and Adams in successive overs. Adams, especially, can be difficult to remove. At 93/3, we had high hopes of another breakthrough. But it wasn't to be. Now, with those two stroke-makers at the wicket, we're going to have to be on our guard tomorrow. Another quiet night. Honest. These Test matches are emotionally and physically draining.

Sunday 30 July Old Trafford

West Indies 314   England 94/4
England won by 6 wickets   Man of the Match: Dominic Cork

What a day – for England and me. If you were writing a fictional account of a cricketer's year like this, nobody would believe it. When my bubble does finally burst, there's going to be an enormous explosion.

How could things get better – even better than a second win over the West Indies? I'll tell you. Today, I took the first hat-trick by an Englishman in a Test match for 38 years. Thirty-eight years! Can you believe it! I still can't. And we're back on level terms in the series. That's a phenomenal achievement after Edgbaston. How did my day start? It started absolutely brilliantly. Athers gave me the ball for the first over of the day. I've never regarded that as a practice or warm-up over or as an excuse to be a little wayward or wild. You should have got rid of all the cobwebs in the morning warm-up beforehand. I always try to run in hard straight from the off. After all, the batsman tends to be a little tentative early on and he's not sure whether the wicket is going to play exactly as it did the previous evening. Richie and Lara had both taken singles by the time I ran in to bowl the fourth ball of the day to the West Indies captain. I wasn't happy or hopeful. It was way outside the off-stump. But the man upstairs was smiling on me again. Richie lifted his bat out of the way, but the ball clipped the top of his pads, bounced up on to his bat and fell back on to the wicket. Richie stood there looking bemused. I don't blame him. I was ecstatic. We desperately needed an early breakthrough. However fortuitous this dismissal was, it was the perfect start to our day. With Richie gone and Hooper pushed down the order because of a broken finger, we now had an end to bowl at. The general feeling was relief as much as anything. I could bowl the same delivery to Richie another thousand times and never get him out again. But that was the one that mattered.

Junior Murray was next in. The ball was reverse swinging. I said to Athers, 'Let's have an extra man on the leg-side. We'll go for a catch behind or LBW. He doesn't get a long way forward.' Such bold and well-thought-out plans rarely work. Unless, that is, it's your day. The ball reversed and Junior missed it right in front of his stumps. I knew instantly it was out. And I knew instantly that he would be given out. There could be no doubt. The ground wasn't that full, but the noise was incredible. Now, for just one solitary ball, the match was not important. Everything was focused on me. I was on a hat-trick.

I wasn't hopeful. Normally one of the lesser West Indies batsmen would be coming out to follow Murray. Not this time. It was the injured Hooper. But his entry persuaded me that perhaps fate was on my side. I already had one first-class hat-trick to my name and that was for Derbyshire against Kent in 1994. And guess who was victim number three on that occasion? You're right. One Carl Hooper! Although he's a class act and a great timer of the ball, Hooper has a tendency to walk across his stumps early on. Athers came over and we had a chat. He put a man in at short extra cover. I asked him, 'Do you want me to bounce him or do the same as Murray?' Because we both felt that Hooper doesn't get out of the blocks early on, we decided on the latter course of action. As I walked back, I kept saying to myself, 'Come on. Get it in the right place.'

I've had hat-trick balls before. Too often that final delivery is a half-volley or down the leg-side – which doesn't even give you a chance of taking the wicket. This time I was going to make sure that Hooper had to play the ball – and play it under extreme pressure. The hat-trick ball was the least of his worries. He was the last recognised batsman they had to stay with Lara who was watching all this unfold from the non-striker's end.

It soon became clear that the last thing Hooper wanted to do was play the ball. I bowled a similar delivery and the ball reverse swung again. Hooper looked as if he was trying to leave it, but it was too late to do anything when he saw the ball coming in at him. He was plumb. I knew he was out. But this time I wasn't sure the umpire would give it. Two LBWs in two balls? It doesn't happen, does it? Cyril was going to give this one much more thought and it seemed to take an age before the finger went up. It does happen! He's done it, I thought. No, *I've* done it. I threw my hands in the air and for a split second didn't know what to do. Should I run around the pitch on a lap of honour? Or leap into the air? Instead, I just sank to my knees, basically because they had turned to jelly. Wake me up, somebody. This can't all be happening to me. Judgey came over and lifted me up. Athers was there. All the boys were round me. A hat-trick in Test cricket! I wasn't staggered because it was the first for so many years; I didn't have a clue about when the last one was at the time. I jut knew that it's a rare feat, especially in Test cricket. Later, I learned that mine was the 21st, and the first by an England bowler since Peter Loader's at Headingley in 1957.

My reaction this time was totally different to the dismissals of Richie and Junior. I didn't think Cyril was going to raise his finger, but when he did, I was gone, absolutely gone. I was drained, empty. I could feel my body shaking. It was so emotional, I was close to tears. The lads were full of the usual tributes – 'Golden Boy', 'Golden B*ll*cks' and 'Let's bow to the new Messiah'. I was lucky it was the end of the over because I didn't have another delivery in me for a few minutes. As I wandered down to the other end, Lara congratu-lated me. I was really struggling to hold back the tears as I went to backward point. I could see Jane just to the right of the pavilion. Because there weren't that many people there, I'd looked up after getting Richie out and she clapped. She did the same when I looked up after Junior had gone. This time I was just shaking my head when I looked her way. I was thinking, 'I can't have just done that. Come on. Wake up. Get out of your dream.'

It was just as well the ball didn't come near me during that next

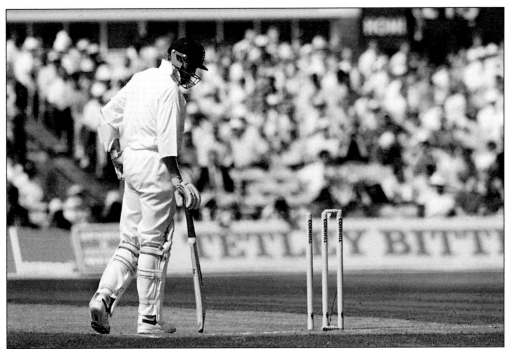

When I first saw the bail on the ground I thought Junior Murray had dislodged it as he rushed up to the wicket. So did Cyril Mitchley; only later with the help of new technology did I realise my lucky escape.

Wickets two and three from the hat-trick. As can be seen, Cyril Mitchley was far quicker giving Junior Murray out LBW than he was Carl Hooper. Hooper must have been doubly annoyed: he'd been part of a hat-trick I'd performed against Kent in 1994.

Surrounded by delighted teammates – none of whom had been alive when Peter Loader took the last English hat-trick in a Test match, in 1957.

over because I was in no state to stop it. I don't even remember much about bowling the next three or four overs. I was in a daze. All I do know is that I bowled rubbish. Nothing was in the right place, especially to Lara, who was refusing to fall under the Cork spell and playing one of the great Test innings. The Windies were almost out for the count. Everything hinged on Lara's survival. I must admit the hat-trick was a distraction and stopped me focusing on what I should have been doing. Now I've had time to reflect, I'm annoyed with myself for losing concentration. The hat-trick may have been the reason I did – but it's not an excuse. I hope I've learned from it. You've got to get rid of your emotions as quickly as possible after the event. You can't ignore them while it's happening. Sport's an emotional business – that's why I enjoy it so much. I would hate to play cricket in a cold, clinical climate. But the hat-trick affected me at the time much more than the seven wickets at Lord's. This was a much more intoxicating 'high'.

I needed a good kick up the arse and got it when I came in to lunch. Peter Lever, never a man to mince his words, brought me down to earth with the loud observation that I'd bowled like a pillock. He was right. It wasn't that I was unaware I was playing into Lara's hands, but I'd felt powerless to do anything about it in the overs that followed the hat-trick. Soon Lara had taken his side beyond an innings defeat and ensured that we had to bat again. He was protecting his tail-end partners superbly and finding the gaps with unnerving and unerring ease. Once the Windies had got in front, we didn't want them to set a target of 50. Once they got to 50, we didn't want a target of three figures. We just managed that. We needed 94 to win. The great man eventually went for 145 when he pulled Gussie, and Nick Knight took a good catch at mid-wicket. Our relief was enormous and understandable. We had just witnessed an innings of the highest quality from one of the masters. It was special not just in itself, but because of the match circumstances. I finished off their innings with a not-too-special delivery that bowled Courtney off his pads.

Against most sides in the world, 94 would be a doddle. Not against this lot. Once again, Trinidad 1994 came sharply into focus. Everyone was praying for a good start. And we got it. Athers and Knightie put on 39 without too much fuss. I started to pack my bag – a fatal mistake and one I'll never repeat. Suddenly, Athers was given run-out on the third umpire. Game on. I thought if I unpacked, everything would be OK. But the damage was done. I even put my whites on. No good. By this time we were 48/4. The situation was even more serious because the Judge was on his way to hospital after being hit in the face by Bishop. It was even money now. We had half the necessary runs – they had half the required wickets. Cometh the hour. Cometh the man. Enter one Robert Charles Russell – known throughout the cricket world as Jack. He's not been happy that the selectors have ignored him for the past year, and saw this as the perfect opportunity to prove a point. So, while Creepy dropped anchor, Jack took the attack to the West Indies.

The England dressing room was fairly fraught place by this stage. Mike Watkinson was sitting down padded up. I was standing. We started counting down in fives. Bishop bowled magnificently and the rest weren't far behind, but Jack kept clubbing them in his inimitable style. When the target got down to under ten, I thought I won't mind going in now. Only when it got to under five did I believe that we would definitely win. Still, I didn't switch off until that winning run.

What a Test match and what a comeback by England. This has been four days of quality cricket. The pressure was immense, even when I was off the field. The cheering and celebrations started at ten to six tonight. This was a better win than Lord's, it was a real team effort. Everyone got stuck in; everyone contributed. The two day and a bit disaster at Edgbaston was a one-off. This proves it. This display shows the real spirit of the England side. It proves that we were strong enough mentally to come back from the Birmingham ordeal. Everyone will remember Ambrose's first ball in that third Test. It will enter cricket folklore. To come from that, and the press reports, and the crowd's hostility, and produce four days of quality cricket is a remarkable achievement. And I've got another Man of the Match award – two in my first three Tests. The important thing is that we're back in this series and I think the West Indies will be worried about the way we've been able to bounce back twice.

Another press conference for me. During it, Illy revealed that he would have picked me last summer if I'd been properly fit. I wish he'd told me at the time. It would have saved a lot of worrying. The only disappointing note came when we learned that the Judge had fractured his cheekbone and will need an operation. He's probably out for the series. That's a big blow. After the match and half a glass of champagne, Jane and I headed for my parents' house in Stoke, where Gregory is. We're staying the night here and will head back for Derby tomorrow. I still can't believe it. Three Tests. Two fantastic wins and one horrendous defeat. Who says Test cricket is boring?

August 1995

Lara Runs – but Athers Defiant

NatWest Trophy Quarter-final
Warwickshire 290/6 Derbyshire 174
Derbyshire lost by 116 runs

Back to reality and Derby! That's our last hope of a trophy gone for this season. Warwickshire certainly showed us why they are cup favourites and the in-form side in the country at the moment. They're a quality side who are tough to beat. Someone always seems to come up with the goods when they're needed most. I wish we had that knack. It's Derbyshire's big failing – and has been ever since I first arrived at the County Ground.

Just a month after Lord's, I'm under the full glare of the media spotlight again. But I'm ready for it this time and not quite so over-whelmed. It's easier for the club, too. Everyone's after another Cork exclusive – what is there new to say? They are pointed firmly in the direction of Jon Holmes's office. Well, nearly everybody. I'll never put myself off limits to our local reporters and radio – they are the ones who support the club and its players through thick and thin. I enjoy radio work. Yesterday afternoon I did a live commentary on Radio Derby, all the more enjoyable because the boys were on top and heading to a big victory over Glamorgan.

There was a much bigger crowd than usual today. In fact, we were packed out. Even though we'd put up extra stands, the spectators spilled over in front of the advertising hoardings. Warwickshire's captain Dermot Reeve decided to bat. That was no surprise. It looked a good track, but we didn't start too badly. Devon got Neil Smith out in the first over and he and Daffy kept it so tight, Warwickshire were 17/1 after ten overs. Daffy was particularly unlucky as he kept beating the edge. I removed Dominic Ostler with my second ball, but 40/2 in the 16th over was about as good as it got for us. It looks like Dermot Reeve will be accepting some more trophies this season. He's one of the most inventive captains around – always trying something new – but, I'm afraid, he's also one of the most annoying. Mind you, he was that way when he was only a player. And I don't just mean because of the nagging way he bats and bowls. Today, I had a typical confrontation with him. I'd had trouble with cramp in my left hamstring and left the field after my spell to have it strapped up. Dermot, who was batting at the time, refused to let us have a 12th man as he felt I was taking liberties. The umpires agreed with Dermot, so I had to rush back with our physio trying to strap me up after every ball. That's Dermot's style. A little later, after I was all strapped up, he said it was OK if I wanted to go off now. Typical Dermot. And typical me. I told him to stuff it. If that's the way he wants to play it, that's fine with me. There will come a day when he wants something. And, if I'm in a position to stop him getting it, I'll remind him of today.

Not that I spent too much time worrying about Dermot. We were getting a pasting – with over 80 runs coming in the final ten overs. It wasn't an impossible target, but we had to get a good start. Warwickshire have a great attack with four seamers, five if you count Roger Twose, plus two spinners. Unfortunately, 29/3 left us with a mountain to climb. Tim Munton bowled brilliantly at the start, giving absolutely nothing away as his figures of 12-6-13-1 show. He's such a consistent bowler. I'm sure he could have had more success at international level, but he's been very unlucky to get injured at the wrong time. I came in with a runner, Chris Adams, and we already needed something like eight an over by then. You always dream of scoring a hundred and pulling a cup tie like this out of the bag. But you know deep down that it's going to be very hard. You've got to play a lot of big shots, and off bowlers like Allan Donald. You can't see him off, then attack the others. The runs have got to come all the time. I hit Donald over his head, tried to do the same again and was caught at long-off. We lost by over 100 runs in the end.

All we can do now is try to get as far up the Sunday League table as possible and as far away from the bottom of the championship. I hate it when teams and players switch off because their season is finished. It's not. I still find it hard when cricketers say they can't get motivated when there's no trophy at stake. Their pride is at stake.

Their professional pride. You are a professional cricketer. There's always your job and career to play for. Even if Test cricket isn't your aim, every championship game should be a winning one. But you can see more and more players switch off as the season progresses. I'm afraid that's because counties have too many on the staff, too many cricketers who will never reach the standard. Others think that the job's done once they get on a county staff. But it's only the first step. You've got to keep working harder, got to keep improving. Otherwise, it's a waste of time. Too many get carried away by the sponsored car, the free accommodation and meal money. They let the county take responsibility for their career and their life. I like to be in control of my destiny.

We've certainly got time to reflect on this season's failure as we've now got a week off. When I was just playing county cricket, I used to find these breaks annoying. Now I'm really looking forward to the rest.

Thursday 10 August   Trent Bridge

Fifth Cornhill Test   England 227/4

A solid start that we can build on. I think the West Indies know they are in a contest now. There's a great atmosphere in the team. I am more determined than ever that we'll win this series. It's funny how little things can add to that desire. I walked out to the wicket yesterday while Geoffrey Boycott was there. He doesn't take too kindly to remarks like, 'I could get you out with an orange.' His stock answer is, 'How many 100s did you get?' Lara was also in the vicinity. Boycs spoke to him: 'Don't let that little twat get you out. With his pace, he'll never get you going back. Get a hundred against him.' I said nothing and just walked off. He wasn't joking. I don't think he's got a sense of humour anyway. I was shocked and very surprised. I was also fuming. This was the man who's supposed to have battled for England over the years. Now he was siding with the opposition. It just confirmed much about what I'd heard about 'Sir' Geoffrey.

I found it sad, because I'd had a good build-up to the Test in my week off. It was great spending time with Jane and Gregory. On Thursday and Friday, I netted with Derbyshire. On Saturday I went down to watch my brother Simon open for Betley. Simon's 31 and a good club cricketer. He might have made it as a professional foot-baller and was offered terms by Crewe Alexandra. But, at 26, he thought it was a bit late and turned it down. Jonathan, my other brother, is two years younger. He might have gone far as a cricketer, but suffered a bad leg injury playing soccer seven years ago. They both played semi-pro with Nantwich Town. On Sunday, we had a barbecue to celebrate my 24th birthday the following day. 'Twenty-four and there's so much more,' so the Neil Young song goes. I certainly hope so.

There were several BBC vans outside my house on Monday as I did a live link with *Midlands Today* from my back garden to discuss the hat-trick and England's prospects for the next Test. I didn't join the side until Tuesday evening, and I spent the afternoon at Kim Barnett's wedding – I'd asked the chairman if I could go while we were at Old Trafford. So I drove to Trent Bridge, dumped my kit and headed for the Church in Breadsall. Kim's best man was our chairman, Mike Horton. I could have stayed overnight, but I didn't want it to look as if I was getting too big for my boots, taking liberties and having days off. We had stayed at the Royal Hotel in the centre of Nottingham for the Texaco match, but you can't open the windows there. After such a hot summer, the chairman decided to move us out of town, so I headed for the East Midlands Hotel, just off the M1.

Our nets session yesterday was dominated by worries about Athers' fitness. Jack Russell, just one Test back after 15 months in the wilderness, was the man nominated to take over. Graeme Hick was back because of Judgey's injury. We aren't likely to see him again this summer. The papers were full of reports of Hick confronting Illy over his dropping at Old Trafford, but if that happened I didn't hear about it. Richard Illingworth returned for Embers, and Alan Wells and Mark Ilott were not required for duty. Neither was Yorkshire's David Byas who was called up because of Athers' problems. We're in confident mood – and not just because the Windies have lost Adams, Ambrose and Hooper through injury. We are really looking to win it from here after coming back twice. I think Richie's side have worked out that we're not going to lie down and be walked over. At the team dinner last night we all felt that one last push could settle the series here. The reports for the Oval are already that it won't be as quick as usual.

We knew that 'Uncle Ron' Allsop wouldn't be producing a quick bouncy wicket here. But batting was still tough and today saw a great effort by Athers, who turned up fit and healthy, and debutant Nick Knight. The pair were still together at tea. During that break I was presented with the hat-trick ball on TV by Tony Lewis. Bob

Taylor had got hold of it at Old Trafford and, as it was Cornhill's 100th Test, he was asked if they could mount it for me with a little commemorative plaque on the ball. A great idea, I thought.

Athers eventually scored the first England Test century of the summer before being run out. Illy batted out the final 40 minutes as nightwatchman. Unfortunately, he got hit on the finger. It's broken and I don't think he'll be able to bat tomorrow. I had a chat with my agent Jon Holmes in the Cornhill tent. Nottingham is where he's based. Gary Lineker was there as well. But it's another of Jon's clients, Will Carling, who's grabbing all the headlines this week over his friendship with the Princess of Wales. I can't imagine what he's going through. I find it bad enough being chased around after doing well on the cricket field. It must be unbearable when the world's invading your private life. I gather Will's actually left the country. I don't blame him.

Friday 11 August   Trent Bridge

England 440   West Indies 25/0

A repeat of our battling batting performance in the Old Trafford Test with everyone chipping in. At one stage, it looked as if we might last through until tomorrow. But 440/7 became 440 all out. Gussie went first ball and Illy was unable to bat after I was caught behind. That left Hickie undefeated on 118 – his first century against the West Indies. Hickie's taken a lot of stick about his ability to face fast bowling, but I believe he's now worked out a technique that works for him. I came to the wicket when he had scored 72 and, as well as making sure we got to 400, I wanted to be there when he reached three figures. He was so in control when I got out to the middle. Some of his shots were pure timing. It's actually embarrassing when you're bludgeoning away and there's a batting genius up the other end. I think it's becoming increasingly obvious that No. five is the right spot for Hickie. He appears to have a lot more confidence and a lot more time. I don't know if he will ever settle all the arguments. As far as I'm concerned, anyone who's scored the amount of first-class runs he has so quickly, must have talent. Whoever you are, that step up from first-class cricket to Test cricket is enormous. Until you do it, you can't appreciate how big the jump is. It's hard to adapt and it takes some longer than others. I've had three great Tests, but I'd be a mug if I believed I'd cracked it. Hickie was probably ready to play Test cricket in 1988, but had to fulfil a seven-year qualification to play for England. That can't have been easy with his ability. And the expectations when he did appear were enormous. I remember everyone expecting miracles and at least 1,000 Test runs in his first summer four years ago. By the end of that West Indies series, Hickie had been dropped. He was marked out as a great Test player before he had played for England. No one is guaranteed graduation before the exam. Now I believe that England will reap the benefits of their loyalty to him over the next six to eight years. He has so many powerful shots in his repertoire and can wipe out any attack in the world.

I wasn't the only one who helped him to the century. Hickie put on 84 with Jack, 57 with Winker and then 60 with me. The Windies weren't used to finding a sting in the England tail. We had 19 overs at them, but couldn't make a breakthrough.

SATURDAY 12 AUGUST   TRENT BRIDGE

West Indies 334/5

Is this man Lara ever going to fail? I didn't think it was possible, but he batted even better here than at Old Trafford. Poor Gussie. Lara cut him three times in a row. The third man was moved wide, then fine in an effort to follow the ball. Unfortunately, he never got near it as Lara stroked the ball to the boundary with inch-perfect precision. Lara's one of those players you can tell means business from the very first ball. If it's there to be hit, it will disappear. I still think we bowled too many balls in his favour. He likes to pull and cut. I've been as guilty as anyone – probably more so. You've got to try to cramp his style. But even good balls go for four. We employed a sweeper, but he was still able to pick the ones and the twos, as well as piercing the fielders on the boundary. Lara scored over a century in boundaries today. I fancied getting him out when he came in. And I did. Unfortunately, he had 145 to his name before he unluckily gloved a ball down the leg-side to Jack. He'd been scoring so freely that we had to employ a bit of leg-side theory to quieten him down. It was a bit negative, but we decided that it was the only way to stop him. He got frustrated and played a rash shot for my only success of the day. However late in the day it was, we were glad to see the back of him. At one stage, with Lara and Richie firing and the Windies 273/2, they looked intent on a reasonable lead. By the close, both sides are hopeful of a first innings lead.

Sunday 13 August

West Indies 417   England 111/2

We were reminded today that it's not only when the West Indies are bowling that life is dangerous. Nick Knight received a sickening blow to the head when fielding close in to Kenny Benjamin. I just remember the silence of the crowd and the sight of him going down. We were all happy to see him moving, but he was completely out of it by the time I reached him. It was a hell of a crack. Benjamin had given it a real thump, trying to smash it over extra cover. Nick was at silly point and not wearing a helmet. I really feared the worst as Nick turned away and the ball smashed into the side of his head. Getting hit is an occupational hazard in this business, but you're taking a real chance being in that close without a helmet. Judgey discovered how dangerous life can be without a helmet at Old Trafford when he had his cheekbone broken. It might not have looked like it, but I believe that Nick was lucky today. I've only been hit once. That was in 1992 at the Oval. Martin Bicknell was the bowler. I turned away and the ball missed my helmet and hit my head. I felt dizzy, but carried on batting. I remember looking at the Oval scoreboard and the numbers being all mixed up. I went to bed dizzy, woke up dizzy and had a week off.

After Nick was taken off to hospital, I was left wondering about two things. Would he be able to bat? And was it going to cause lasting damage? Not just physically, but mentally. A lot of bat-pad fielders are pretty good until they've been hit. Afterwards, they are never quite the same. Nick is a brilliant close fielder. I hope he doesn't lose it.

We took half the day to get rid of the last five West Indies wickets, but they only scored 83 runs in three hours, so we led by 23. I got Dhanraj out with a good bumper that he could only fend off to Nick at second slip. But my final bowling figures were 2/110, my second successive century with the ball for England. Our best bowler was Richard Illingworth, all the more impressive because of his broken finger. It was his right hand, but he still had to field with it. One ball was driven straight back at him just after he started bowling, and he didn't flinch. That's typical of the uncompromising attitude of this side. Creepy opened with Athers because Nick was in hospital, but was bowled without offering a shot again. He was very annoyed with himself. Hickie also went cheaply, but Athers and Thorpey saw us safely through to the close.

It's going to be odds on a draw, but we need a good first session tomorrow just to be sure.

MONDAY 14 AUGUST   TRENT BRIDGE

England 269/9 declared   West Indies 42/2
Fifth Cornhill Test drawn
Man of the Match: Kenny Benjamin

A comfortable draw in the end on paper, but we had a few nervous moments today. We lost Athers and Craig White early before the Windies went up for an LBW shout against Thorpey. I don't think anyone in the dressing room would have been surprised if Cyril Mitchley had raised his finger. Jack and Nick, who had got off his sick bed, soon followed. We were starting to count down the overs. I didn't stay long. I smacked Ambrose straight back to the boundary. Then, attempting to play confidently, I tried to force one from Kenny Benjamin off the back foot. I was caught by the wicket-keeper, an exact repeat of my first-innings dismissal here. Benjamin then claimed Gussie's wicket for ten in the match and we were in strife at 189/9. We needed Illy to stay with Mike 'Winker' Watkinson for at least half an hour. That looked to have gone out of the window when Winker chipped a simple chance to Sherwin Campbell at mid-wicket. The West Indies would have needed 213 to win in about 50 overs at that stage. I was just starting to work out the odds of those calculations when there was a groan from the crowd. Campbell, somehow, had let the ball evade his grasp and hit the ground. Instant relief. You could sense the tourists knew they had let a golden chance slip through Campbell's fingers. Our last pair never gave them another sniff and were still there an hour and a half later. Winker was on 82 and deserved his century, but Athers had to declare. The target and scoring rate had soared dramatically. The Windies now needed 293 to win in 20 overs. Even at 250, I hadn't felt safe. Not with Lara around and in this form. Go on, go on. Don't just make the game dead. Kill it stone dead! It was a tense day in the dressing room, but there were some moments of great hilarity with impersonator Rory Bremner around. He was taking off our chairman. Rory kept asking Ray to say 'moisture' over and over again, as he tried to get it right. They say that imitation is the greatest form of flattery. And I think Illy was flattered.

I took one of the two wickets to fall today. There was no chance of a result, but you don't just go through the motions. This is a Test

After being dropped for Old Trafford, Hicky gave the selectors the best possible riposte at Trent Bridge. I was pleased to be on hand to congratulate him on his century.

Sadly I was also on hand as Brian Lara matched him at Nottingham.

Our batting heroes from Trent Bridge. On the last day of the Fifth Test, Richard Illingworth (*left*) and Mike Watkinson (*below*) came together with 189/9 and the West Indies having high hopes of winning the Test, but they managed to bat the tourists out of the game with an undefeated stand of 82, that showed the side's fighting spirit. Illy's performance was all the more impressive because he'd bowled and batted with a broken finger.

match. Your figures and performance are in the book for ever. I had knocked Campbell off his feet the ball before – it wasn't his day. I've noticed more and more with their batsmen that, if you do something like that, you are almost guaranteed that the next shot is a big one. It's almost a macho thing, as if they've got to keep proving themselves. So I bumped him again. He went for the hook, but only managed to glove it to Jack. Gussie got rid of Lara and it was all called off after 11 overs. All square with one to play. The Test fizzled out in the end, but you can't get a Lord's or an Old Trafford finale every time. My fourth Test – and my first draw. There can't be many cricketers who experience the most common result in international cricket last of the three options. It could have gone against us today, but I felt we could easily have won because we had the better of this contest for the first four days. Without Lara, the West Indies would have struggled and I'm sure we could have forced a win.

One great thing about going home after Trent Bridge is that it's not too far – the nearest of the Test grounds for me. The NatWest semis are tomorrow and that doesn't involve Derbyshire. It'll give me a bit of rest before getting ready for the Oval showdown. I'm convinced we aren't going to lose this series now.

THURSDAY 17 AUGUST   BRISTOL

Derbyshire 336/4 v Gloucestershire

A record day for Kim. He's completed 1,000 runs for the 12th time, equalling Denis Smith's county record. It was Adrian Rollins who provided the backbone of the innings with a career-best 129. It's the best I've seen from him. Adrian is a good long-term prospect – he's prepared to work and has a good temperament. Sometimes being slow is not such a bad thing, especially in our side. We've got too many crash, bang, wallop merchants. What we haven't got enough of are performers who spend time building an innings. Adrian's primary claim to fame in cricket is that he has the biggest feet in the county game – size 15!

FRIDAY 18 AUGUST BRISTOL

Derbyshire 463   Gloucestershire 248/5

Adrian carried on the good work, batting for over nine hours for his double hundred. Yet the innings of the day was Gloucestershire's Andrew Symonds'. He's the English-born Aussie who scored a century for Queensland against Athers' side last winter. At the time, he declared that he had no ambitions to play for the country of his birth. But it seems that he might have changed his mind. There's talk of him making one of England's winter tour sides or even England's World Cup squad. I don't suppose you can blame him for keeping his options open, but I can't imagine playing for a country just because they've asked you. He must feel either English or Australian. Judging by what he said last winter it would seem to be Aussie, and that's the country he should opt for. If he goes against that, I believe he'll regret it at a later date.

The boy can certainly bat. He hit 71 runs out of 93 in only 18 overs. His partner was Mark Alleyne, not normally reduced to a watching brief. Our day finished well with both Symonds and Alleyne departing on their closing score. We still have hopes of making them follow-on. I'm not sure if we'll see Tony Wright again after he got hit on the forearm by Devon. We'd already lost Jack Warner, who was hit in the jaw mis-hooking Gloucestershire's Indian fast bowler Javagai Srinath.

SATURDAY 19 AUGUST BRISTOL

Gloucestershire 351 & 78/4   Derbyshire 104

Another typical Derbyshire day. Kim was ill, so I took over the captaincy. Me against Jack Russell. Great. I tried to bump him with the first ball I bowled to him last night, and ran down the wicket and just stared. Jack's great. He simply stood there. No emotions, just looking at me. But I know that, underneath, he was getting worked up.

I didn't bowl this morning. Daffy turned to his off-breaks. Not bad, either. The ball was turning square. Gloucestershire quickly avoided the follow-on, although I'm not sure if we would have enforced it. Then the old Derbyshire failing. So far in front, we started playing big shots. Once it starts, we seem incapable of stopping. All out for 104. It could have been worse – at one point we were actually

78/9. It was all a bit pathetic. It was Srinath who did most of the damage, finishing with 5/25. I was one of his five victims, padding up. That left us 28/5 and emergency calls were made to Kim back at the hotel. Even he couldn't stop the slide and Gloucestershire were left needing 217 for victory. Our Jack has given us a fighting chance by taking four wickets.

Devon and I dined with the opposing captain at his house tonight. Now I know where he lives and, if he doesn't behave himself, I'll let people know. Jack is paranoid about his privacy, even with his team-mates. It was good to see another side of him with his family.

SUNDAY 20 AUGUST   BRISTOL

AXA Equity & Law   Gloucestershire 138 (38 overs)   Derbyshire 142/2 (37.2)
Derbyshire (4pts) won by 8 wickets

Our sixth Sunday League win of the season, but I still found it an intrusion into what is a very good four-day game. There's been talk of changing the starting day of the championship matches to a Wednesday. I wouldn't argue with that. I don't know of any other country's cricketers who have to stop mid-game and play another. And you have to switch from a four-day to a one-day mode. We bowled well and kept it tight. Grizzly and Kim gave us a good start and I joined Kim for the run-in. Another four points. We've got to try to get as high up the table as possible.

MONDAY 21 AUGUST   BRISTOL

Gloucestershire 217/7
Derbyshire (8pts) lost by 3 wickets

I'm back in charge. Kim returned for the Sunday League game but had a relapse on Sunday night, probably because of his exertions in the heat during the day. Their Jack had the last laugh today as he and Tim Hancock put on 85 for the seventh wicket that took them within two runs of victory. It was our own fault. Hancock was dropped early on and it wasn't the last chance we let slip through our fingers. Tim Tweats hurt his knees missing that first chance and went off. Our 12th man, Paul Aldred, was already on for Kim, so I waved at Jack's, signalling for one of his players to help us out. Gloucestershire's coach Paul Romaines came out and told me one was on his way. For the next half hour, I waved and moaned, but still no sign of the replacement fielder. Eventually, I was told one wasn't coming. 'We don't play games to help the opposition out,' was Jack's explanation. I don't mind friendly rivalry, but I thought this was out of order. Gloucs have been charging up the championship. Jack was worried that one of his young players might take the catch that cost them the victory points – not only for the effect on the team, but also on the player. I was quite annoyed. It was just a case of common courtesy as far as I was concerned. Jack entered the fray – and I mean fray – when I had Andrew Symonds caught at short mid-on. He obviously knew what to expect because I've never seen a batsman with so much protective gear on. He knew how I'd react to his snub. And he was right – I had him dancing to some chin music. I'd asked the umpire about it. Jack was technically within his rights but the umpire agreed that it wasn't the friendliest of gestures from an England colleague. It did little for my state of mind that Jack took his side to the verge of victory, especially as we dropped other chances. The damage had been done by our batting in that second innings. It was crazy.

THURSDAY 24 AUGUST   THE OVAL

Sixth Cornhill Test   *England 233/5 v West Indies*

The prophecies about the Oval wicket have proved correct. It's playing as true as ever, but it's not as quick and bouncy as in recent years. We shouldn't lose from here, but it's going to be hard to bowl the West Indies out twice on this track. Still, you never know what the pressure of a big first innings total can do, and Mr Lara is due for a failure. Alan Wells' Test debut has been a long time coming. Unfortunately, he suffered that worst of fates on any batting debut – a golden duck. Alan had waited 15 seasons for that moment. I felt so sorry for him as he walked back. Getting out first ball is a fact of cricket life. You just pray it doesn't happen on your Test debut in front of a packed Oval crowd. I gather he was given some words of consolation as he crossed the field at the end of the day from Sky TV presenter Charles Colvile. 'I got a first-baller here myself earlier in the season.' There the similarity ends, I think. Alan was caught Campbell, bowled Ambrose. I've found out that Colvile's dismissal was caught Rory Bremner, bowled Bill Wyman, who had a cigarette in his mouth at the time.

Back to serious matters. Our visit to the Oval brought back two previous match-winners, Devon and Phil Tufnell, who spun the Windies to defeat here four years ago, to the Test squad. Tuffers didn't make the final line-up, but Devon has been recalled for our first Test together, as he was dropped after the Headingley defeat at the start of the series. It's hoped that Dev might repeat his efforts against Australia and South Africa in the past two years here. I'm not sure this track will suit him quite as much. Nick Knight dropped out with a damaged finger and Jason Gallian gets another chance. Wells came in for Craig White. The Windies have welcomed back Ambrose and Hooper.

This was an important toss to win. Richie called wrong for the fourth time in my five Tests. The side losing was always going to field. The Oval was packed, even before the start. The interest in this final showdown was incredible. The more experienced lads told me that they have never known tickets so scarce. The first morning at Lord's was obviously special, not only because it was my debut. But there was a real buzz around the Oval this morning. Intent as we are on winning this Test, there was definite feeling in the camp in the two-day build-up that making sure we didn't lose came a very close second. We don't want our supporters to forget all the hard work we have done to get in this position. None of us wants 'England lose another Test series' headlines.

I feel we have a great chance, because you can tell we're beginning to annoy the opposition. Whatever they might have heard about England being an easy touch, the Windies have found out that is not the case. Drawing the fifth Test in such a courageous way brought the team closer together, and everyone was keyed up for this one final assault.

Winning the toss was only the first step. The Oval wicket might be slower than usual, but the Windies' pace attack is quick on any wicket. The second ball from Ambrose thudded into Athers' rib-cage. That would unsettle a few I know, but not the England captain. It merely strengthens his resolve to resist. Jason went early, but Athers, Creepy, Thorpey and Hickie took England to 192/3. The only setback was losing those two wickets in two balls, but Hickie and Jack made sure there were no further problems.

FRIDAY 25 AUGUST   THE OVAL

England 454   West Indies 50/1

Yet another position from which we shouldn't lose. This 454 follows
on our 437 at Old Trafford and 440 at Trent Bridge. It's much easier
playing Test cricket when you have scores like that behind you. Our
heroes today were our overnight batsmen, who put on 144 for the
sixth wicket. Both deserved centuries – both got out in the 90s. To
think that Hickie was dropped for the fourth Test and only made it
back because of Judgey's injury. And Jack. What a return after over
a year in the wilderness.

The rest of us chipped in as we did during the second half of this
series. I made 33, although I tweaked a hamstring pushing off when
I had about eight. Eventually, Ambrose got me with a good yorker.
I'd already had a little dust-up with him when he tried to push me
out of the way as I was running. It probably looked worse than it
was. I've great respect for Curtly as a player and a bowler. The
traditional West Indies image is a laid-back one. Not Ambrose. He's
one of the fiercest competitors I know. I was obviously frustrating
him. He's not too keen on even the best batsmen in the world hanging
around when he's bowling, so when the likes of me occupy the crease
for more than a few overs, Ambrose takes exception. Often, he bowls
deliveries that are wasted on people like me. If I'd been any good, I
might have got a nick. He just stares down the wicket at you, leaving
no doubt as to what he's thinking. Ambrose was coming to the end
of a long tour and didn't fancy too much resistance from me. He
was trying to ruffle me up. At this stage, I was rather delighted that
the Oval track was less bouncy than usual. I felt confident facing
him as I didn't think the ball would misbehave. The trouble started
when I slapped him for four. I wandered up the wicket and tapped
it down, then returned the stare that was being directed my way.
The next ball I ran down to third man, looking for two. You've got
to put fielders under pressure, even in Test matches. That's when the
collision took place. Basically, Ambrose stood his ground, trying to
make me run round him. When I didn't, he pushed me, and told me
to get out of his way. I replied that I had the right to run when I
was batting. It all sounds rather dramatic now, but it was just one
of the countless confrontations that take place in the sporting field.
Honour was even. Neither of us gave way. It was over and forgotten
before it had begun. The only important part of these little flare-ups
is not to back down. The matter ended up in match referee John

Reid's domain. He wasn't bothered about it. I was looking for two runs; Ambrose was frustrated after a day and a half in the field. That was what it was all about.

Our total should ensure that we don't lose. An absolute minimum score on this track was 350. One West Indies' wicket tonight was all we could have expected. It's going to be hard work tomorrow.

Today was a special day for Courtney Walsh who took his 300th Test wicket at last. He needed just three after our first innings at Old Trafford to become the third West Indian to reach that landmark after Lance Gibbs and Malcolm Marshall. But three England innings only brought him two wickets at Trent Bridge. Winker was his special victim, caught behind. That means that Walsh has 277 more Test wickets than me. I wonder if I'll ever get that far?

SATURDAY 26 AUGUST   THE OVAL

West Indies 424/4

That man Lara again. For a third successive Test Saturday, the little left-hander has held centre-stage. It's bad enough bowling to him in this form when the wicket is doing something, but this placid Oval track ensured a day of torture for those of us employed with the task of getting him out. Now I know what the lads felt like at Antigua last year.

My best chance came with his very first ball at the wicket after I'd had nightwatchman Kenny Benjamin caught in the slips by Athers. Enter the world's premier batsman in top form – on a wicket that was a batsman's paradise. Yet he almost gave his wicket away with an enormous wha-hoo to that first ball outside his off-stump. The delivery missed the edge of his bat by a whisker. What a shot to play. I couldn't believe it. I would have been delirious if he'd edged it, but Lara would have committed a great sin to his craft and his team if he had been dismissed like that. My disappointment was all the more painful because I knew it was unlikely to happen again. His only other narrow escape came when he should have been run out in his 30s.

The rest of the day has been carnage as Lara and Campbell, then Lara and Richardson enjoyed the conditions. Our only relief was Lara's departure near the end of play. As at Trent Bridge, I thought he might threaten his record 365. But once again, the left-hander seemed to get tired. What a series he's had, though. I remember reading one of Geoffrey's pieces for the *Sun* before the third Test, suggesting that Lara was 'burnt out'. Spot on, Boycott! Of all his knocks this summer, the one I have the highest regard for was the Old Trafford century. That was a real fighting innings, that gave his side a fighting chance. At Trent Bridge and here, there was no denying the majesty and precision of his stroke-making, but Lara played too many indiscreet shots. Anyway, the game situation was not as critical. Still, his 179 came in just 206 deliveries – quick scoring for Test cricket. Most of our day was spent trying to stem the flow of runs rather than take wickets. It's not much fun bowling when the only close catcher is the wicket-keeper, but Athers had no other choice. Anything slightly off target was dispatched hard and fast. It was a day when my bowling figures took a battering and there was very little I could do about it.

SUNDAY 27 AUGUST   THE OVAL

West Indies 692/8 declared   England 39/0

Only the West Indies can win this series now. And that is highly unlikely after the way we negotiated the final 19 overs tonight. Had we lost a couple of wickets, then the Windies might have fancied their chances tomorrow. But Athers and Jason held firm and, as long as there are no disasters in the opening session, this Test match will be drawn. Another sell-out crowd enjoyed another great day of batting in the sun. I didn't. Four of us conceded over 100 runs – Winker's figures were 0/113, Gussie's 1/155, Devon's 3/160 and mine 3/145. And one of those was a rather fortuitous dismissal. The first ball I bowled today was slapped by the West Indies captain straight to Hickie at backward point. Richie was just seven short of his first century of the series and must be sick of the sight of me after that other unlucky dismissal at the start of my Old Trafford hat-trick. That was our only success for hours as Hooper and Chanderpaul put on 196 for the sixth wicket. Hooper played the shot of the innings when he lifted Gussie straight back over his head for six. I don't think I've ever seen anything quite as effortless. Even in the midst of getting a pasting like this, you have to admire genius. His century was well-deserved. That gave the Windies a lead of 238, enough of an advantage to cost us dear if we batted badly. My groin was bothering me, but I don't think even a super-fit Cork would have made much more of an impact here.

As the tourists rolled on relentlessly, I began to wonder just how long I was going to be left stranded on the Oval outfield. Lara's run gluttony reminded everyone of Viv Richards' feats in England in 1976. Master Blaster actually scored 829 runs in only four Tests in that series – compared to Lara's 765 in six this time. That must have been something to see, but my memories are rather hazy as I was only five at the time. But I do recall the picture of Tony Greig on his knees at the Oval. He had launched the series with that bold prediction that England were going to make the Windies grovel. England are still waiting to do that, although we've won six Tests against them in the 1990s, unlike the sides in the '80s who didn't win a single match in five series. And, if we stand firm tomorrow, than we'll match the 1991 England side who drew 2–2 with Richards' West Indies.

Even with a day left and the knowledge that we mustn't relax, there's a growing sense of anti-climax around the dressing room. We were up for this and could have won this series. We've been beaten in that quest by this wicket as much as anything. I think the crowd, too, wanted a showdown, a fight to the finish like the Rocky movie, and a winner. Over the past 24 hours, we've lived with the realisation that it's not going to be us.

MONDAY 28 AUGUST   THE OVAL

England 223/4
Sixth Cornhill Test drawn   Man of the Match: Brian Lara
Cornhill Series drawn 2–2   England Man of the Series: Michael
Atherton   West Indies Man of the Series: Brian Lara

After the odd worrying moment this morning, this Test and the series ended in a draw, to no one's surprise. Actually, in my five-Test series against the West Indies, I came out a 2–1 winner. Nobody seemed much interested in this fact when I mentioned it. The sense of anti-climax which began on Saturday increased throughout the day as it became obvious that there would be no breaking the stalemate. Danger lurked when Jason and Creepy went in the morning session and Thorpey followed shortly after. We were still over 100 runs adrift.

Ambrose, especially, was awesome on this final day as he pulled out all the stops to try to snatch this one out of the bag. It was the mark of a great competitor, as well as a great bowler. Never the most demonstrative of men, Curtly gave the crowd a wave as he came off early. That's probably his final Test appearance in England. He couldn't budge Athers. Once again, our skipper stood firm and

Left: a great moment for Courtney Walsh. Watkinson becomes his 300th Test victim – a feat I'd love to emulate, although I'm going to have to wait until the 21st century!

Athers asks for something special on the placid Oval wicket, but once again Brian Lara reigned supreme.

was as surprised as anyone when he was caught down the leg-side on 95 near the end. It's not the first time he's been out in the 90s – nor was he the first in this Test. He was the fourth! Hickie had been with him for most of the day and stayed to the end. But Athers' disappointment did at least allow Alan Wells the chance to score his first Test runs – all three of them. And that was it. A subdued end to what had been a sensational series, not just for me. You would have had to play badly to lose on this wicket. My award-winning summer came to a shuddering halt when they gave the England Man of the Series to Athers. Strange, that. I'm just one place behind him in the batting averages and I don't even see his name in the bowling list! Seriously though, it had to be our captain because his determination and character were at the core of us coming from behind twice in the series, then making sure we didn't slip up again. A very modest man, Athers. A fierce competitor, but an unselfish one. He gets as much pleasure out of one of us doing well as from his own performance. A team man, through and through. Athers has been especially generous to me all summer. It's important for a bowler to know his captain is 100 per cent behind him. I believe this England side has made real progress over the series, even allowing for the Edgbaston defeat.

It would have been nice to have relaxed with lads tonight, wound down and reflected on a record-breaking (receipts-wise) series. That's not the way of an England cricketer. I jumped in my car and pointed it eastwards for Derbyshire's four-day championship match against Essex which starts tomorrow. Impressions of my first Test series will have to wait. I'd actually forgotten we were playing tomorrow. Athers reminded me. I had to send an emergency SOS back home to get Jane to bring down my Derbyshire kit. Normally, championship games begin on a Thursday, but they've been moved forward a couple of days because of the NatWest Final on Saturday.

TUESDAY 29 AUGUST   CHELMSFORD

Britannic Championship   Essex 315/9 v Derbyshire

Just what I needed after two days in the field getting whacked all over the place by Lara and company – another day in the field, getting thumped by Goochie and Mark Waugh. I must admit my mind kept drifting back to the West Indies series today. There it was in the papers this morning – Dominic Cork top of the England bowling averages with 26 wickets, ten ahead of the next man, Gussie, in average and in total. No. 7 in the batting wasn't bad – 197 runs at 28.14 to be precise. A few rash shots, sure enough, but I was as pleased with the way I coped with the Windies' quickies as with the number of runs. I didn't back off.

It seems amazing that I was worried about ever playing Test cricket less than three months ago. So much has happened. Those seven wickets, the hat-trick, the 50. And two Test wins. Of course, those personal milestones wouldn't count for much if the side had been getting trounced.

I'm more tired physically than mentally, which surprises me. The psychological pressure's been intense, but those two final Tests at Trent Bridge and the Oval were hard work for the bowlers. I think being on such a high kept me going. You don't get tired when you're winning and enjoying it. And I have enjoyed it. My agonising wait was the key to that. I was determined that if my chance did come, I was going to give it everything and enjoy it. I was going to throw myself into the game the way I've always done. Test cricket was all I imagined it would be. The atmosphere, the tension, the elation, the despair. It was well worth the wait and my life would not have been complete without that experience. That said, or written, it's only a start. And cricket life is not all Test matches, as I've found out today, although admittedly we were on the receiving end from Goochie and Waugh, two of the best batsmen in the world. Our day started badly when Kim went down with a stomach bug before the start. Daffy took over as captain. He responded to that challenge and was our best bowler with five wickets. Our bowling attack is carrying various injuries and Essex have the right sort of batsmen to take advantage of that.

WEDNESDAY 30 AUGUST   CHELMSFORD
Essex 326 & 40/1   Derbyshire 290

Daffy had to rush off late today to his five-year-old daughter's hospital bedside. She's been badly scalded in an accident at home. Details are rather vague, but it sounds horrendous. It made the cricket seem rather irrelevant. Daffy had been our star performer again, blasting 91, including a sixth-wicket stand of a century with me. Most of the lads chipped in with a few runs, but Essex extended their advantage to 76 runs by the end of the day.

THURSDAY 31 AUGUST

CHELMSFORD

Essex 386/8 declared   Derbyshire 38/3

We're in trouble. The victory target is still 385 away and we've effectively lost four wickets because Daffy won't be returning. The news from the hospital is still not clear, but they hope Alexandra will make a full recovery. Those men, Goochie and Waugh, did the damage again. Waugh matched his first-innings 121 exactly. Goochie managed to miss a century by getting out to part-time bowler Rollins. Paul Prichard was also dismissed in the 90s. Such and Childs, who took nine of our first-innings wickets, gave us a hard time too. Childs actually claimed his 1,000th first-class wicket yesterday.

SEPTEMBER 1995

A First Winter with the Big Boys

FRIDAY 1 SEPTEMBER   CHELMSFORD

Derbyshire 166
Derbyshire (6pts) lost to Essex by 256 runs

We held on till mid afternoon, which wasn't bad considering all the calamities we'd suffered in this game. Grizzly and Tim Tweats took us from 43/4 to 130/4. Once they went, the rest of us capitulated rather too easily, with the two Essex spinners doing the damage again. Only two Derbyshire wickets didn't fall to them in the match. Not that the early finish did me much good, as we've got to hang around for the Sunday League game. Sometimes, you wonder if the fixtures are pulled out of a hat. I was supposed to be going to the Cricket Writers' Dinner tonight in London and joining the Sky table. But I've pulled out. I'm absolutely shattered. As much as it's given me, I'm really looking forward to the end of this season.

SUNDAY 3 SEPTEMBER   CHELMSFORD

AXA Equity & Law *Essex 196/7 (40 overs)* *Derbyshire 172 (38.2)*
Derbyshire (0 pts) lost by 24 runs

Not a very productive visit to Essex for us. We were outplayed in the championship match, but we should have won today. Kim and Grizzly put on 101 for the first wicket, leaving us needing another 96 for victory in 16 overs – exactly six an over – with all ten wickets left. In effect, we were bowled out for 71. Derbyshire at their finest!

Goochie stole the show. Age doesn't seem to dampen his talent or spirit. The Golden Oldie hit an undefeated 63 in 53 balls, took two wickets and held three catches, one a brilliant caught and bowled to remove Colin Wells for a duck. After it was all over, I was able to head for home for the first time in nearly a fortnight.

All the Sunday papers were full of predictions of England's squad for the tour to South Africa. D-Day is Tuesday. If I read the phrase 'automatic choice' one more time, I'll scream. Sure, I'd ask for a stewards' enquiry if I'm left out, but let's just wait for the official announcement. Middlesex's Richard Johnson is widely tipped as the surprise bowling choice, although I gather he has back problems. The batting arguments revolve around whether England will take a third opener – Jason Gallian or Nick Knight – and which one or two out of Creeps, Ramps and Nasser Hussain will miss out. Ramps has got a pile of runs since his pair at Lord's. Every time I look in the papers, he's got a century or double century. His 111 against Northants last week was his seventh ton of the season. I would imagine the selectors will stay loyal to the players who have served England so well this summer. Goughie's working his way back after his foot problems. I'm sure he's pencilled in. But, as I've written earlier, let's wait for the official announcement. It's all speculation at the moment.

Thursday 7 September Edgbaston

Britannic Championship *Warwickshire v Derbyshire*
No play

Rain and day off. Dermot Reeve's dressing room seemed much more worried about this inactivity than ours. I don't blame them. They're the championship leaders and they could take the title with a win against us, provided Middlesex don't beat Leicestershire. Warwicks were relieved to hear that the rain was also hampering Middlesex's challenge.

The touring squads were released on Tuesday morning. I switched on Ceefax to see that after four winters on A tours, I've finally graduated to the big-time. It was a predictable line-up. No third opener, no Nasser and Richard Johnson has his chance. The A squad was also named. They're off to Pakistan under the captaincy of Nasser. England's World Cup squad won't be named until near the end of the South African trip. That makes sense. There are seven one-day internationals against South Africa in January to prepare us (I hope it's us). Why commit yourself to a line-up when there's so much cricket to be played?

The Lord's Test

At last my first Test for England: straining to get the last ounce of pace.

Below: miracle of miracles, a champagne finish as Man of the Match. Around me are Roger Knight, MCC secretary, Bob Willis, the Man of the Match adjudicator, Cornhill's Ray Treen and smiling Sky commentator, David Gower.

The hat-trick

Left: bad luck for Richie Richardson, as the ball ricochets from his body on to the wicket; *below:* none was needed as next ball Junior Murray is plumb LBW.

Above: I wasn't convinced Cyril Mitchley would raise his finger for another LBW but he did. Carl Hooper was on his way, and the celebrations *right* began.

Above: this picture shows that neither Junior Murray nor I was aware that I had dislodged a bail as I set off on an all-run four.

Left: acknowledging the crowd on reaching my first – and as yet, only! – Test fifty.

The great Geoffrey Boycott told us
after the Lord's Test that Brian
Lara was 'burnt out' – but the
Trinidadian left-hander showed
little sign of being ready for the
scrapheap with a trio of brilliant
centuries in the final three Tests.
Below: it might only have been
two. I was convinced I had Lara
caught behind early on at Old
Trafford. This time Mr Mitchley
did not see things my way.

Eating out at Port Elizabeth with the one and only Ian Botham.

Teaching Gregory how to appeal in the Cork fashion. Jane has seen it all before.

With Goughie at Johannesburg Zoo. Two young English lions meet the South African real thing.

Helping the South African captain on his way. Cronje caught behind by Jack Russell at the Wanderers Stadium, Johannesburg, in the Second Test.

More smart work from Jack. Cullinan is stumped off Illingworth during the Fourth Test at St George's Park, Port Elizabeth.

The highlight of the tour for Athers, Jack and all of us. The pair defied the South African bowlers for most of the final day of the Wanderers Test.

Donald uses a double-finger farewell as he removes Mike Atherton in the first innings of the Second Test.

Despite Graham Hick's brave century in the First Test there was no doubt that the South Africans had unearthed a special talent in Shaun Pollock, latest in a great cricketing family.

To the victors the spoils... Unfortunately, as this photo shows, that was not England in Cape Town.

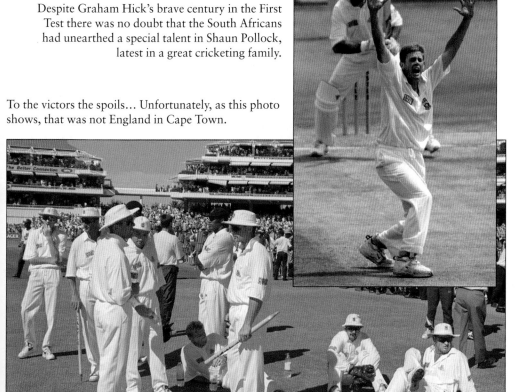

New haircut, new beard, old knees, same old story as England's dismal one-day form continued throughout the World Cup.

We went out to Sri Lanka in the quarter-finals. It didn't surprise me that they should cause the biggest upset in Cricket Cup Final history. *Below*: Ranatunga lifts the trophy that England never even got near.

I'm not sure Derbyshire are going to get much here. The forecast is not good. Dermot will be worried if we don't start tomorrow.

FRIDAY 8 SEPTEMBER   EDGBASTON

Derbyshire 268   Warwickshire 19/1

We might not need the rain to halt Dermot's charge to the title. Ours is a good total on this wicket and it was a real bonus when I trapped Nick Knight LBW for a duck at the death. It's thanks to our overseas star for our healthy position as he came out on top in his duel with his South African team-mate, Allan Donald. Donald had put us in trouble early on with his pace, but Cullinan showed all his class. His fifth century of the summer – 121 – contained 20 fours, a six and even a seven. His driving through the off-side was especially powerful. I helped the tail wag a bit, so we recovered well after being 86/4. The rain abated at Uxbridge, too. What a surprise – another Ramps century has put them in a better position than Warwickshire are tonight.

SATURDAY 9 SEPTEMBER   EDGBASTON

Warwickshire 387/8 declared   Derbyshire 31/3

We've done it again. As I've written before, these Warwickshire batsmen find the runs when they most need them. The champions were struggling at 124/5 before Trevor Penney and Dermot went past our total with a stand of 168. We only had ourselves to blame because Penney was dropped on 41. Everyone chipped in and Dermot was able to declare to give himself – or rather Donald – a few overs at us. Donald claimed three wickets in eight balls and we may have handed Warwickshire the title. Middlesex are struggling. Unless Leicestershire are willing, there seems little chance of a result there.

SUNDAY 10 SEPTEMBER   EDGBASTON

AXA Equity & Law   Derbyshire 81/5 (25 overs) v Warwickshire
No result   Derbyshire 2pts

The rain has ended Warwickshire's hopes of a third successive treble. Kent are four points ahead and the pair meet next Sunday at Canterbury. But even if they lose, Kent's superior run-rate will give them the title. The state of the game made the home side doubly disappointed when the rains came, especially when it could hit them where it hurts again tomorrow.

MONDAY 11 SEPTEMBER   EDGBASTON

Derbyshire 122   Warwickshire 5/0

A day full of drama, with little input from us. Dermot bettered Donald's Saturday night three-wicket haul in eight balls with three in six this morning. I was victim number three. We threatened briefly when Grizzly and Cullinan more than doubled our score to take us to 80/4. The collapse that followed was all too typical and we only just managed to make Warwickshire bat again. Nick Knight hit the winning runs and left the field to a standing ovation.

Everyone was convinced those runs had given them the title, us included. But I gather that the fun was only beginning. As we left, the champagne was on ice as they waited for confirmation from Uxbridge that Middlesex would not be able to catch them. That looked on the cards when Middlesex set Leicestershire 251 to win after yet another Ramps century. That was his eighth in 13 championship innings and took him just 69 balls, and past 2,000 runs for the season. The Middlesex declaration gave them two sessions to bowl Leicestershire out. At 131/2, the visitors were well on course. Then they collapsed to 204/8 and Middlesex looked home and dry. The ninth wicket fell with 14 runs needed, but Adrian Pierson and Alan Mullally were set to break Middlesex hearts with nine balls left to get the two runs necessary. Get them in singles is an old maxim, but Mullally went for a big-hit finish. Phil Tufnell was the bowler and John Emburey the old man running around the midwicket boundary to take the catch, ensuring Middlesex's sensational one-run victory that kept the championship race alive. I swear I could hear the Warwickshire groans in Derby as that champagne was put back in its box.

THURSDAY 14 SEPTEMBER   DERBY

Britannic Championship *Derbyshire 267   Lancashire 134/8*

A very busy day. Kim became the second Derbyshire player to go past 20,000 runs, Adrian Rollins was awarded his county cap and Grizzly had his request to be released turned down. Over 400 runs were scored and 18 wickets fell – five of them to me, including four England colleagues – Athers, Gally, Creepy and Winker. We might have been batting again. Lancs were 51/7 before Ian Austin came in and clouted the ball around in the fashion Daffy had done earlier. The news of Daffy's daughter Alexandra is much better and it is hoped that there will be no permanent scars from the scalding. His relief was obvious in his batting. He was only six short of a century when he ran out of partners.

Friday 15 September   DERBY

Lancashire 155   Derbyshire 161/2

Saturday 16 September   DERBY

Derbyshire 325   Lancashire 19/0

I've got to take all ten wickets in Lancashire's second innings if I want to receive 100 for the season. Fat chance, really. But the way my summer's been going, who knows? I finished up with 7/61 on Friday, including another England scalp, Peter Martin. But for Austin's undefeated 80 off only 51 balls, Lancashire would have been routed completely. We batted less frantically second time out and set Lancs a 438-run target.

Sunday 17 September   DERBY

AXA Equity & Law   Derbyshire 119/4 (10 overs) v Lancashire No result – Derbyshire 2pts

The end of our Sunday season. We finished eighth. Kent, Warwickshire and Worcestershire all tied on 50 points, with Warwickshire winning at Canterbury and rain ruining Worcestershire's chance of going clear at the top. Kent's run-rate, the best in the league, gave them the title for the fourth time. We started two matches today. Kim put Lancs in and they were 12/0 when it began to rain heavily. That match was abandoned. All we could manage was a ten-over contest. We looked in good shape after Colin Wells hit 66 from 26 balls, including six sixes. But Lancs never got to the wicket. Another storm broke and all bets were off.

MONDAY 18 SEPTEMBER   DERBY

Lancashire 155   Derbyshire (22pts) won by 282 runs

TUESDAY 19 SEPTEMBER   LONDON

No 100 wickets for me. I didn't get close. In fact, I didn't get any. It was Jack who grabbed the glory with a career best 6/21 as Lancs folded. Creepy and Athers were the only ones to offer resistance. The final seven wickets went for 47 runs. So we've finished the season like we started it, with a massive win. It was just the in-between that caused us a few problems. We have finished in 14th spot, an improvement of three places on last year. Another eight points and we would have moved up another three places. What might have been! When I think of the number of games we threw away, the ones that slipped away, it's ridiculous. Apart from that flying start and sprint finish, there were only two other Derbyshire wins in the 15 other championship matches. Those wins were against Hampshire and Glamorgan. Another interesting statistic is that I didn't play in either! Maybe it's my fault. The title went to Warwickshire after all and Dermot's side were clear leaders over Middlesex, who could only draw at Somerset. You have to take your hat off to Warwickshire. Following the achievements of 1994, this year was always going to be tough. But Donald for Lara was a fair swap and no one could argue with 14 wins in 17 matches, apparently the highest win percentage in the history of the championship, a few percentage points better than the 1955 Surrey side. Worthy champions, they defended their title well.

After the match, we headed to London for the annual Cricketers' Association Dinner at the Café Royal. I was surprised to receive the Reg Hayter award – for the cricketers' Player of the Year. I thought Northants' Anil Kumble might have got it for his 100 wickets. But I was delighted. It was four years ago that I got the Young Player award.

October 1995

Mandela Greets the Destroyer

My first senior England tour starts tomorrow. I can't wait. The schedule suggests that we've had a month's rest, but it hasn't worked out that way. The past few weeks have been really hectic, what with trying to catch up on things, as well as cramming in as much time as I can with the family. We are home for such a short time between the South African tour and the World Cup – if I'm picked for that.

One day was spent in Nottingham. I've signed a new three-year contract with Gunn & Moore. I've also been on Gary Lineker's Sunday radio show and received an award from the Commonwealth Institute. My new-found status took me to India for five days last week to film a Pepsi-cola advert for the World Cup. Maybe they know something that I don't. It wasn't easy going off so near my tour departure, but it's great money and they are a huge international company to be associated with. The new Derbyshire captain has been announced. It's the Australian Dean Jones. He's a typical Aussie and I'm sure he'll bring a competitive attitude and edge to the County Ground next summer. It doesn't bother me that the club felt the need to look outside. It's a job I'd like to do at some stage of my career, but not now. I don't think that's being selfish, just realistic. I've got enough on my plate establishing myself in the England team.

I see in this morning's papers that South Africa have warmed up for our visit with a seven-wicket win over Zimbabwe in Harare. That victory was no surprise, nor were the figures of Allan Donald – 8/71 – in the second innings to win the match. Fanie de Villiers is out with injury, but the left-armer Brett Schultz, who missed the tour to England last year with knee trouble, had a good first Test back. It looks a pretty good pace attack to me.

I was in London yesterday to receive the Whyte & Mackay

Cricketer of the Year award, judged by a distinguished panel consisting of Geoff Boycott, Alan Knott, Ted Dexter and John Lever. Individual prizes in a team game? It doesn't bother me. It's inevitable. I don't believe any cricketer who thinks he can do it on his own. Anyway, most awards go in the team pool. The lads reckon one of the best awards to win is the Whittingdale Young Cricketer of the Month. The player receives a Gucci watch for his trouble – with a case of champagne going to the team. Something for everyone.

I'm driving down to the Excelsior Hotel at Heathrow with Devon tomorrow. He picked up a pre-tour bonus yesterday when the High Court awarded him substantial damages over that 'Is it in the blood?' article. The judge even wished him luck on the tour and said he hopes he's going to repeat his 9/57 match-winning feat against the South Africans at the Oval last year. He's not the only one. Illy's also in the news this morning. He's announced that he's scrapping the traditional tour selection committee. 'I'll have overall say this winter,' declared our chairman. 'I can't play for the players, but I'm sure I'm going to be judged on what happens this winter.' Fair enough.

Thursday 19 October
Sandton Sun Hotel, Johannesburg, South Africa

My first injury and I've been in the country less than 12 hours. I can't believe it. I was just throwing a few balls to Jack. Then I decided to bowl one. I'm not sure how I did it, but I managed to rip the thumb-nail off my bowling hand. I don't know what was dripping more – the blood from my thumb or the sweat as I realised what I'd done. It's not that serious, but I think I'm struggling for the opening game on Tuesday.

The questions at today's lunch-time press conference centred on the relationship between Illy and Athers. The *Sun* ran the 'Boycott and Illingworth Tapes' for a couple of days before we flew out. I presume Boycs insisted his name got first billing. As these two Yorkshiremen considered England's many cricket problems, much of the blame appeared to lie at the door of the skipper and his team. It doesn't affect me, but it doesn't seem fair that we've been gagged by Illy from doing our diaries and columns, while he has no such restrictions. Even if we are allowed to express an opinion, it still has to be passed by the tour management first. So much for the freedom of speech and right to reply!

There were no restrictions at the Excelsior Hotel before we left yesterday when I gave dozens of interviews to papers, TV and radio. Dozens of interviews – all asking the same question. 'Do you feel under extra pressure after the summer and how are you going to cope with it?' My standard reply is that it's not a problem, because I don't feel I *am* under extra pressure.

It was tough saying goodbye to Jane and Gregory, especially as he's so close to talking and walking, but at least they'll be out at Christmas. The BA flight was very comfortable. It's only when that plane takes off that you really feel you're on tour. The new South Africa looked very similar to good old England when we landed. It was pouring and rain's predicted for the next few days. It's the first wet weather they've had here for nine months. We were given a traditional dancing and drumming Zulu welcome at the hotel, which is one of the poshest places I've ever stayed in. Yet danger lurks not far away, as we were warned this evening. Representatives from the British Consulate and the security forces advised us of the 'dos' and 'don'ts' in one of the world's most violent cities. Basically, the message was 'Don't go out!' They focused on the combi vans that are used as taxis to transport locals from the city centre to the townships – a definite no-go area. We've also been banned from hiring cars because this is the car-jacking capital of the world. Despite the warnings, I went for a run with Jack and the doctor, Philip Bell, to try to get acclimatised quicker. It's funny how you're full of these mad ideas at the start of a tour.

MONDAY 23 OCTOBER   JOHANNESBURG

How the other half lives! My first contest of the tour was partnering the chairman in Nicky Oppenheimer's Golf Day. He's the Diamond King of South Africa and is reputed to be the second richest man in the world. I can believe that after today. Illy and I won our match on the Riverside course, definitely designed for millionaires, despite the fact that the pair of us put our balls into the lake in front of everyone. Thorpey and Goughie took first prize, but I did detect a slight look of disappointment on their faces at the prize-giving. I suspect they couldn't understand why Oppenheimer's diamond connection meant they each received a wildlife video. There are stories that a couple of the Kiwi cricketers were spotted on film pocketing the odd diamond last year. No charges were pressed and the diamonds were returned.

After golf, we headed for our host's house where he had laid on a barbecue, although it bore little resemblance to my back-garden efforts. Even his books are well looked after – his library is kept at a special temperature to preserve them. I'm looking forward to seeing his cricket ground tomorrow, although I'm disappointed it will only be as a spectactor to give my thumb another day to heal.

I think we've all settled in well. We've trained hard every morning. I've noticed how quickly the altitude has you gasping for air, but even after only five days it's beginning to ease. As soon as we arrived, it was emphasised that playing cricket was not our only job on this trip. We'll have to do our bit as cricketing and political ambassadors. Friday night was spent at the British High Commissioner's. These diplomatic affairs can be rather heavy-going, but the lads let their hair down this time and had a great evening. My hero, Ian Botham, was there and it was great to get some words of encouragement from him. The music livened up when our resident guitarists – Mark 'Ramble' Illot and physio Wayne Morton – took over. Plenty of Billy Bragg, Bryan Adams and the Beatles. I'm sure it won't be the last we hear from them on this trip.

The affluence of the Hyde Park suburb contrasted dramatically with our trip to Alexandra on Saturday afternoon. It wasn't a first visit for me – the A team played there two years ago – but time hasn't dulled the horror of the deprivation and despair. Anyone who thinks all South Africa's problems have been solved with Mandela's elevation only has to spend a few minutes here to realise that life's not that simple. We went there to mark the opening of a new pavilion, but most of the kids just wanted a look at Devon. Obviously, he's a key man for us on the field. But I've gleaned that, as England's only black player, Dev's got an important part to play elsewhere. At the High Commissioner's, it was Dev who drew the winning ticket for the raffle. At Alexandra, the photograph everyone wanted to take was Dev and the kids. I've read in the papers that the South African cricket supremo, Dr Ali Bacher, has met with Illy to make sure Dev plays in our opening first-class match at Soweto on Friday.

TUESDAY 24 OCTOBER   RANDJESFONTEIN

England 242/5 declared   Oppenheimer's XI 130
England won by 112 runs

WEDNESDAY 25 OCTOBER   SPRINGS

Eastern Transvaal 261/5 (50 overs)   England 264/5 (49 overs)
England won by 5 wickets

Three firsts for me today. First England game on tour, first day/ nighter and first in coloured clothing. Make that four. My first England win on tour. It was a close-run thing as Eastern Transvaal made

SOWETO CRICKET OVAL

President Nelson Mandela gave the match authorities just seven minutes' warning before arriving by helicopter for our game in Soweto. Despite all that had happened to me in 1995, meeting this great man is the moment I'll treasure most.

The sun shone on the President that day but rain dominated our early weeks in South Africa. At one stage, I was spending more time on the golf course than at cricket grounds.

us work hard for the runs. For some of the lads it was a second win in two days. Yesterday, they beat Oppenheimer's XI by 112 runs at Randjesfontein. Stewie top-scored with 74 and Richard Illingworth took five wickets. Fittingly, the first wicket taken by an England bowler on an official South Africa tour for 31 years went to Dev. Yesterday's atmosphere was very sedate, reminiscent of a traditional English country-house setting, although Oppenheimer's private pavilion was worthy of any Test ground in the world. Today, at Springs, was rather different, especially once the lights were switched on. Yesterday the result was unimportant to the home supporters. But we were certainly never in any doubt that there was a game going on today. We had a mishap on the way to the game. One of the coach's rear tyres exploded. After all the warnings we've had, one or two brave lads already had their heads well down!

Eastern Transvaal shouldn't have reached 261/6 in their 50 overs, but we shelled a few chances. That would have improved my figures of 1/48, but I felt reasonably happy with this work-out, although I feel tired. That might be due to all the hard running in my partnership with Mark Ramprakash that took us to victory. At 165/5, we were in some trouble. Athers told me to run our singles quick – so that's what I did.

FRIDAY 27 OCTOBER   SOWETO

England 285/7 v   South African Invitation XI

A historic day for Soweto – their first-ever first-class cricket match. And one for us, too. We had been told that the leader of the Rainbow Nation was scheduled to make an appearance on Sunday, but President Nelson Mandela surprised everyone by turning up this morning, and the place went wild. The game had actually started when the news was relayed to the match authorities that the most famous man in South Africa, and possibly the world, would be arriving by helicopter in seven minutes' time. Cricketers, like most sportsmen, are a fairly cynical bunch. Not too much impresses us – well, not so as you'd know. But the lads are in genuine awe of this man and were really excited as we lined up to meet him. I can't imagine any British politician getting such an affectionate reception as Mandela received from his home crowd.

The President is well known for saying the right thing at the right time, and he certainly made Devon's day today, saying 'I know you. You are the Destroyer,' as he shook our fast bowler's hand. I could see Dev's chest swelling from down the line. He'd already captured the great man's arrival on his camcorder. Dev doesn't say much at the best of times, but he's a bowler who needs confidence, the occasional pat on the back and word of encouragement. The President has been a great motivator for South African sport. Remember his appearance at the Rugby World Cup final in a Springbok jersey? This time, though, his words may just rebound on his country's fortunes if Devon fires properly. All the schoolkids in Soweto were given the day off today. Two special stands have been built for them, but they hardly sat down. Instead, they used them as giant climbing frames.

We travelled from Sandton to Soweto by coach with a police escort. We knew what to expect, but it was still strange to come across the cricket ground – the only grass wicket for the whole of Soweto. Soweto is totally different from Alexandra, and less intimidating. In Alexandra hundreds of thousands of people are crammed into a tiny area, whereas here millions are housed over a huge area. This is a city that serves a city, and right in the middle are the giant towers that provide most of Johannesburg's electricity. It's only fairly recently that this facility has been extended to the people who live in the shadow of those towers.

Tuesday 31 October   East London

Out of Johannesburg at last. The Sandton Sun may be luxurious and adjoining the undercover Sandton City shopping centre, but it had the feel of a giant prison. I don't mean to be ungrateful or critical, but most of the lads have complained of feeling trapped. The only time we got out into the fresh air was during our practices at the Wanderers Stadium or at the match. On Sunday, we headed for Centurion Park near Pretoria because the Wanderers was unfit.

Devon joined us, despite the fact he was playing at Soweto. I gather the management are trying to get him to change his action slightly. The press appear to be making a big deal about it. I don't know why. Apparently, Illy and Plank – Peter Lever – held a press conference on Monday and whatever they said certainly excited our media. They keep asking us what's going on. How should I know? I've not been party to their intimate discussions. I must admit that I can't see Dev making too many adjustments at this stage of his career. He's always been a bit hit and miss. That's his strength and his weakness. He's here because of what he did to the South Africans at the Oval. From what I hear, the South African batsmen weren't too keen on facing him that day. There aren't many bowlers who frighten world-class batsmen – England is lucky to have one. It would be suicidal to do anything that affects Dev's pace or undermines his confidence before the Test series starts. It would be letting the South African batsmen off the hook. I'm not the only one looking forward to that confrontation. We bumped into Brett Schultz at the Centurion Park nets on Sunday. He's raring to go and was promising to do all sorts of nasty things to our batsmen. He might do at Centurion Park. When we were here with England A, one delivery of Goughie's went straight over the keeper and had one bounce to the boundary.

The Soweto game ended in a draw. We had looked certain winners on Sunday night. The South Africans needed 380 runs to win with nine wickets left, but the rain had the last word as the final day was abandoned before the scheduled start. Our relief at leaving Johannesburg soon vanished during one of the bumpiest flights I've ever been on. We dropped in at Port Elizabeth on the way to East London. 'Dropped in' is about right. The pilot gave it a real thump on landing. East London's weather wasn't much better than Jo'burg's; it was really windy. In true fast-bowlers' fashion, we started discussing who would be charging up the hill into the wind.

Hard luck, Gussie! He's my room-mate here. Quiet bloke. No trouble. It was the same in the Sandton. 'H' was my roomie. 'H' is Richard Illingworth. He was Illy – until Raymond returned to the scene. Now he's 'H' again – as in Harry Worth! Another quiet guy. East London is a port, and it's much safer than everywhere we've been so far. It's great to be able to walk around like a free man again. Most of us didn't have any choice because we were waiting for our luggage to arrive. The plane was so overloaded that we had to leave much of it behind. When it did turn up, one of the Doc's cases was missing, so his size seven feet have been walloping around in Hickie's size ten flip-flops.

I rang Jane. She told me that Kim has decided to stay at Derbyshire. I'm pleased and relieved about that. The place wouldn't be the same without him.

Hanging Around and Splashing About

THURSDAY 2 NOVEMBER BUFFALO PARK, EAST LONDON

England 218/4 v Border

My opening first-class match, but I haven't got out of the pavilion yet. Play was delayed until after lunch because of rain. It seems to be following us around. It was pouring when we woke up and, if it had been England, I would have turned over and gone back to sleep because there would have been no chance of play. John 'Creepy' Crawley and Mark Ramprakash dominated the two sessions. I'm next man in. All the media attention concerns two players not involved here. Thorpey has flown home to be with his wife, Nicky, who is sadly recovering from an operation to terminate an ectopic pregnancy. And the Devon affair rumbles on. I gather it's been all over the back pages back home. Even Kim Barnett has got involved. It's not the first time he's spoken out against the way Devon has been treated by England. It was reported in the papers here that Plank said about Devon, 'He has just one asset – pace. That apart he is a nonentity in cricketing terms.' Whatever truth there might be in that verdict, it's a view I don't think should have been made in public – certainly not before anyone has bowled a ball in anger at the South Africans. The lads are playing it down. Devon has certainly enjoyed being the star attraction here and, to those who don't know him, it might appear that some of the adulation has gone to his head. But that's not his style. We don't see it as a big issue. I'm just surprised it's an issue at all at this stage of the trip. We don't need to be seen to be squabbling amongst ourselves. That really is shooting yourself in the foot. I'm sure a few wickets from our fast man will put it right. I wouldn't mind a few myself – when I get the chance.

There is a really good spirit in the side. It was especially noticeable when we had a North v South fielding practice match yesterday. There's nothing like a little competition to get the lads running around. It was a public holiday because of the local elections and most of the place was closed up. In the afternoon, Goughie and I took the money off the old timers – Illy and Edie (John Edrich) – on the golf course. It was an exceptionally hilly course and we had to carry our own clubs. The over-60s had no chance. The rain came and we had to call a halt after ten holes. We'd all driven over a hill on one hole, but couldn't find a single ball when we got over the top. Apparently it's a local rule. If you don't hire the local caddies, then your ball is almost certain to go missing at that spot.

SATURDAY 4 NOVEMBER   BUFFALO PARK

England 351   Border 153/6

A proper bowl at last – after 18 days of the tour. Yesterday was another wash-out, so it was back to being a mountain goat. I'm getting more golf than cricket at the moment. This time Hickie and I lost to Goughie and Creepy. There's a local saying that, if you can see the hills behind the hotel, it's going to rain. If you can't, it's raining already. I'm sure I've heard that somewhere before.

You never seem to get the rest periods when you want them. Suddenly, the first Test isn't too far away and everyone is desperate for practice. But then it rains and you're left to make do as best you can. The limited time puts pressure on you to perform. Most cricketers need to play to find their best form. There are one or two exceptions who can just turn it on, but the Laras and Tendulkars of this world are few and far between. The rest of us mere mortals need to get on the park. In some ways, it's tougher for batsmen. One mistake and you're out. Judgey, playing his first cricket since that Old Trafford injury and operation on his cheekbone, has managed just 49 runs in five knocks out here. With Creepy, who completed his century today, and Ramps scoring well, and Athers, Stewie, Hickie and Thorpey assured of places, it doesn't take a mathematician to work out that three into two places won't go. Judge will be hoping for a bat tomorrow. I'm sure that if he shows any sort of form, he'll start in the Test line-up. And that's as it should be after all he did last summer and his long-time Test success against the best pace bowling in the world. Pleased as I was with my 43 runs, my three wickets were much more important. There was a strong, cold wind out there. I'd expected the sun to be on my back for most of this trip. It was also nice to keep Cullinan quiet in the final session – he only managed 15 runs in over two hours.

Rang home again and got my first 'Dada' from Gregory. He appears to be the only one from the Derby area who hasn't commented on the Devon situation.

SUNDAY 5 NOVEMBER   BUFFALO PARK

Border 166 & 132
England won by an innings and 53 runs

A win – and well deserved on a wicket that was pretty lifeless. It would have been easy to have used the final day for batting practice after so much time had been lost to the weather. But Stewie, skipper with Athers sitting this one out, appreciates that nothing beats the winning habit. The first wicket was mine and it was for the Derbyshire lads. I trapped Darryl Cullinan LBW. I wasn't surprised to learn that he is about as popular in the Border dressing room as he was in ours. It got better when they followed-on and I smacked him on the chest, adding, 'That one's for Krikk'. Amazingly, the ball hit the wicket but the bails stayed on. I suppose this might all sound a bit childish, but if I can irritate Cullinan and put him off his stroke, then it will be to England's benefit. I finished with eight wickets in the match, Ramble (Mark Ilott) got six and Goughie five – the other was a run-out. Our resident guitarists were back in action tonight, with the added attraction of Hickie on the drums.

WEDNESDAY 8 NOVEMBER   KIMBERLEY

Our final warm-up match before the Test. Unfortunately my good form against Border means I'm only 12th man, while the other bowlers are given a last chance.

There seems no end to the Devon saga, as far as the media are concerned. The press put on a poolside reception for us on Tuesday night. That's one big difference between the A tours and this winter – I've never seen so many journalists in one place before. The press pack from the UK already numbers more than 30 and that is expected to double around the time of the Test. I've got to know them a lot better over the past six months. So far I've had nothing but good times since I started my Test career, so I can't say I've been on the receiving end. I basically treat them all the same, try to be as helpful as I can, confront them personally if they've upset me and cut them adrift if they 'dag' me unfairly. Anyway, they put on a good party and it was nice to see them dipping into their expenses on our behalf for once. Thorpey arrived back in time for the party – it's good to have him back.

Kimberley is a quiet town. Quiet, but wealthy. It's the diamond capital of the world and it boasts the 'Big Hole'. That's exactly what was left after they extracted the diamonds. We've spent the past two days practising at the school ground. The bowlers enjoyed it, as the wicket was quick and bouncy. All the batsmen were hopping around with the ball flying about. My feet blistered during the Border game, so I've broken in a new pair of boots since I got here.

Our bowling coach Peter Lever hasn't had the best of days. First, Plank thought he was keeping a local lad in business by buying a paper off him. Only after he'd parted with his money and put his specs on did he realise that the only words he could read on the front page were 'Michael Atherton'. The rest was in Afrikaans. His bad day continued when he was drenched by water poured from the fourth-floor walkway while he was sitting in the lobby. My lips are sealed.

FRIDAY 10 NOVEMBER   KIMBERLEY

South Africa 470   England 127/4

Have we met the new Shane Warne? In recent weeks, we've been hearing and reading a lot about an 18-year-old left-arm spinner with a peculiar action – Paul Adams. Today, the lads had their first taste of the real thing on a flat pitch that saw South Africa's A side rattle up nearly 500 runs. Tonight, he's tucked up in bed with the wickets of Stewie, Thorpey and Hickie added to his growing collection, so I'm sure he's sleeping like a baby. He took a bit longer than Warne did to dismiss one of England's top batsmen, but only just. We've all been comparing his second-ball googly which was too good for Stewie with the 'Ball from Hell' that Warne delivered to Gatting first up in 1993. Adams certainly has the strangest action I've ever seen. As his left arm comes over, his head is ducked down and facing backwards. The other remarkable thing about the youngster is that this is only his second first-class match. Apparently he wasn't con-sidered good enough for the South African Schools squad that toured England last summer. They got that one wrong. And his dismissal

Peter Lever is reported to have called Devon Malcolm a 'cricketing nonentity' – but then he called me a 'pillock' at Old Trafford. Our bowling coach has a way with words.

Below: The amazing Paul Adams, who teased us at Kimberley but, more damagingly, tormented us at Cape Town.

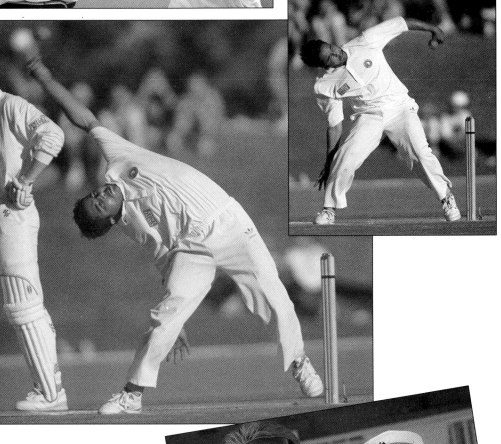

Gough and I roomed together in Bloemfontein, reviving horrible memories of our winter together in New Zealand several years ago.

of Stewie was no fluke. Thorpey was caught at silly point and Hickie – my roomie – patted a full toss back to the bowler. It was another famous England collapse – 55/0 to 59/4 before the skipper and Judgey steadied things. Athers, especially, handled Adams well and we'll need a big knock from him tomorrow to ensure no disasters here.

Incredibly, the rain has even followed us to Kimberley. I checked about the weather when we reached the hotel after our experiences in Johannesburg and East London. Rain? There will be no rain here until March at the earliest. Don't you believe it! Plant two sets of stumps in the ground and fly in the England cricket team and the heavens will open. The start was delayed yesterday because of a sudden downpour. Our spirits, especially those of the bowlers playing, had already been dampened by the news that our esteemed skipper had lost the toss and the opposition were batting. As Goughie complained at the end of yesterday's play, it looked like they could build a motorway through the pitch it was so flat. He said he's never been so tired after a day in the field as yesterday. It was hot, boiling hot. I felt it as I ran regularly round the boundary with drinks to keep the bowlers going. Gussie looked wiped out, and even worse after learning that he'd lost over half a stone during the day. The bad weather has certainly affected our preparation. The bowlers are short of match practice, so everyone playing here is trying as hard as they can. On this pitch, it's almost impossible for the quick bowlers to make an impact. But they can't afford one mediocre performance, so they try harder in conditions that are taking a lot out of them.

We had our official team photo taken this morning, which is also used on the Christmas cards. That's hard to imagine with the temperature soaring over the 100 degree mark. Thinking of Christmas also adds to the homesickness which has hit me badly over the past few days. I told Jane yesterday to get on the next plane out here. Only 41 days to go. 41 days! Fred Swarbrook, an old Derbyshire stalwart, is the groundsman here. It's good to talk about the old place with him. Fred was a useful bowler who totally lost it. He told me about how, in desperation, he went to see a gypsy healer, who gave him a stone to keep in his flannels and rub before every ball. That was going to do the trick. Unfortunately, Fred's first delivery in the very next game flew over the keeper's head for four byes, the second bounced 12 times and the third sailed miles wide. That was enough for team-mate David Steele, who bellowed, 'Hey, Fred, why not rub the ball and bowl the stone?'

After the day's play, Goughie, Ramble and I joined the South African police and headed for the shooting range. No airguns here.

They let us loose with machine guns, automatic rifles and shotguns. Then we travelled back in a Nyala – one of those anti-riot wagons. I tried to imagine what it must be like for troops in Ireland, Bosnia and Kuwait.

Another haircut today. The hairdresser must have got out of the wrong side of bed, he was so miserable. Didn't do much for my looks, either. Tonight, we wet the baby's head. It's Wayne's third – Ethan. The same as the John Wayne character in John Ford's classic western *The Searchers*.

SUNDAY 12 NOVEMBER   KIMBERLEY

England 308 & 309   South Africa A 148/4
England lost by 4 wickets

Not the ideal preparation for the first Test. We have to hold our hands up and admit that we were all beaten. Adams finished up with nine wickets in the match and the South African papers have been clamouring for him to be included in the Test squad that was picked a week ago. That's up to them. I certainly didn't expect to be discussing a spin bowler in the build-up to the Test series here. The lads believed that they handled Adams better second time around, although he did pick up one more wicket than the first innings. This has been our first real opportunity to see what a South African crowd is like. For most of the match, the smell of burning meat wafted over the ground as they all tucked into their barbecues – or *braais*, as they are known here. There's a fair amount of banter from the crowd. I can't really call it banter, because there's nothing clever or responsive about it. Most of it is about as subtle as an air raid. They all think they're terribly funny. I hope it's not the trend for the rest of the tour. One or two of the lads gave them a few words back. It doesn't achieve much other than releasing some tension. You can't really win with this lot. There's not much call for rapier sharp wit on the Highveldt.

I played golf today. Creepy and I had little trouble taking the money off two of the Sunday press boys, James Mossop and Peter Hayter. Always a nice feeling, that. By the time we got back to the ground, the temperature was 115 in the shade. England were in trouble, too. The highlight of our batting today was an undefeated 48 from Devon, of all people. His second-highest knock ever included six sixes and gave us just a glimmer of hope. But the South Africans stayed in control as they had been all match. Losing is part of the game, but we'd been trailing from the first day to the last. That's not much of a confidence booster before the Test.

The two teams had a good drink and sing-song at the Keg pub this evening. Steve Jack bought Goughie a drink for being his 200th first-class victim. Goughie was caught behind, Jack was appealing for LBW! There was nearly a bit of trouble after a few inane comments to Devon from a local redneck, but the loudmouth was so drunk it wasn't worth the effort. You've got to ignore it and turn away. It's not just words, though. They are great touchers here – jabbing, barging and pushing, as if that makes what they say even more important.

WEDNESDAY 15 NOVEMBER   JOHANNESBURG

The waiting is over. Tomorrow all the talking stops, thank God. We flew back to Johannesburg and the Sandton Hotel on Monday morning. Illy moaned about our choice of music on the bus from the airport. It's generally rave and dance. He's pulled rank and threatened us with a week of Johnny Mathis. Johnny who? Later, the chairman gave us the benefit of his thoughts at a team meeting, especially on our Kimberley performance. He's right. We shouldn't have been bowled out twice on that wicket. Afterwards, we had a fines meeting – a sort of kangaroo court with lots of laughs and jokes. Wayne was in charge, with Winker (Mike Watkinson) and Ramble as the officials. The chairman got done twice – once for an appalling pair of socks, which he later proudly admitted had been bought during the 1970/71 Ashes tour; secondly for being the first player to take 500 wickets and score 1,000 runs on the tour. Well, that's how many he's told us about, so far. Jack was given the Olympic Torch award – he never goes out. Judgey owned up to being the only player not to lose weight on the trip. Amazing that, after the humidity of Kimberley. The Doc brought the house down with his quip, 'I'm not surprised, the amount of time you've spent at the crease!'

I'm rooming with Creepy. We toured Australia together with Young England. His feeling all week has been that he won't be playing in the Test. Although he's averaging 65, he would only come in at the expense of Judgey, and Illy told the press at Kimberley that Robin had done enough to win his place. I know Creepy feels very frustrated. He's playing well and it's not really his fault that he's missing out at the moment. It's amazing how the atmosphere changes as a Test approaches. Our net sessions were good. Everyone was trying to be positive.

We had an official function last night – the pre-series dinner at Centurion Park, which will be hosting its first-ever Test match tomorrow. I tried not to be too friendly with the opposition. I don't like anything that might affect my competitive edge. There were speeches from Illy, Jack Bannister, Mark 'gin & tonic' Nicholas and an impersonator who did a very good Nelson Mandela. The rest of his act mainly consisted of other politicians speaking Afrikaans, so it was lost on me. It went on too long. The rain is here, too. We arrived in a thunderstorm and, by the time we left, the ground was flooded. If this had been England, that would have been curtains for the Test. But the organisers seem to have no worries about Centurion draining.

The practice today was less intense. The talk was focused on the possible bowling permutations since the batting line-up appears settled. The pitch was bouncy here on the A tour a couple of years ago, although the spinners have been getting wickets this season. The chairman wasn't too happy to find the strip being watered this morning. Yesterday, Illy was pretty confident that his namesake would be a key player in this Test; now he's not so sure. He's chosen a thirteen with the Lancashire trio of Winker, Creepy and Digger missing out. That wasn't much of a 27th birthday present for Digger, but Winker lightened spirits with a witty, dry speech. I'm glad Devon's in. I hope he gets a game. At the moment he feels his best and, probably, only way of setting the record straight is to take some South African wickets in the Test. Dev had a knee operation in September and he's had some fluid drained off it since he's been over here. Now he's raring to go. After the team dinner, we talked about the South African team. I was honoured to make my contribution. My mate Cullinan, of course. I don't think any of the England lads are in any doubt about what I think of him as a player and a bloke. The two bowlers we studied most on video were Brett Schultz and Shaun Pollock, the son of the SA chairman of selectors, Peter.

THURSDAY 16 NOVEMBER   CENTURION PARK

First Test   *England 221/4*

Round one to the tourists. And two and three, I think. We've got runs on the board, we've recovered from a dodgy position. More importantly, the South Africans appear to have made a mess of selecting their team and reading the pitch. We've had to put up with a lot of talk about their professional and thorough approach and preparation. Well, they've had months getting ready for today, yet their coach Bob Woolmer and captain Hansie Cronje made a right pig's ear of it. These are only views for my diary and I wouldn't make them public now – there's a small matter of 29 days to go in the series. You've got to keep your powder dry in a sporting contest that lasts a couple of months. Yet, the opening exchanges are vital. Let the initiative go on the first day and you might never get it back. That's been the story of England's Ashes battles in recent years.

Ramble kept us waiting this morning. He thought he was answering his early-morning call, but it was our liaison man Dougie telling him that we were all on the bus. He's on the 20th floor and the lift stopped 20 times. He was fined heavily.

There wasn't a massive crowd to watch Centurion Park become the newest Test ground on the circuit. It's an interesting stadium. Half is one huge stand which sweeps round in a semi-circle. The other half is just grass banks where fans can set up their barbecues. It's not unknown for smoke to stop play here. The crowd built up during the day, but the South African authorities are hoping for bumper crowds on Saturday and Sunday.

The South Africans made two astonishing decisions before the start. They picked five quick bowlers – Donald, Schultz, Matthews, Pollock and McMillan. Five! If the pitch is that quick and bouncy, then four is more than adequate. If it's not, why would you want five quicks in the first place? That flawed strategy forced them into another. With such a fast-bowling battery, they had to invite the opposition to bat if they won the toss. Cronje did. And for that to work, we had to be all out – or as good as – by this evening. The fact we're not is due to a typical gutsy knock by Athers and a punishing innings from Hickie. Had either gone early in the afternoon session, England would have been in trouble. The morning session had gone reasonably well, but the balance tipped towards South Africa when Thorpey was out to the last ball before the break. It was probably the best delivery of the day, bowled by the new boy, Shaun Pollock. In fact he was South Africa's best bowler by some way, extracting more life out of the wicket than even Allan Donald. It might be a flash in the pan, but they may have found Donald a partner. They'll need one after a disappointing return by Schultz. There were fitness doubts about him before the Test. He got the first wicket to fall, but looks as if he's struggling.

I don't think I've seen Athers bat better in a Test match. His concentration was immense. I particularly remember him digging out a Schultz yorker. After lunch, the skipper realised it was

Devon and Illy: the saga that started on the first week of the tour and was still going strong after Devon's return home, when he went into print about the way he felt Illy had treated him.

I've never seen thunder and lightning like that experienced at Centurion Park.

imperative that he didn't give his wicket away. The South African bowlers didn't make life easy for him, hitting him on the helmet three times. He was out for 78 just before the close. But it was worth a century of anyone's money. Hickie's knock was different. Full of power and aggression, with a little bit of arrogance, it was the perfect foil to Atherton's solid dependency. When you see Hickie carve the ball around like this, you wonder how anyone can doubt him. He was world class today. He's often accused of making his runs when the pressure's off. Not today. It was stand up and be counted time. Hickie stood up and smacked the South Africa quicks all over the place. He's normally an undemonstrative bloke but, after the cut off Donald that brought up his 100, he punched the air in delight.

The day had started with Devon and Ramble being left out, which had widely been predicted. But I'd hoped that Devon might be given a chance. Lunch was a fairly quiet affair – 64/3 is a precarious position on the first day of a Test series. Gussie and I went up to the Sky commentary box after lunch to look at a few replays, and we ended up being there all afternoon. Cricketers are a superstitious lot. When a partnership starts to build, the players off the field tend to stay where they are, in case any movement breaks the spell. Gussie and I returned to the Sky box after tea as Athers and Hickie continued their stand. I'm still in awe of Beefy, Gower and Willis, who are all here commentating for Sky. I just can't believe that Ian Botham actually chats to me about a Test match in which I'm playing. He's great. Always encouraging the lads, always being positive – unlike one or two former players who take great delight in being negative and putting you down. Bad light brought proceedings to an early end and I popped into the South African dressing room for a drink. They are a bit subdued. Good. We can win after this start.

Friday 17 November   Centurion Park

England 381/9

The weather is threatening to ruin our great start. I've never seen a thunderstorm like the one that washed out play today and flooded Centurion Park in a matter of minutes. Actually, the players came off because of lightning. Umpire Cyril Mitchley told Jack Russell that he couldn't take responsibility for the players' safety. Cyril told me afterwards that two of his friends had been struck and killed by lightning, one on a golf course and the other on the cricket field. It was the only sensible decision. The violent electrical storm cost us

30 overs when we might have made serious inroads into the South African batting. Still, we're in the driving seat and there's plenty of time to force a win. The South African tactics and players took a fair amount of stick from their own media after the first day.

Unlike yesterday, I knew I would have some part to play today. Athers got the lads together before the start. His message was simple – make sure yesterday's effort is not wasted. Hickie, not quite as fluently, and Judgey carried on the good work. Eventually, I joined Jack at the crease with England 320/6. Still work to be done. I walked out to a standing ovation. It wasn't for me, but for Hickie, who was out for 141. I felt good until I hit a ball from McMillan straight to Craig Matthews at square leg. Another careless shot. The delivery had four or six written all over it. Instead, I was out for 13. Goughie and Illy both got ducks, but Jack was in typical belligerent mood. He reached his fifty with help from Gussie just before the storm.

Kim is here with a tour party. He came up to the England balcony, but he was a bit embarrassed because of all the fuss over Devon and what he said about Plank. Kim's entitled to his opinion. It doesn't bother me. After play, I went back with him to his hotel for a drink. I'm glad he's staying at Derbyshire. It will seem strange with a new captain, but it would have been sad if he'd retired or gone to another county.

SATURDAY 18 NOVEMBER   CENTURION PARK

Play abandoned

England lost to South Africa today. Not here, but at Twickenham where the home side was outplayed. They have been trailing the rugby for the past couple of weeks here with an advert which shows someone dressed up in Will Carling's No. 13 jersey sneaking into Princess Diana's room. When he gets there, he is confronted by the Springboks and runs away. It's the sort of 'kick-you-in-the-nuts' South African humour that we're getting used to. I hadn't expected to get the chance to watch the Twickenham game, but the rain has all but finished our chance of pressing for a win. With two days left, it's going to take something special to bowl them out twice. I can't see the South Africans making a game out of it. They'll be happy with a draw after what's happened here. Illy is confident that we can still cause some damage. We have nothing to lose, so I intend to charge in and give their batsmen a real working over and a taste of what they can expect in the weeks ahead.

It was raining this morning when we got on our bus for the half-hour journey to Centurion. We're staying in Johannesburg, although the venue is in Pretoria. There's a hotel opposite the ground, and I suppose it would have been too logical to put us in there. The pitch was remarkably dry when we arrived, but the rain appeared every time it looked as if we might get out there. Hanging around in dressing room is part of cricket life. Illy and Athers took on the Doc and the scorer at bridge. The best moment came when Illy was shuffling a new pack and some of the cards fell to the floor. 'First time I've put down anything in my life – I held 500 bloody catches, you know.' The dressing room was in stitches. Every ten minutes or so, he bellowed 'Turn that music down.' Down it went, then the volume was slowly raised until the chairman objected again. Most of the rest of us played Pictionary. Brian McMillan invited Goughie and me to a single-wicket competition in Cape Town after the tour, but I don't think I'll be able to fit it in. Many of the lads are ploughing through Mandela's autobiography, *Long Walk to Freedom*. Jack keeps beating Ramble at chess. The highlight of our day came when one of our security guards, Rory, asked Wayne for a rub-down. Our physio was only too happy to oblige. Only he didn't use liniment. Instead, he rubbed whitener all over Rory's body. He was not amused and is promising retribution. Knowing these South Africans and having been threatened by one myself, I know he means it.

The umpires called the day's play off just in time for everyone to get back to the Sandton Sun and settle down to watch the live TV broadcast of the rugby. How convenient! The news about Stoke is better. They drew three-all at Portsmouth after being three-one down. That's 12 goals in the past three games. Later we had drinks with our bowling and batting coaches, who are about to leave us. Edie will rejoin the party, but Plank's work is finished.

Sunday 19 November   Centurion Park

Play abandoned

I won't ever give Derby stick for its weather again. Some of the lads are even talking about building an ark! I don't know why we bothered getting on the bus today. It was pouring in Johannesburg, pouring all the way up to Centurion and pouring when we got there. The bowlers are especially frustrated. The batsmen have done their bit. Now it's our turn. Well, it would be if the rain relented for a few hours. We hung around the ground for four hours, pretending there was some hope of starting play. The fans weren't fooled. Nobody was there apart from a few Brits who have paid a lot of money to visit the Rainbow country. It's well named. There should be a monster one when all this lot finishes. The players are very bored, and we started throwing grapes at the crowd. Players have a tendency to get up to mischief when they have time on their hands. Stewie and I wandered into the library. There was a live TV interview taking place with David Gower. Just for fun, Stewie and I wandered behind Gower in camera and started taking books off the shelf and reading them. A bit childish, I suppose, but we thought it was funny. So did the lads in the dressing room watching the TV.

Since that storm on Friday night, six inches of rain have fallen here. The Hennops river bursting its banks hasn't helped – it borders the ground. It's not just a blow for us. Dr Ali Bacher's cricket board are also counting the cost. The Northern Transvaal has spent a six-figure sum on getting the ground ready and it's rumoured that they are not insured for loss of income. They had budgeted for around 30,000 cricket supporters visiting this weekend and it's been a complete wash-out.

MONDAY 20 NOVEMBER   CENTURION PARK

First Test abandoned   Man of the Match: Graeme Hick

Something extraordinary nearly happened at Centurion Park today. We were within five minutes of playing cricket there. I kid you not. The rain abated, the drainage was good and the stumps were returned to their slots for the first time since Friday night. There was no chance of forcing a result, but a two o'clock start meant that we could have a few hours making life uncomfortable for the South African batsmen and scoring a few points for the remainder of the series. I started to warm up, looking forward to the new ball which Athers told me I'd be taking. I was really going to charge in. After three days of twiddling my thumbs, I had a lot of excess energy to get rid of. But I had been lulled into a false sense of security. As the umpires put on their coats and prepared to walk out, the heavens opened again. This time, there was no delay. The first Test with England on South African soil for 31 years was abandoned as a draw. Looking out a few minutes later, I couldn't believe it. The sun was shining. We could have play after all. No chance. As we headed back on our new coach, it was raining again. Fortunately this coach did not leak. Every morning, we found the other coach had got wetter and wetter, inside and outside. Life was miserable enough without having to park yourself on wet seats. I'm not sure we're going to escape the rain, either. Bloemfontein is the next stop and the reports confirm that it's had more than its fair share of water, too. But it's not all doom and gloom around here. The farmers, who were caught in the middle of a crippling drought until the England cricket team arrived, are holding celebration parties.

Our tour management now has a problem. The Test bowlers haven't bowled an over here and there's only one game before the second Test at the Wanderers. Does Illy give his Test line-up a much-needed run out? That would give the understudies no chance of pressing a claim. The South Africans have named their squad for the second Test. Schultz is out. He has been criticised for breaking down so quickly and it's been claimed he didn't have a proper fitness test. Merryck Pringle, who took a hat-trick against us at Soweto, returns and the popular view is that the spinner who was left out here, Clive Eksteen, will play. No place for young Adams. Hickie is named Man of the Match. No arguments about that. England are ahead on points. But there is a real feeling in the England camp that if the positions had been reversed after two days we wouldn't have seen a drop of rain. Moral victories will count for nothing at the end of the series.

Thursday 23 November
Springbok Park, Bloemfontein

England 316/4   Orange Free State 36/0

Still waiting for a bowl, although I'm lucky to get a game. Gussie and Goughie have missed out. Mind you, if I wasn't so desperately short of bowling practice, I wouldn't come anywhere near a wicket like this. It's a batsman's paradise, typical of all the wickets we've encountered outside the Test. It's all very well spreading the word around South Africa, but when you're playing away from the big towns and centres, it's only fair to the touring side that they are provided with a decent wicket. A wicket like this hampers batsmen and bowlers alike. The batters suddenly find the margin for error is drastically reduced just when the pressure's on – in the middle of a Test match – after preparing on a featherbed. And it does the bowlers' confidence little good to get no response from a wicket that dictates that you concentrate on not giving away runs rather than taking wickets.

This is a three-day game now, with Sunday's play switched to a one-day contest to give everyone in the squad a run out. I've got two games. Good. The change was decided when we arrived after the short flight to 'Bloem' – with a two-hour delay at Johannesburg Airport, where we met that well-known cricket enthusiast Sir Tim Rice. He was passing through on his way to speak at a dinner in Cape Town. The lads were more interested in some inside info on Madonna with whom he's working on the film and album of *Evita*. Another tribal welcome. Illy got on the phone to Ali Bacher who gave his approval for the new schedule. I can't imagine Lord's moving as quickly or as flexibly. Then the bad news. I've drawn the short straw. I'm sharing with Darren 'Barnsley Chop' Gough. It brings back memories of a winter together a few years ago when we shared a flat in New Zealand. We were playing for East Shirley in Christ-church, and it was the first time either of us had ever been away from home at Christmas. The Odd Couple – and I was the one with the apron. Goughie was happy to let me do all the washing, ironing and cooking. Christmas day was spent on the beach, though we did manage a traditional dinner, which Goughie smothered in tomato ketchup as usual.

We weren't able to use the nets yesterday because of the rain. We were put through a heavy fielding and training session in the morning, then a group of us headed for the cinema in the afternoon to watch *The Net* with Sandra Bullock. The hotel has a pinball machine, so I've spent most of my tour allowance on that.

I felt stiff this morning after all that training. Once Athers had won the toss, I thought it unlikely I'd be called upon to bat, especially as Allan Donald was being allowed to rest between Tests. Athers actually went for a duck, but the Surrey duo of Stewie and Thorpey scored centuries. Thorpey needed the runs. Since his trip home, he's not found his touch. Someone had a fax copy of the *Daily Telegraph* which had played out the rest of our first Test on a computer. England won by 165 runs, although I wasn't too happy with my first innings bowling figures of 0/75. I was just about to call it all a load of rubbish when I saw my other figures were 3/29. That's more like it. Gussie was delighted with his 7/112! Alongside this report was yet another proposal on changing the structure of the English game. You don't have to be a genius to work out that little will be cured by these plans. David Graveney expressed his disappointment that players weren't consulted. Quite right, you can hear the old codgers preaching. Players, players! What have they got to do with the game? My favourite quote came from a Test and County Cricket Board official who confirmed that secrecy had been a deliberate policy. 'We don't want the press helping people make up their minds!' I wonder if they ever read their own statements and realise just how they appear to outsiders.

FRIDAY 24 NOVEMBER   BLOEMFONTEIN

Orange Free State 245/9 declared   England 121/1

Once again the difference in attitudes to youth has been brought to the fore. While the English are very protective, fearing that a real talent may be destroyed by an early setback, the rest of the world works by different rules – 'If you're good enough, you're old enough.' Paul Adams wasn't shy to take his chance. Today it was Hendrik Dippenaar, whose entry into first-class cricket has been delayed by exams. He was the outstanding batsman on the under-19s tour of England in the summer. Today, 42 of his 46 runs came in boundaries and he belted one of Devon's attempted bouncers into the trees. It was his attitude as much as his runs that I found impressive. We might be Mighty England and I might be the famous Dominic Cork, hat-trick hero of Old Trafford, but if the ball was in the slot to be hit, he hit it. Annoying as it is to be thumped around by a schoolboy, I have nothing but admiration for his guts. It confirms a belief I have that we are too nice, too respectful; we don't upset people enough. The other point of note today was the battle between Ramps and Creepy. It's not over because both are still at the crease. Illy has stated on the record that Ramps will be given two Tests to prove himself. I agree. It would be unfair to drop him after one knock at Centurion Park. But life is not proving very fair for Creepy at the moment. He's in great nick, but is kicking his heels until someone fails. And, occasionally, there's talk of playing Jack at No. six and five bowlers, which would give Creepy even less chance of making the Test side. Illy is certainly impressed by Creepy's commitment and improvement. All the chairman can say is that when he does finally get his chance, he must make the most of it.

My highlight of the day was knocking Hansie's poles out. I opened the bowling this morning and the ball was reverse swinging. But it went out of shape and was replaced. It was the new one that did for the South African captain. Because of the rain, it was a few days late for me.

The lads spotted the *Daily Telegraph*'s cricket correspondent Christopher Martin Jenkins bare-chested on the grass bank today. Afterwards, he admitted that it was the first time it had ever happened at a first-class cricket match. No wonder the game's in turmoil. What would Swanton have made of it?

SATURDAY 25 NOVEMBER   SPRINGBOK PARK

England 239/4   Orange Free State 110/3
Match drawn

If I've ever had a more boring day's cricket, I can't think of it at the moment. You can't blame Athers. He put preparing for the Wanderers Test in front of going for a win. It was the sensible thing to do. But it killed the game for player and spectator alike when our motives became clear. The real excitement came before the start when Illy searched out the BBC *Test Match Special*'s producer, Peter Baxter, to give him a rollocking. Illy was woken up at 11 o'clock last night by someone working for *The Parkinson Show* in London, looking for Judgey. The chairman wasn't too pleased to hear it was that late or that Judgey wasn't in his room. Not surprisingly, he declined a request to speak to Parky in Judgey's place. It wasn't Baxter's fault, but he works for the BBC and that was good enough for Illy.

We scored 60 in the first session, during which Judgey struggled over a 30-ball duck. Creepy fell ten short of another century, although he had more than made his point. I found myself filling the England No. 5 spot again, though with much more optimism than I'd done at Edgbaston. It wasn't one of my more dashing knocks, my undefeated 67 coming in 115 balls. Richard Illingworth retired hurt with a back strain, but was able to bowl seven overs later in the day. Devon got a wicket with his first ball after tea, but it was a rare moment of celebration and the biggest cheers came when the umpires decided to end the contest with 16 of the allotted overs left. At least that gave us plenty of time to prepare for the players' barbecue back at the hotel. Gussie and Hickie were the chefs and not a bad job they did.

SUNDAY 26 NOVEMBER   SPRINGBOK PARK

Orange Free State 201/8 (50 overs)   England 202/3 (41 overs)
England won by 7 wickets

On with the coloured clothing, although this was not a day-night contest. We'll be back here in January for that. The crowd was about 7,000 – five times the number that came yesterday. The bigger the *braais*, the greater the abuse. Bloemfontein was not much different from Kimberley in that respect. I've yet to understand why hurling abuse is considered hilarious over here. I'm happy to acknowledge a clever remark at my expense. But shouts of 'Cork – you're a big ******!' leave me cold. Perhaps I'm missing something.

Hansie won the toss and batted. They were going well at 106/2 in the 24th over, but lost their way when they decided to slog our spinners, Illy, Mike Watkinson and Ramps. Their total was a good 50 runs short of making it a contest on this track, even though Donald returned to their line-up. He only bowled three overs, which cost 25 runs. Even the quickest and best in the world struggle to get any life out of this wicket. Athers, Stewie and Ramps were never in trouble and we won easily. A fight broke out at the close and somebody nicked the stump with the camera in it. As he was chased, he threw it into the crowd, and unfortunately it stuck in someone's leg. Supporters like a drink in England, but I've never seen incidents degenerate into brawls like this. It's strange, but you always feel that an argument here is likely to end up in a fight. As a result, we're keeping our distance from local fans to be on the safe side.

WEDNESDAY 29 NOVEMBER   JOHANNESBURG

Another team dinner. It feels as if we are starting the series all over again. We have picked the same XIII again, although I can't judge whether we are going to play four quicks or include a spinner, as we did at Centurion Park. That's where we've been practising today. Or were supposed to be. We headed there because the net facilities are better, but would you believe it? The England cricket team arrived and the heavens opened again. Back on the bus and we drove to see if the Wanderers was any better. It was. I hope we're not going to have another five days hanging around the dressing rooms.

The Sandton Hotel is becoming very familiar. Our physio was certainly relieved to see it after our flight from Bloemfontein. Rory, our security guard, finally got his revenge. Wayne was stopped by the airport security guards and accused of bringing in drugs. It was very convincing, especially when he was hauled away to another part of the terminal. There he was searched, fingerprinted, handcuffed and thrown in the back of a paddy wagon. I gather Rory had a word with the driver and told him to throw the van about. Wayne was white as a sheet by the time he got to the Sandton, and feeling very sick. He was honest enough to admit that it was not a pleasant experience. The back of the van was completely dark and he wasn't able to control his movements with his hands tied behind his back.

In the afternoon, Goughie and I headed for the zoo for some promotional pictures for Tetley's with lion cubs. They seemed cuddly enough until I caught sight of mum and dad having dinner. I wasn't going anywhere near them. The visiting Press XI let us down by losing the media match to the South Africans under lights on Tuesday night. You can never rely on cricket writers!

THURSDAY 30 NOVEMBER   WANDERERS STADIUM

Second Test   *South Africa 278/7*

I'm exhausted. I've bowled one ball short of 28 overs in five spells in the day. That might have been a short burst for the likes of Fred Trueman, but it's the most I've ever delivered. At one stage after tea, South Africa were 211/2 and our decision to invite the home side to bat was looking rather silly. But we kept plugging away and three wickets at the death have brought us right back into the match. The locals were surprised that we chose to bowl and left out our spinner. The side batting first has a tradition of winning Wanderers Tests, or at least not losing them. Time to end that. Devon got the nod at last. Great. It was his pace that picked up the wickets of centurion Gary Kirsten and wicket-keeper Richardson in the space of four deliveries. The other England hero is Jack, who has taken five catches and must be hoping for more the way the wicket is playing. He caught my old mate Cullinan off Hickie – his 100th Test catch. Cullinan rode his luck yesterday and should have brought some welcome relief to Goughie, whose first spell of three overs went for 21 runs. But Jack's one blemish robbed Goughie of his wicket. We finished on a high when I trapped McMillan plumb LBW in my final over. They say if you put a side in, you've failed if you haven't bowled them out by the end of the first day. I don't really go by those rules. The South Africans made a good start, better than we did at Centurion Park – but we're better placed than they were at the end of that first day. All teams look great when things are going their way. They didn't for us today. But we dug deep and fought hard. I would say honours were even by the close of play.

December 1995

Stalemate – with Glory

South Africa 332 & 5/0   England 200

My delight at my second five-wicket haul for England quickly vanished when our first innings collapsed and our last eight wickets contributed only 91 runs. We were not helped by a bad umpiring decision that removed Thorpey, who was going along nicely. Eksteen's first ball ballooned off his pad. We were astonished when South African umpire Karl Liebenberg raised his finger for the catch. We rushed to watch the replay. Thorpey was nowhere near the ball. Maybe that decision affected us more than it should have. Having fought back on the first day, we continued this morning. In all we claimed the final seven South African wickets for 72 runs. I was just as pleased at Devon's four wickets as my five. His form has certainly been nothing special up to now, but that's Devon. He seems to be able to pull it out on the big occasion more often than not. The press have made much of a quote I gave at last night's press conference – 'I'm tired now – I'll have a meal, go to bed and have a bath.' They fell about. OK. Not in that order.

Our reply started badly when we lost Athers, who left one from Donald that he shouldn't have. He shouldn't have because it shaved his off-stump. It was a misjudgement of the tiniest proportion and one which would not have cost him his wicket on the more docile pitches we have been encountering outside the Tests. Enter Ramps. It was painful watching him struggling to get off the mark. There is such a talent there that he just can't release at this level. Eventually, he cut a ball from Donald to the boundary. You could feel the tension ease in the dressing room. Now Ramps could get on and show this crowd what he was made of. Two balls later, he was back with us after playing round a full-length delivery and losing his middle stump. Ramps knows better than anyone that he now has one innings left to redeem himself and his Test place – on this tour at least. Stewie, who escaped when Pollock dropped an absolute sitter that would have given Donald his 100th Test wicket, and Thorpey took us past the century mark. Once they had gone, only Judgey stood firm. Their spinner Eksteen took 3/12 in 11 overs and tied us down. I'm not sure he's that good a bowler or this wicket is particularly receptive to spin. But we let him and South Africa take the initiative and that has cost us dear today. I batted with Judgey and felt confident. Once again, a loose shot proved my downfall. I'm always writing here that I must not throw my wicket away at these crucial times. But it keeps happening. My main job is to take wickets and some look upon my runs as a bonus. But I don't want it to be that way. I want to become a better Test batsman and a better Test bowler.

Being behind by 132 runs on the first innings is not a healthy situation. I can't believe how one bad session in Test cricket can put you on the back foot. We mustn't ignore the reality of our position, but we mustn't let it get us down. The lads had a drink in the team room, well aware that it had not been a good day but determined to put it right tomorrow.

SATURDAY 2 DECEMBER   WANDERERS

South Africa 296/6

The situation is much more serious than it was last night. The South Africans are over 400 runs ahead and, as usual when England are in trouble, there's no sign of the rain that was forecast this weekend. I don't think we bowled that badly today, but Athers was in a Catch-22 position – stopping runs was as important as taking wickets, probably more so. I was surprised that the South Africans came off early for bad light. That would suggest that they will bat on tomorrow. The longer they do, the less time we have to survive. There are some captains who might have had us batting again tonight. We raised our glasses to one of our own after the match. Jack Russell took ten catches to equal Bob Taylor's world Test record. Amazingly, their keeper Richardson didn't take a single chance in our innings. Catch number. ten was extra special as he took a one-handed effort low to his right to dismiss Jonty Rhodes. Bob Taylor, a former Derbyshire stalwart, is at the match and he was one of the first to congratulate our keeper. We did need something to raise our spirits tonight.

It was always going to be a tough day. There was never any doubt the South Africans were going to rub our noses in it. After getting rid of the openers cheaply, the rest all dug in. I accounted for Hansie and Cullinan, who pulled a long hop to Goughie at mid-on. It's almost as pleasing to get him with a ball that he should have smashed to the boundary as with a good delivery. Goughie did well to make it today. He was smashed on the arm on Friday and had an X-ray before being cleared to play. The bandage on his arm had a message on it: 'No pain, no gain. Be strong'. Devon got a bit of stick when he came back with a new ball. McMillan smashed him for a couple of huge sixes. That's what made their decision to come off for light all the more strange. Having been kept tied down for most of the day, they had broken free and the ball was certainly running their way. But I've noticed that safety first is the order of their day. Not so much in the way they play, as in the tactical decisions they take. We can't disguise the fact that we're in trouble here and it will take something special to avoid defeat. The match referee Clive Lloyd issued a statement tonight saying that SA coach Bob Woolmer's criticism of the dismissals of Dave Richardson and Graham Thorpe had brought the game into disrepute. Woolmer was strongly reprimanded.

We've heard reports that Boycs was caught on the back foot yesterday. *Test Match Special* is not providing continuous ball-by-ball coverage and Jon Agnew used the opportunity well.

Agnew pretended he was on air and said, 'Donald is bowling fast, Geoff. You'd be raising the white flag and backing to square leg.'

Boycs: 'I don't know about that.'

Agnew: 'Is it true, Geoffrey, that you were the most boring batsman in history?'

Boycs: 'I was only doing my job.'

Agnew: 'They said that Ian Botham emptied bars. You must have filled them.'

Boycs: 'Well, how many Test matches did you play?'

The great man had finally cracked. I wish I'd been there.

SUNDAY 3 DECEMBER   WANDERERS

South Africa 346/9 declared   England 167/4

We're still alive and kicking. There's a long way to go, but Athers looks determined to stay the course. If England go down, it won't be for lack of effort on his part. But our last two recognised batsmen are at the crease. We can't afford any more mistakes. Yet I think the South Africans are already regretting batting for so long. They thought this Test would have been more or less over by this evening.

We took the field today to the National Anthem. I like that idea – it's another reminder of why we are here and what it means. Another drink for Jack tonight, to celebrate another world record. He took the eleventh catch that took him past Bob Taylor. Eksteen was the victim and I was the bowler. That was my ninth wicket and I should have had my first ten-wicket haul in Test cricket. But for some reason umpire Liebenberg did not share my utter conviction that the ball would have hit McMillan's middle stump if he had not got his pad in the way. The South African was on 99 at the time and the wicket would have made no difference to the match situation, but I was hopping mad. It *was* out. Absolutely no doubt. He might still have been stranded on 99, but he went for a risky single that would have seen Donald run out if Ramps had hit. That marked the South Africans' declaration, setting us 479 to win or rather, survive, in five sessions and 20 minutes. I felt stiff this morning and worked out I'd finished up bowling nearly 60 overs in the match. But I knew every minute fielding was one less to bat. McMillan, especially, took his time to get going this morning and we were in no mood to hurry him up. It didn't take a genius to work out that Athers was the key to our survival. A win, I'm afraid, was always out of our reach. If we had four good sessions and reached 350 for the loss of two wickets, we might have thought about it.

Ian Botham's been down to the dressing room a few times. It's great to have him around. He's got England out of a few scrapes and worked the odd miracle himself. His presence reminds us that such escapes are possible. I was only ten when England won the Headingley Test in 1981 against the Aussies, but winning that match from an impossible position has always been one of my cricket inspirations.

We knew we needed a good start and we didn't want wickets falling in bunches. Athers and Stewie provided the first, putting on 75 for the first wicket. Ramps walked out knowing that his England future was going to be decided over the next few hours. It was decided in two balls as he played down the wrong line and was bowled. We really needed him to stay there. Initially, I felt annoyed that he'd let the side down, but that soon gave way to sympathy for his predicament. Ramps has the talent, is desperate to succeed and is trying like mad. You could see by the way he walked back to the pavilion that he knows it's back to the drawing board and a long spell in county cricket after this trip. Thorpey and Athers were still together midway through the final session. Two wickets down at the close would be a result. But Thorpey and Hickie went quickly and the final overs were spent making sure that we didn't lose a fifth wicket that would surely have signalled the end. Mind you, the locals think we're dead and buried already. If we need any more incentive for pulling this one out of the fire, it's to remove the smirks from their gloating faces. I see where Cullinan gets it from. They're an arrogant bunch. What gets me is that they think their players are angels, who would no more question an umpire's decision than resort to sledging. When we react, we're accused of being bully boys. They don't even try to hide the fact that they think victory is a formality and have begun celebrating already, even around our hotel.

Tomorrow is a big day for Athers, and not just on the field. Ian Botham has laid down a 'Cane & Coke' challenge. Athers had made sure Beefy got to hear of his remark that, once they reach 40, the great drinkers are past it. One I. T. Botham, just 40, was rather predictable in his response. If – and only if – Athers is still batting tomorrow night, then we'll find out just who is past it in the drinking stakes. It's typical Athers – increasing the competitive environment and edge. We just wish him luck, hoping that we are not going to let him down ourselves.

MONDAY 4 DECEMBER   WANDERERS

England 351/3
Second Test drawn

TUESDAY 5 DECEMBER   PAARL

Apologies for being too drunk last night to record the historic events of the day. That's not quite true. I did write a few lines, but I cannot read a single word. I can just about make out 'Athers' and 'fantastic' and '****ing unbelievable.' Rather brief, but it does say it all. Athers batted for nearly eleven hours to score 185 not out. The runs weren't important. He saved the Test for England with more than a little help from our own terrier, Jack Russell. Jack joined the skipper 45 minutes before lunch and for the rest of the day my prayers were answered as the South African bowlers failed to separate them. I was praying hard because I was padded up and the next man in. I went through four pairs of batting gloves. I'm exhausted. And all I did was sit on my backside all day. At first, I asked for Jack still to be there at lunch. It was obvious to all and sundry at the Wanderers that the South African bowlers wouldn't get Athers out if they bowled until Christmas. Get through to drinks in the afternoon, Jack. I can last three hours, I hope. But once there, tea became the key. If we could have five wickets intact going into the final session, then we would have a real chance. But Jack had been in this position once before – at Barbados in 1990, when he looked to have saved the game for England. Then the new ball delivered by Ambrose shot along the ground and he was gone. England lost their final wicket with 12 minutes left. Jack kept telling Athers, 'I'm not going through that again. I'm not going through that again.' Then there was an hour to go and I knew I wouldn't be batting. It was a matter of pride now. Athers and Jack weren't going to give the South Africans anything – not even a consolation wicket. I was so proud of them. The South Africans were going to have to live with the fact that they hadn't won the second Test after all. Hard cheese, as they say.

We knew that we were watching history in the making. But that wasn't what mattered to us. It was about team spirit and refusing to surrender. England teams have gained a reputation for folding in recent years, but I have found no evidence of this. Edgbaston was a freak pitch and occasion. In my other Tests, we have fought the Windies all the way and beaten them twice. We had the better of the first Test here and now we've fought one of the greatest rearguard actions ever seen by an English team abroad. Jack was in tears and the Barmy Army was going crazy. The champagne started flowing, but we were high without it. I've never waited for five hours with my pads on before – and I never want to again. Nobody argued with the Man of the Match award – a joint presentation to Athers and Jack.

But Athers had one more ordeal – the Botham Challenge – to survive. Both men were still standing, if rather unsteadily, in Vertigo's in the early hours of this morning. Not that I was much of a judge, by that stage. We gave it some serious tap. And why not? Somehow your head doesn't seem that bad the next morning when you've been celebrating something worthwhile.

We were a pretty motley crew as we checked out of the Sandton for the third time this morning. Not that Athers looked any different. He's always a mess first thing. The lads were glad to be moving on, especially to the Cape wine region of Paarl. Today's been a continuation of yesterday. I spent most of the flight down to Cape Town up at the back of the plane with Judgey. He was flying before he got on. There was a permanent idiot-grin on his face. Anyone he knew – and a few he didn't – was greeted with, 'You've got to be strong' and a none-too-gentle jab to the chest. There was a group from a religious sect on board. They had never flown before. They had certainly seen nothing like the Judge. But no one took offence. We went by coach from Cape Town airport to a winery that had organised a barbecue lunch for us. Most of the lads were just topping up. The hotel is set in a beautiful location, surrounded by mountains. This is the place where some of the New Zealand touring team were caught smoking dope last year, but we were all on cloud nine before we arrived. The papers are full of England's historic fightback. Because you're so wrapped up in the game, it's only afterwards that you appreciate the scale of the achievement.

THURSDAY 7 DECEMBER   PAARL

England 263/8 v Boland

FRIDAY 8 DECEMBER   PAARL

England 402/8 declared   Boland 129/4

A good one to miss. The pitch is the dullest of the dull. No pace, no bounce, no grass – perhaps the Kiwis smoked it all. Illy and Athers are getting fed up with being expected to prepare batsmen and bowlers for Test matches on flat ****heaps like this. Amazingly, this square is the same as the one that saw last year's New Zealand tour game abandoned because it was too dangerous after 22 wickets fell on the first day. Not this time. You might get a result in a four-week game. Survival is a piece of cake. You could bat all day in this wondrous setting. But scoring runs is another matter, the ball is coming on to the bat so slowly. Nearly all the batsmen got out trying to up the tempo. Most of the bowling was done by the Boland spinners – just the workout the lads need to get ready for Donald, Pollock and McMillan! Why should I worry? Tomorrow Ramps and I are off to Cape Town for the weekend, staying in Daffy Defreitas' flat. Athers told me on Wednesday that he wanted me to rest up after the Wanderers. I couldn't argue. It took a lot out of me. Athers is also sitting this one out. No one's worried about *his* form.

On Wednesday afternoon groups of us went sightseeing in cars. That's a rare event on cricket tours these days. My Derbyshire team-mate 'Daffy' is among the opposition. He's trying to impress Illy with the World Cup coming up. In his second spell on Thursday, he took the wicket of Peter Martin and conceded no runs in eight overs. The Test No. 3 spot has opened up for Creepy, but he chose today for his first failure of the tour. It's always the way. Still, unless England play only five batsmen in the third Test at Durban and move Judgey up the order, Creepy will get his chance there. Jack's at No. 6 in this match and once again he came to England's rescue with a career-best undefeated 129. That's over ten hours he's batted against South African bowlers this week and they still haven't got him out. I missed most of the first day's afternoon session as I was training at the local Health & Racquet Club. You can't sit out these matches, do nothing and expect to roar in a week later. Put some in, take some out. The lads went to a reception at the Nederburg Winery last night. We'd been told it was a low-key affair – a few drinks around a barbecue. But it was the full works. One or two of the press boys were definitely underdressed. Nothing unusual there.

To gain my weekend pass, I've been on 12th man duties today. It was quite a busy day. Doing 12th man duties is not a day off. Batting is slightly easier. There are only two blokes to keep an eye on and the rest of the squad will soon tell you if you miss a signal for new gloves or a bat. Fielding is a different proposition. Of the five remaining players, a few are often given leave of absence to allow them a complete break. Today, Athers and Gussie headed for a tour of the wineries. The guys on the field were thirsty, too. It was very hot in the middle, and I was on and off dozens of times. And Goughie, trying to find some form, limped off after less than four overs with a damaged hamstring, we think. He returned briefly, but didn't appear after tea and is waiting on the specialist's report. The Barnsley Chop is not having the happiest of tours. He's dreading repeating his experience of last winter in Australia and returning home early. You can't blame the wicket directly, but Goughie knew that he had to put in something extra on this track and that might have led him to straining too hard. No such problems for Jack – he's batting like Brian Lara at the moment. What a week for him. A world record, a record Test-saving partnership with the skipper and now a career-best with the bat. And his wife, Aileen, is here. She's never been on tour before. Jack knew nothing about her visit. He returned to his room at the end of the second Test and there she was. True romance! Not a dry eye in the house.

SATURDAY 9 DECEMBER   BOLAND PARK

Boland 288   England 33/2
Match drawn

SUNDAY 10 DECEMBER   BOLAND PARK

England 244 (49.4 overs)   Boland 170 (42.4)
England won by 74 runs

What's going on? My weekend break turned into an away-day. I thought the lads were pulling a fast one when the phone went in Daffy's Cape Town flat yesterday and we were ordered back to camp. Because of the docile nature of the pitch and general apathy, the four-day match was being cut short a day early and Sunday was now being turned over to a one-day game. Pardon? How does that affect me? You're playing! Too late I tried the old answering machine trick – 'You are through to Dominic Cork. Unfortunately, he can't take your call at the moment. Please leave a message after the tone. He'll try to get back to you after the weekend. Beep, beep, beep . . .' Instead, Winker found himself stuck with me again.

Apparently, the local lads had mentioned the possibility of ending the first-class game early. Just at that point, the plastic chair which Illy was sitting on, leaning against the clubhouse wall, broke in half. Illy banged his head against the wall and found himself sitting on the ground. Enough was enough. Were the local lads being serious? Yes. Right, this match ends tonight. Athers was out with our tour manager, Trout, fly fishing for the first time in his life. He returned to the hotel for our liaison man Dougie's birthday gathering, and a relaxing dinner of the fish he had caught. He didn't look best pleased when he found out that not only was a one-day game arranged, but he was playing. Ours is not to wonder why.

There was always hope of a result yesterday while Boland struggled to save the follow-on. Once that target was passed, thanks to a typical Daffy 50, the proceedings slowed almost to a halt. Their score of 288 took a grand total of 135 overs to amass. There was some confusion about whether England would come out to bat again. If they hadn't, that might have put Jack's career-best in doubt as the

Jack equals the world record – his tenth in the match was this catch to dismiss Jonty Rhodes off my bowling.

The Wanderers' Second Test: Athers couldn't have wished for a more determined ally than Jack, and together they batted from 45 minutes before lunch till the close of play.

match might not have been regarded as first-class. Jack, who'd been leading the side with Stewie off the field with an injury, was going out regardless, with one of the crowd or press if necessary. But it wasn't. Creepy and Judgey made their way to the wicket for the final few overs. The most significant event of an insignificant game from a tour point of view was that Goughie was unable to bowl and will certainly miss the Durban Test. Athers, as usual, recovered his composure and hit an unimpressive 77 today. Our total was always going to be too good for Boland. It was an easier wicket to bowl on when you didn't need to take wickets and stopping the runs was the main priority. All the other bowlers know there's a place up for grabs with Goughie out. Digger Martin was especially impressive today, picking up four wickets. It's been a pleasant respite here on the Cape, but it's not done much for our preparations for the third Test. Spirits are high. I feel that our performance in the first Test and refusal to capitulate in the second gives us the edge on this series.

WEDNESDAY 13 DECEMBER   DURBAN

Not again! There's a good chance the rain is going to disrupt this Test match as well. I can't believe it. Paarl apart, every place we've been, it's rained. But for once I might read the wicket right. The Kingsmead groundsman is my old coach at Derbyshire, Phil Russell. If the weather holds, he's positive there will be a result. It was a long flight from Cape Town, but most of the England team travelled business class and it was a comfortable journey. As we flew over Durban, I remembered being here on New Year's Eve two years ago on the A tour when there were 300,000 people on the beach. Heavy rain throughout Monday night meant the nets were rather sporty yesterday. The batters normally have things their own way, so it was nice to find the ball flying around for a change. The Test wicket looked green and had a lot of moisture in it.

I've had trouble with the nail on my big toe. Wayne can't decide whether it should come off or not. Every first ball I bowl in a spell crucifies me. Wayne has cut away the dead skin and says the nail will come off when it's good and ready.

There was a positive atmosphere at tonight's team dinner, more confident than in Johannesburg. It's a big day for Judgey tomorrow. This is his home town – after he was dropped for the South Africa series in England last year, he thought he might never play against the country of his birth. I'm not sure whether he will bat No. 3 with Creepy or No. 6 – or vice versa. Jack meanwhile is in seventh heaven.

He's been up to the Zulu battlefield of Islandhlwana and the mission at Rorke's Drift, where a handful of soldiers held off 3,000 Zulus. It was the setting for the Stanley Baker/Michael Caine movie *Zulu*. Jack's paints went with him, of course, and we'll no doubt be seeing another masterpiece, valued at around £10,000! I'm in the wrong game.

The only two members of the squad not under consideration tomorrow are Goughie and Ramps. Illy has stated that Winker may be used as a spinner and/or seamer and Ramble may get a chance because the ball is expected to swing. Whoever gets picked is going to enjoy bowling on this wicket. Illy's missus has pitched up. Unfortunately, her luggage has not. Good to see the chairman under the cosh for once.

THURSDAY 14 DECEMBER   KINGSMEAD, DURBAN

Third Test   *South Africa 139/5*

We're back in charge. At one stage the South Africans collapsed from 54/0 to 89/5 before Rhodes and McMillan steadied things. Then bad light and rain ended the day prematurely. It's been a day of shocks. Devon and Gussie were left out for Ramble and Digger. I hadn't seen that coming. Hansie Cronje's decision was no surprise, though. After the opposition had been inserted in the first two Tests, it wasn't likely to happen a third time. This was one toss it was better to lose. The South Africans set off at a rate of knots, especially Hudson who's been short of runs so far. It looked a great toss to win and there were some worried looks at the scoreboard when the home side had reached 51 without loss after only an hour. That's quick going on the first morning of a Test match. I couldn't quite find my rhythm. I thought the ball would have swung more. Digger had a bad start. After three dot balls, Hudson hit the next four to the boundary. But after he switched ends, Digger found Gary Kirsten's edge and we made the breakthrough. Hudson went in the next over. The delivery from Illy bounced off his pad and hit his glove as he had his bat raised out of the way. Some might call it unlucky. We didn't. Our third wicket before lunch was the South African captain. He made a horrible mess of coming down the wicket and trying to drive Illy over the top. Digger got the next two wickets, including Jack Kallis on his debut. That wasn't a bad ball. We'd taken five South African wickets for 35 in 22 overs. Despite some confident shouts, that was our lot for the day. We would have settled for that at the start. It's an early start here, too. The light went towards the end of the afternoon, so kick-off time tomorrow is 9.35. Durban is like Blackpool with its long front, hotels, night clubs and restaurants. It's not the quietest of spots.

FRIDAY 15 DECEMBER   KINGSMEAD

South Africa 226   England 123/5

This one is going to be close. We should have been in front by now, but Pollock and Donald frustrated us with a last-wicket stand of 72. There's nothing so frustrating at the best of times, but this was heartbreak after we had them 153/9. That last-wicket partnership cost us more than runs. Creepy has torn his hamstring and it looks like the management are sending for a replacement. He was almost in tears when we got to him. He's worked like a dog to get fit and get back in the Test side. This was his big chance and it's disappeared in a fielding mishap. The South Africans' total isn't huge, but we could be forgiven for thinking our position is not as strong as it should or could have been. Donald made it worse with the quick wickets of Athers and Thorpey. Stewie and Judgey, watched by his folks on their 40th wedding anniversary, repaired some of the damage, but Matthews took three wickets to put us on the back foot again. At that point, I walked out to join Hickie. There was only one thing on my mind – stay there. And that's what I've got to do tomorrow, and give Hickie as much support as possible. There are strong warnings of a cold front and rain for the weekend, but this Test is so far advanced already on a bowler's wicket, we could lose a day or even more and still get a result. That last-wicket stand is still nagging me. I should have bowled better with the second new ball. The selectors got the other bowlers right – all ten South African wickets were taken by bowlers who didn't play in the Wanderers Test.

Both teams are staying in the Crowne Plaza, so you can't help bumping into them in the bar. Had a drink with Ian Botham, Stewie and Allan Donald. AD's been a slow starter in this series, but, worryingly, he's approaching his best. Another South African hero was with Beefy – Joel Stransky. He's the man who dropped the goal that beat the All Blacks and won the Rugby World Cup for his country in the summer. People haven't stopped buying him drinks since. Beefy's been flying home after each Test to do *A Question of Sport*. He had some trouble getting down to Durban. Flights were being cancelled or delayed from Johannesburg, so he picked up a sponsored Mercedes for the 400-mile journey. He made it in four hours, despite stopping for a chat with a traffic policeman!

SATURDAY 16 DECEMBER   KINGSMEAD

England 152/5

I've lasted a whole day. But only because a total of seven overs and four balls and 32 minutes' play was possible in two visits to the middle. Hickie and I added another 29 runs, so we are only 73 runs behind. If I could guarantee two whole days' play, we'd get a result. I can't. The forecast for tomorrow is rotten. Players don't like hanging about. Neither do the fans. Hundreds of England supporters have paid thousands of pounds to come here, thinking there'd be no danger of the weather disrupting the cricket in a holiday spot like Durban. One elderly gent summed it up in the lobby: 'I don't have to come here to watch it rain.'

Jason Gallian is coming here as Creepy's replacement. The management wanted someone to fill one of the top three Test spots. They've almost guaranteed Jason a Test place, saying that Ramps will not be considered at the top of the order. Creepy was padded up and would have been next in, if we had needed him. It's felt he can't damage his hamstring any further and he's desperate to play some part if we need him.

SUNDAY 17 DECEMBER   KINGSMEAD

Rain – no play

We'll need a miracle to get a result now. I'm into my third day of batting and I've still only scored 23 runs. There was never much chance of play today. Umpires Steve Bucknor and David Orchard called off play just after noon. Both teams are frustrated because both feel they have (or rather had) a chance of winning.

There was some excitement this morning. The *Mail on Sunday*'s Peter Hayter accused Craig Matthews of ball-tampering and his accusations were backed up with pictures from Sky TV. You can imagine what it would have been like if that had happened in England. Not here. Clive Lloyd, the ICC referee, studied the pictures, spoke to the participants and announced his decision. That's actually against ICC regulations, I believe. The referee isn't supposed to read out his own statement. That way, if any questions are asked, the official there can't answer them because it's not his statement. But Lloyd and the South Africans wanted this cleared up as soon as possible. Lloyd decided there wasn't a case to answer. Then the South Africans brought in Craig Matthews himself, and coach Bob Woolmer. Matthews talked to the press as he repeated the actions that were under question. It was interesting that after he had allegedly tampered with the ball, he bowled a practice delivery. The best quote came from Woolmer, who said that the two bowlers in the world he knew who were incapable of ball-tampering because they were hopeless at it were Matthews and Warwickshire's Tim Munton. I'm not sure I would have taken that as much of a compliment. The British media were astonished. The whole matter had been raised, discussed, decided on and killed in a matter of hours. 'They're hopeless here,' one told me. 'If this had been Lord's, this story would have run for weeks and weeks. I suppose we'll have to go back to covering the cricket!' Not here you won't! The weather is really beginning to depress me, although the realisation that Jane and Gregory will be here in a matter of days is beginning to occupy my thoughts more and more.

I went up to the Sky box while we were hanging around. I wanted to look at my action and see if there are any problems to sort out. Sky are always helpful and the new spin vision – the 'slo-mo' – can pick out the smallest errors. I wasn't worried, but I think it's a mistake to wait until you're in trouble before using these modern techniques. Every little helps and I'm not foolish enough to think I've learned a tenth of what I need to know in order to stay in international cricket.

Monday 18 December   KINGSMEAD

No play, Third Test abandoned as a draw

Someone mentioned this morning that in the history of Tests in South Africa, which goes back 100 years, there have been 11 complete days lost to the weather. Well, I've sat through five of them! Now there's everything to play for in the Port Elizabeth and Cape Town Tests. The locals tell me that PE is a certain banker for a draw, so it's all going to hinge on the fifth and final Test. Judgey, Stewie and Jack were with England in Guyana, when the Test match was actually abandoned without a single ball being bowled. The umpires and ground authorities did the decent thing and called it off very early this morning. The rain hadn't stopped and there was no point in prolonging the inevitable. Much as I'm looking forward to seeing the family, I hope the weather perks up. I've promised them sea, sun and sand. Two out of three won't be much of a result. But there's little suggestion that it's going to improve. We're supposed to be commuting to Pietermaritzburg, but the reports from there keep referring to flooding. Suggestions of switching the SA Universities game to Kingsmead are complicated because of a one-day game here on Friday involving Natal. Most of the lads just want a game, anywhere. The trouble is that Creepy and Goughie apart, 15 lads are after 11 spots. With back-to-back Tests after this, all the bowlers are trying to prove a point. Does Illy pick his Test line-up for the Universities to give them much-needed practice, which is basically hanging the other bowlers out to dry? Or does he give those who missed the Durban Test a run-out? Not easy. Considering we've been here two months, we seem to have played a ridiculously small amount of cricket. Goughie's injury means Daffy's been added to our squad for the one-dayers. The press are charging around about another addition – this time to the South African party for the next two Tests. Young Paul Adams, 35 wickets in five first-class games, is included. It's the right way to go. It will probably take something special to break the deadlock – and he's something special and different. One notable feat today. I broke my roomie Thorpey's heading record of 117 in the dressing room and reached 182!

WEDNESDAY 20 DECEMBER
JAN SMUTS STADIUM, PIETERMARITZBURG

SA Universities 253/6

THURSDAY 21 DECEMBER   JAN SMUTS STADIUM

SA Universities 269/8 declared   England 186/2

The best morning of the tour so far. I'm not normally at my best at six a.m. but it was absolutely delightful to be thumped around the head by Gregory, who wanted to play. Back home, there's a tendency to give him a bottle, put the cartoons on, turn over and go back to sleep. Not out here. He and Jane arrived yesterday. I've spent most of the past few days wondering what he would look like, would he remember me. And then there he was, walking brilliantly, and with a flicker of recognition for me. He's almost talking, too. Most of the lads spent Tuesday moving rooms, so that all the families could be accommodated. That doesn't mean we've forgotten why we're out here. I thought it was to play cricket, but there's been precious little of that in the past month. I don't know about the other wives and girlfriends, but Jane knows where my priorities lie when I'm a member of the England squad.

Gally arrived on Tuesday and he was able to fill us in on the successful A tour. Then he was taken down to the beach by the snappers. They always react to a different face. Gally had a nightmare 30-hour journey here from Peshawar, via Faisalabad, Karachi, Dubai, Bombay and Johannesburg, to Durban. Mum and Dad called to tell me they had arrived safely in Port Elizabeth and I'll see them next week. Both Gussie and Devon were left out of the Universities match, along with me. I made noises like 'You never know.' You don't. But this must mean their series is over. Devon played just that one Test – at the Wanderers – and I don't think he bowled too badly. For whatever reason, we haven't seen or got the best out of him on this tour, and that's a great shame as far as I'm concerned. Nobody was too happy yesterday morning. Having left Durban at seven-thirty a.m., the coach broke down on the N3 motorway to Pietermaritz-burg. We spent 40 minutes on the hard shoulder waiting for a replacement and the game started half an hour late. The lads showed no ill-effects and the Universities were quickly 23/5. Those of us not playing were allowed to head back to Durban at lunch-time to see our families. The rest must have missed us because they took only one wicket in the rest of the day as the Universities went past 250. Today was a bit better. Stewie and Athers got runs, although Gally only managed three. Once again, the rains came and play ended three overs after tea. That's finished any hope of a result. I imagine we'll use tomorrow for batting practice. Creepy's girlfriend, Kate, arrived later than the rest. She forgot to change planes in Johannes-burg and ended up in Cape Town. I was excused Pietermaritzburg duty today. A few of us practised in the morning and then I went Christmas shopping with Jane and Gregory. That's no different to England. The shopping mall was mayhem. Why does everyone leave it to the last minute? We had a meet-the-families barbecue at the hotel tonight. It was supposed to be round the pool, but, as ever, the rain interfered with our arrangements and we had to move inside. But it didn't dampen the spirits or the atmosphere. A good time was had by all.

MONDAY 25 DECEMBER CHRISTMAS DAY
PORT ELIZABETH

The rain has gone. But it's left its mark, with me at least. My throat is very sore and I feel as if the flu is coming on. That's why I missed our pool-side *braai* this afternoon. I hope a spell inside might help me shake it off and I don't want to pass it on to the others. Being a cricketer, you get used to Christmas Day in the sun, round the pool or on the beach. After Gregory had opened his presents, we went round to the house my folks are renting. We left Gregory there, so Jane could sunbathe without having to keep a permanent eye on the wee lad's antics. He's a real handful now he's mobile.

I was right about the Universities game going nowhere. The heavens opened on Friday and the match was called off in the morning. This tour has certainly tested my word power. How many ways are there of saying it's been raining again? Also on Friday, I learned that I'd received the East Midlands Sports Personality of the Year award jointly with Nottingham Forest's Steve Stone. Very honoured.

The move here from Durban was something else with all our cricket kit, the families and hundreds of Christmas presents. The Port Elizabeth hotel is the Summerstrand, which is no longer part of the Holiday Inn Garden Court Group. It's under new management, and they have no previous experience of running a hotel. It shows. Mind you, I wasn't expecting much. I stayed here with the A team two winters ago and it was a bit of a shambles then. We went out with my mum and dad on Saturday night to celebrate their 34th wedding anniversary.

Yesterday morning we had a good hard practice session. Jack got one in the throat from a net bowler. I remember when we played here two years ago there were a lot of LBW decisions as the ball kept low. Apart from Gally replacing Creepy, it looks like being the same Test line-up as Durban. Last night, Christmas Eve, we had our big Christmas dinner. Everyone agreed that it was better to spend today focused on the Test. Wayne organised a karaoke evening – duets, but with someone else's partner. Hilarious, but I think that's where I began to lose my voice. For some reason Stewie and I were partnered. The highlight was Ramps and Jackie Hick's rendition of 'Hey Big Spender'. Despite the welcome distractions of the family and Christmas Day, it's impossible to escape thinking about the task ahead. I still think we've shown the better form in this series and I'm sure we have the bowling capabilities to expose their batting.

Tuesday 26 December
St George's Park, Port Elizabeth

Fourth Test   South Africa 230/4

That man Cullinan is causing me and England problems. After losing the toss, we were in sight of a good day when the South Africans struggled to 89/3, but Cullinan and Rhodes took them past 200. I'm not happy with my bowling. I'm going to have another look at my action in the Sky van tomorrow morning. The ball isn't swinging as it should and I want to know why. My figures of 2/57 in 23 overs aren't bad and the ball that found Hudson's edge did all the right things, but I've lost something since the Wanderers. Cullinan was at his annoying best. I'm never one to duck a challenge, but he got the better of me today. Still, there's always tomorrow. He is a class player. No doubt. Although he's still only 28, it's 12 years since he became the youngest South African to score a first-class century, a record held by Graeme Pollock. Two years ago, he made South Africa's highest-ever first-class score – 337 – for Transvaal. I just wish he didn't get under my skin so much. I've heard similar stories about him out here and I've read articles which reveal he has a problem fitting in whatever team he's playing for. Still, there was no denying he was the class act on show today. We need to get rid of him quickly tomorrow. Our trio of one-day experts turned up today – Neil 'Harvey' Fairbrother, Dermot Reeve and Neil Smith. Dermot was quickly into the swing of things, keeping everyone amused with his impersonations, including his famous X-rated Imran Khan. We needed some light relief. It was a hard day in the field.

Wednesday 27 December   St George's Park

South Africa 426   England 40/1

South Africa are in the box seat now. We're not in trouble by any means, but we would have been better placed if we had held on to the chances that went begging. If you put 400 on the board in the first innings of a Test match, you don't expect to lose. But at least I got my revenge on Cullinan. My first ball of the day denied him that century he desperately wanted. That was the best Christmas present I've had. Sadly, it was our only success of the morning. It didn't help that we lost Ramble with a thigh strain and he's struggling. That leaves me and Digger as the only pace bowlers.

Richardson looked set for a century until Jack took a marvellous catch in front of the wicket, then our little terrier stumped Matthews for his fifth victim. What a series he's having. And he played an important part in running out Adams. The youngster got a fantastic welcome from the crowd and the band in the old grandstand struck up 'When the Saints Come Marching In'. All the South African batsmen chipped in, as we did against the West Indies last summer, and that makes a respectable total an intimidating one. Athers and Stewie had 18 overs to negotiate. The vice-captain only lasted two before playing a shot that he regretted, even before Richardson took the catch. A tough baptism for Gally, but he kept his nerve and his wicket intact and lives to fight another day. I'm wiped again after 43.2 overs, but I was happy with my four wickets and happier with the way I bowled today. I'm not complaining. There's nothing like bowling for your country, but that doesn't make it any less knackering.

THURSDAY 28 DECEMBER   ST GEORGE'S PARK

England 250/7

Athers got a shocker today. He and Hickie were coasting at 163/3 and Athers had batted untroubled for five hours when he tried to turn a ball from Adams to leg. It hit his pad and went into Richardson's gloves. Nothing unusual in that. The South African went up. Nothing unusual in that. But Athers looked astonished when Cyril Mitchley's finger went up. We all turned round in the dressing room to watch the replays. The 'slo-mo' camera suggested his bat was nowhere near the ball. It was easy to understand Athers' dismay because it looked a poor decision. What hit Athers harder was that he knew it put us in trouble. While he was there, matching the South Africans' total was a probability. But, as so often with England, one out – all out. Judgey went cheaply and then Hickie got a questionable LBW. I only added to all the dismay with a dreadful swipe at a wide half-volley. I seem to lose all common sense when I get out there with the bat at the moment. I've taken backward steps on this tour in my bid to become a genuine all-rounder.

The crowd gave young Adams a great cheer when he came on to bowl. Athers was his second wicket. The ball that got his first – Thorpey – didn't deserve one either. Thorpey smashed a long hop straight to mid-wicket. But good luck to Adams. You won't hear me complaining about bad balls getting wickets. Jack (once again) and

Illy came to our rescue after my rush of blood and have put on 50 for the eighth wicket. Out with the folks again tonight, plus my brother Simon and his wife, Christina. I tried not to dwell on the day's events, but it appears the rub of the green is going against us at the moment.

FRIDAY 29 DECEMBER   ST GEORGE'S PARK

England 263 & 20/0   South Africa 163/9 declared

Welcome to Bodyline, 1995-style. Athers did a brilliant job today. With us trailing by 165 runs and down to three front-line bowlers, the skipper reduced the South Africans to 69/6. With a little luck then, we might have bowled them out for less than 100 and been halfway towards victory by now. But the South Africans were saved by a seventh-wicket stand of 66 between Gary Kirsten and Shaun Pollock. There's a great spirit in this side and it was never more evident than today. Athers was very determined – not least because the local papers had made a big deal of his whacking a dressing-room chair with his bat. There seems to be little privacy anywhere for an international cricketer these days. And little room for expression, either. McMillan and I have been spoken to about making gestures on the field and the match referee reminded Illy and Woolmer about the players' responsibilities. Cricket's an art, not a science. We all have our different ways. Cricket is not a game for robots. I'd be a lot less effective if I couldn't express myself.

The home side wiped out our last three wickets in next to no time. Many sides would have gone on the defensive, simply making the South Africans work for their runs without worrying about wickets, hoping to survive the final day. But now we have a chance of winning – and a better one than the South Africans with one day left. As we got ready to go out to bowl, Athers asked for lots of determination and guts. Ramble came out with us. That was a great effort, but after a couple of overs in the field it was evident that he couldn't go on. It can't have helped the thigh strain and it might have ruined his World Cup chances. Yet it showed what we are all prepared to sacrifice for England. It really hacks me off when people say that we don't care. If that sort of comment is made in my hearing, you'll soon find out whether I care or not. Digger bowled a magnificent spell of seven overs, seven maidens and two wickets. I wasn't going to miss the fun and bowled a spell of 20 overs, with only a break for lunch. I got rid of Rhodes, McMillan and Richardson in quick

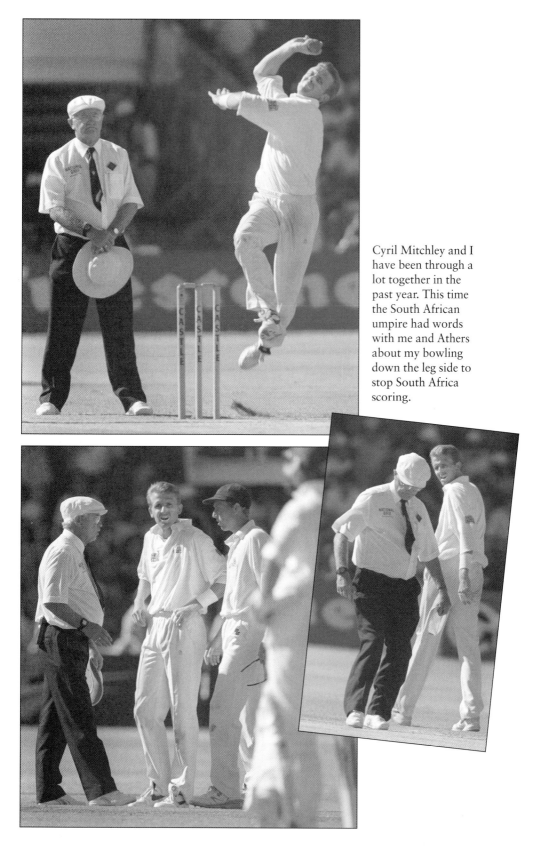

Cyril Mitchley and I have been through a lot together in the past year. This time the South African umpire had words with me and Athers about my bowling down the leg side to stop South Africa scoring.

succession. In fact 16 balls for no runs, according to our scorer, Malcolm Ashton. We needed one more wicket and we were through, but it proved elusive. That's when Athers and I decided to concentrate on the leg-stump, with a leg slip and long leg. I've never seen myself as Harold Larwood and I would have loved his pace. It was a legitimate tactic, although Cyril did signal the odd wide and voiced his concerns. I was asked about our conversation at the post-play press conference. 'Well,' I told them, 'we talked about the weather. And I told Cyril how I wish we had one of those bands at Derbyshire. That would double the crowd.' Most of what is said on the field should stay there. It's said in the heat of battle. Out of context, it can tell a totally different story. The main thing was that we hadn't given up trying to take wickets, but we would have thrown away all that early good work if we hadn't tried to tie Kirsten and Pollock down.

I think some folk believe that Test cricket bears some relation to the game played on the village green. This is cricket war – unforgiving and cruel. I love it! The sheer pleasure of shutting up a South African crowd was immense. At 69/6, there was almost silence. Even the popular St George's band put down their instruments for a while before the strains of 'Stand By Me' were heard for the umpteenth time. I don't mind them. We could do with more of a festive atmosphere at the Test grounds of England. But then, you don't want to wake up the members.

My 'Bodyline' impersonation didn't go down too well with the crowd. I was given more than the odd mouthful while fielding on the boundary. No problem. Speak your mind. Now we need 308 runs to win in 90 overs. Not impossible. And who better to dine with before setting out on such a quest than the greatest man in cricket history – Ian Botham. I was really tired, but I didn't think the great man would take too kindly to me nodding off. No danger. It was a night I'll always cherish. The day I watched him smash the Aussies all over Headingley was the first time I thought: 'That's it. That's what I want.' I was ten and I knew what I wanted to do with my life. The following summer, I begged my folks to take me to see Somerset play Shropshire in a NatWest game so I could get his autograph. But I bottled it. I couldn't get out of the car. My dad had to go and get it. I got into a lot of trouble at school because all I wanted to do was play cricket, and it's all Beefy's fault. It's always been a great source of sadness that I was responsible for Beefy leaving the field as an England cricketer for ever. One of my shorter balls was pulled violently by Pakistan's Ramiz Raja in 1992. Beefy injured himself trying to stop it and had to go off – never to be seen again. What I love about him is that he's always positive, whether about cricket or life. He's larger than life and I don't think my body could stand up to a Botham lifestyle, but the fact that I now consider him a friend is about the greatest thing that's happened to me in my sporting life. I accepted his invitation for a night-cap in the bar. But only one. The key to surviving life with Beefy is quitting while you're ahead. I gather he stayed on and safely negotiated about 20 rounds of spoof. I look forward to the time he's chairman of selectors. Hopefully, I'll still be on the scene.

SATURDAY 30 DECEMBER   CAPE TOWN

England 189/3
Fourth Test drawn   Man of the Match: Gary Kirsten

We flew to Cape Town tonight for a Newlands showdown with the South Africans in the final Test. The PE Test fizzled out into a draw, with neither side keen on giving anything away. Once again, we fought back well and I feel we must be favourites for the decider. It won't be a draw. Everyone is expecting a result and the weather forecast is good. Before play started today, the match referee Clive Lloyd showed me a fax he had received from a D. R. Bennett from Durban. It read 'When are you going to fine the England bowler, D. Cork at least his entire match fee and preferably his series fee for his ugly, over aggressive, unnecessary, nasty, shitty, brash, confrontational attitude? He is swearing at and harassing SA batsmen in a completely unnecessary and unsportsman-like manner with great regularity. He should be fined and banned for life, at the minimum. Thank you.' And it was signed by the man himself. I think I know where he stands.

Stewie played himself back into form today with a patient 81 and he was very disappointed to miss out on a well-deserved century. He and Athers started at a fair rate, but it did not take many runs for Cronje to put the brakes on and abandon thoughts of winning if it meant giving us a chance of losing. I can't believe how negative the South Africans are. They batted far too long at the Wanderers. Here again, safety-first was the order of the day, which made for a disappointing finale for the thousands of spectators. Athers batted for another three hours and Gally not much shorter. We were never in real trouble, although always some way short of the runs and platform needed to push for victory. Scoring a hundred a session might not sound like much, but it was a tall order on this pitch with bowlers of this calibre. Stewie tells me this is the most disciplined attack he's ever faced – and that includes the Aussies and the West Indies. They don't have a bowling weak link. Adams is the newcomer, but all the rest are talented performers and each is capable of picking up five or six wickets if the conditions suit – and Donald and Pollock will take them whatever. The bottom line is that out of four Tests, the South Africans have had two chances of winning and haven't managed to break us down. In the two others, our advantage was nullified by the weather – not South Africa. It was a buoyant England squad that flew to Cape Town tonight (Jane and Gregory went this afternoon). We know there are going to be hundreds, probably thousands of England supporters, there. We can't let them down.

January 1996

Cape Town Catastrophe

A New Year. I must admit that I'm rather sorry to see the old one disappear. Whatever 1996 has to offer, I can't believe that it will match 1995. But this is not the time for reflection. We're one Test short of winning a full series away from home for the first time since Mike Gatting retained the Ashes at Melbourne in 1986. The word is that, in the bid for victory, Jack will bat at No. 6 and we'll include five bowlers. Creepy, Goughie and Ramble are all excluded on the fitness front, while Ramps is paying the price for his early Test failures. Five of the lads will leave the official party at the weekend – Creepy, Ramble, Gally, Devon and Gussie. Craig White has been added to our one-day squad. That's 22 players in all – just as well we have two dressing rooms here. Gussie has been named in the preliminary World Cup 18. As the other 17 are staying and he's going home, he's rather doubtful of making the final 14. Judgey has asked to bat at No. 3. That's the spot that's been causing England problems for years. With the way he plays quick bowling, I'm surprised that the Judge hasn't moved up earlier. Most countries bring their youngsters in at No. 5 or 6 – we pitch them in higher up the order. Maybe that's why we've got a problem. The mood in the squad is very good. There's certainly a great sense of anticipation here in Cape Town. It seems that half of England is here.

New Year's Eve was spent relaxing, preparing for the fight ahead. The family enjoyed a leisurely Sunday lunch down on the waterfront. I must confess that I've spent livelier New Year's Eves. It was part of our official programme to attend a party at the British High Commission. Unlike our early "official" function in Johannesburg at the start of the tour which was great fun, this occasion was rather formal and stuffy. It didn't help that we were outside for our meal and it rained. I hope the wet weather goes out with the old year. All the lads wanted to do was let their hair down, but we felt on show and our best behaviour. It wasn't a relaxing evening.

Another hard net practice today. You could feel the tension. This is the one that neither side can afford to muck up. There'll be no second chances at Newlands. Another English groundsman – Andy Atkinson, formerly of Chelmsford and Edgbaston – is in charge here. Athers hasn't too high a regard for him since he prepared a bunsen burner for the 1993 Birmingham Ashes Test. It was Athers' first game as skipper. Unfortunately, the wicket was perfectly suited to the talents of Shane Warne and Tim May, and England got thumped. The wicket here is expected to turn and bounce. Gussie and Devon are delighted to have a real chance of a game as they have played very little cricket since the Wanderers Test. Gussie, especially, is a bowler who needs to bowl to get in a rhythm. Blame the weather and the tour itinerary. I'm as excited about this match as I was about my first Test. The setting of Newlands is magnificent, with Table Mountain as a backdrop. It's got the edge over Derby in that respect.

TUESDAY 2 JANUARY   NEWLANDS, CAPE TOWN

Fifth Test *England 153* *South Africa 44/2*

Disastrous as that scoreboard may appear, we are not out of this one. If we bowl as well as Donald & company and keep the South Africans under 200, we have a chance. But we can't afford to bat like we did today. There is more bounce in this wicket than all the rest we've played on here put together. We did go in with five special-ist batsmen, leaving Gally out. Illy's side injury meant Winker got his chance at last and Devon and Gussie were recalled. Three of our five-man attack have played little part in the series so far. The South Africans went the other route. Seven main batsmen and three front-line bowlers, although you have to regard McMillan as the fourth. If the South Africans gambled, it has certainly come off. If you bowl the opposition out for 153 in the first innings of a Test, then you'll kick yourself for not winning, supposing the weather doesn't intervene. Also, the South Africans have employed the services of the best sports psychologist in the business – Nelson Mandela. Every time he pitches up at a sporting event, whether in François Pienaar's jersey or Cronje's cap, he works miracles. The papers have pictures of him meeting the team, putting an arm round young Adams and saying the right things as usual.

Athers won the toss and batted. He departed after 25 minutes without scoring, then Stewie chopped on. Judgey and Thorpey were still together at lunch and I thought we had weathered the storm. But Thorpey went first ball after the break, Hickie followed and we were in trouble again. Judgey and Jack came to the rescue again – 103/4 wasn't great, but it wasn't a disaster. Pollock struck twice and then the final four wickets disappeared for 12 runs. Our only hero was the Judge. He was second-last out for 66. I scored 16 before Donald bowled a yorker that I have no hesitation in saying was far too quick for me. I don't actually think we batted that badly. But, on a receptive pitch, the South Africans bowled and fielded brilliantly. McMillan in the slips is something else. This SA side are good at putting pressure on the batters. Yet, that assessment gave us hope. Athers told us we had to go out and do what they had done. And so far we have. I thought I was in trouble in the second over when I collided with Winker in the covers and bent my ring finger back. At first I thought I had dislocated it, but an X-ray tonight revealed no break. Fortunately, it's not my bowling hand, although batting might be difficult. The new ball jagged about and I was able to get rid of Hudson and Hansie. The second found its way to Jack – victim No. 24 for him, equalling Alan Knott's England record for a series. But, like me, he's worried that all the hard work of the past three months could be thrown away in one bad session. We've started badly and can't afford any more mistakes.

Ramble, Goughie and I and our other halves dined at Morton's on the waterfront with the *News of the World*'s cricket correspondent. Glad to see him pushing the boat out at last. Jane and I left early. I've no doubt that tomorrow is going to decide which way the series goes.

WEDNESDAY 3 JANUARY   NEWLANDS

South Africa 244   England 17/1

I know how Scott of the Antarctic felt when he wrote, 'It seems a pity, but I do not think I can write more.' I've never known such emotion or fluctuating fortunes in a day's cricket. Inch by inch, wicket by wicket, we hauled ourselves back into this Test match. Then, just as we were about to reach our goal, we slipped and now we're right back where we started the day, probably in a worse position. It's not often I feel helpless on a cricket field, but I did this afternoon. We bowled magnificently today and when I had Donald caught behind (Jack's 27th victim) with the new ball, the South Africans were 171/9 – only 18 runs ahead. We had them. A reasonable score on this track and it would put them under so much pressure, I was in no doubt that they wouldn't cope with all the expectations. All through this series, their attitude has been negative and defensive. I had the new ball in my hands and the young schoolboy, Paul Adams, was walking to the wicket. New ball, new boy. No trouble. The South Africans had had their last-wicket heroics at Durban. It doesn't happen twice in a series. Half an hour later and the South Africans had broken our spell. After forcing them to live on bread and water all day, suddenly there was a feast of runs. Poor Devon. Four overs went for 26 runs. I might have even started the rot with a wild overthrow that went to the boundary. Even those four runs were riches to the South Africans at the time and you could sense a slackening of the stranglehold we had had all day. Suddenly, the script had changed. The South Africans weren't searching for runs. England were desperate for wickets. Well, just one. Bowling, not batting, was now a problem. I don't know if we panicked. We certainly might have tried too hard, straining all the more as we saw all that hard work go to waste, and the Test and series go South Africa's way. That South African lead swelled to 91 runs and we seemed powerless to do anything about it. Digger and Hickie finally ended the agony. Three months' frustration boiled up and some fairly tense England cricketers retired to the dressing room. Illy wasn't happy. Athers wasn't happy. Nobody was happy. It wasn't the time or place to apportion blame, if blame is the right word. Everyone's out there trying their best. You have good days and bad days. This was a bloody awful one.

Worse was to follow. We lost Athers, our anchor and inspiration. It might have been better if South Africa had batted through the day. Athers, as he did at Port Elizabeth, had got us back in this game with his captaincy. He's been criticised for leadership on the field, but he's worked wonders out here – batting-wise at Centurion Park, the Wanderers and St George's and captaincy-wise at Wanderers, St George's and now Newlands. What do people expect? At 153/9, Athers was a hero. At 244, he was a villain. B*ll*cks. This bloke has sweated blood for England out here. We let him down today. We didn't mean to, but it happened. He must be wondering what else he has to do to make England into a winning combination.

We've started to show ourselves as a much more resilient bunch

Three important wickets for us: Cullinan is caught off Peter Martin; while I get Allan Donald LBW and dismiss Cronje, caught by Jack Russell.

in the past six months. But today, it was the South Africans who held their nerve, not us, and they've got one hand on the prize. We had done so well to haul it back. Only one wicket came in the morning session, although we made them fight for every run. At 125/3, we would have settled for bowling them out for 244. But not after taking six wickets for 46 runs. Only that man Cullinan batted with any real authority. Much as I hate to admit it, he's been their key batsman in this series. Gussie and Digger really kept the pressure on. Between lunch and tea, they only mustered 38 runs for three wickets. I hit the stumps from cover to remove McMillan, but it was a throw that missed the stumps and went to the boundary that I'm reflecting on tonight. It will take a great effort to lift us after what happened today. But that's what good sides do. And we can't afford not to – otherwise we will lose.

THURSDAY 4 JANUARY   NEWLANDS

England 157   South Africa 70/0
England lost the Fifth Test by 10 wickets
Man of the Match: Allan Donald
England lost the series 1–0   Man of the Series: Allan Donald

Defeat and disaster. A day I will never forget. This scoreboard will not look good in the record books, but it's not the whole story. If you thought yesterday was frantic, wait until you work your way through today's proceedings. First up – we were well beaten. No arguments there. When the pressure was on, Cronje's side played the better cricket and took their chances. I don't believe they have been the better side in this series, but they have the trophy and the prize money. Again, I feel a bit like Scott did after he had trundled halfway across the Antarctic and found the Norwegians had got there first. At this precise moment, it seems like three months' work has just gone down the spout. There was a bit of a scene in the dressing room afterwards. The lads were standing at the presentation ceremony when we heard on the tannoy that England are to play Western Province here on Saturday. That was the first Athers had heard about it – and it wasn't the first time on this tour that decisions affecting his team were made without his knowledge. When you've just lost a Test and a series, you're not thinking about tomorrow or the next hour. You're not thinking about anything. Athers had a few words to say about the rearranged fixture when he got back to the dressing room. It was more to himself than anyone, but it was Illy's

The final nail in England's coffin – the controversial Thorpe run-out. South Africa's appeal was initially turned down by umpire David Orchard who did not signal for the third umpire. The groans from the crowd who saw the replay – plus some persuasive talk from Hansie Cronje – changed his mind.

cue. He had a real go. But then Illy has always said what he thinks. He's not got a reputation for plain-speaking for nothing.

It was a miserable end to a miserable Test. The day started badly. Stewie and Gussie, our nightwatchmen, went cheaply. Thorpey and Judgey looked in little discomfort until we got another shocking decision. Judgey was given out caught behind off Adams – the same dismissal that accounted for Athers at Port Elizabeth. The TV replays suggested that Judgey was about as near the ball as Athers had been. It looked like a matter of missing by inches. The umpire's reaction – this time David Orchard – was the same. So, for the third time in the series at a crucial time (don't forget Thorpey at the Wanderers), an England recovery had been disrupted and destroyed by poor umpiring judgement. And Judgey has something else in common with the other two – he was given out by the home umpire. I'm not questioning anyone's loyalties. It's a simple statement of fact. Being sawn off at the best of times is annoying. When you're fighting for your cricket life, it's heartbreaking. Worse was to follow. Aussie Steve Randell, who had turned down several good shouts from both sides, decided to give his finger some exercise for a half-hearted LBW shout against Hickie. Having recovered from 22/3 to 66/4 (thanks, Mr Orchard), then to 138/5 (thanks, Mr Randell), it was now all down to Thorpey. England reached 47 runs ahead and we fancied that anything over 150 might test the mettle of Cronje's men. No chance. Enter Mr Orchard again. Winker called Thorpey for a quick run after our left-hander had turned Adams to Hudson at short fine leg. It was not the most sensible run in the circumstances and Thorpey was always struggling. It looked very close and I couldn't believe it when Orchard didn't call for the third umpire and decided not out. You beauty. Maybe he had seen something we hadn't. But, as the replay was shown on the hundreds of TV sets around the crowd, a huge groan went up as they realised that Orchard had made a horrendous error. That evens things up, I thought.

That's when the fun started. Enter one Hansie Cronje, contrary to ICC regulations, asking the umpire to call for the third umpire. Orchard knew he had got it wrong, but initially stuck to his decision. Cronje then asked Thorpey if it wouldn't be better if the third umpire was called upon. Thorpey regards it as one of the daftest requests he's ever had. 'Why? I've been given not out.' Cronje had another go at Orchard. I'm sure Cronje would not have tried to exert such pressure on Randell. That's another reason for having two 'foreign' umpires. But, to be fair to Orchard, I'm sure an experienced

Although Allan Donald was named Man of the Series there is little doubt that Shaun Pollock is going to be an outstanding force in world cricket over the next decade – not only as a bowler but as a hard-hitting batsman. Here he twice bowls the Judge during the series.

umpire would have called for the TV replay in the first place. So poor old Thorpey, who had thought escaping here had balanced out his Wanderers' dismissal, had to go. He had been batting so well. It was a bitter blow and the final nail in our coffin.

Cricket's always been about taking the rough with the smooth. Orchard made two questionable decisions today – once against England, Judgey's caught behind, and one against South Africa, Thorpey's run out. Two wrongs can make a right in cricket. But, because of the influence of the South African captain, who I'm pleased to see had been fined for dissent, England lost out twice. Add Hickie, and three of England's senior batsmen got a rough deal today. It was all over bar the shouting as Pollock cleaned up the tail. England all out 157 – a grand total of 300 runs in the Test. South Africa's winning target of 67 was a formality – 167 might have been a different matter. In the end, South Africa won by 10 wickets, although we thought we had got rid of Hudson in the second over when Devon wrapped him on the pads. But umpire Randell felt differently. It was not our day. I'm not saying that would have triggered a South African collapse, but even one wicket would have made my Derbyshire colleague feel a lot better.

I can't believe we've lost. And I can't believe we've lost so quickly. In ten Tests for England, there have been six draws, two wins and two defeats – and both those losses have come inside three days! Today ended an England Test run of seven matches without defeat. Goodnight.

SATURDAY 6 JANUARY   NEWLANDS

England 196 (49.5 overs)   Western Province 200/7 (49 overs)
England lost by 3 wickets

TUESDAY 9 JANUARY   NEWLANDS

South Africa 211/8 (50 overs)   England 205 (49.5)
England lost by 6 runs   Man of the Match: Shaun Pollock

As much as I love Cape Town, I'm glad to be seeing the back of Newlands. We've just had England's third defeat here in less than a week. It was a disastrous way to start our World Cup build-up because we handed the match to South Africa on a plate. It would have been a small revenge for the Test defeat, but it's worrying the way we capitulated again so easily. The South Africans got 20 to 30 more runs than they should have after being 107/6. That was thanks to a blistering 66 from Pollock. It was our fault – he was dropped on 29. I picked up two wickets and thought I'd got a third when McMillan gloved it to Stewie behind the stumps. But once again, I was denied his scalp. We were coasting at 155/3, but suffered from the domino effect again. It wasn't even a careless shot from me this time, more a careless run-out. Once again the South Africans coped better under pressure. Athers summed up the mess: 'I thought we did pretty well to lose.' This was my first day/nighter for the full England side. My last one was for the A team against India in Ahmedabad. The difference in the quality of lighting was incredible. They would have been better dimming the lights after our performance. We dominated 90 per cent of the game and lost because of some very poor cricket.

Our one-day campaign did not get off to the best of starts three days ago with a three-wicket defeat by a Western Province side that did not include their five representatives in the South African squad. We started badly. Athers, Thorpey and Ramps departed to leave us 13/3, but newcomers Dermot Reeve and Craig White took us just short of 200. It looked all over when the home side were 132/7, but some big hitting saw them home.

I didn't play Saturday. The early end to the Test gave Jane and me some extra time, so we hired a car and drove around Cape Province. Gregory has been ill and can't sleep at night. If the Test had been going on, I would have had to get another room. I'm saying goodbye to them tomorrow, but this time only for a couple of weeks.

THURSDAY 11 JANUARY
SPRINGBOK PARK, BLOEMFONTEIN

South Africa 262/8 (50 overs) England 265/5 (48.2)
England won by five wickets Man of the Match: Mike Atherton

That's more like it. A much more professional performance. Springbok Park was just as flat as it had been a couple of months ago and the home supporters were just as obnoxious. I thought we were going to be beaten – by the floodlights, when a blow-out at the local power station plunged the stadium into darkness. We were off for three-quarters of an hour and there were murmurings from the England dressing room of sabotage! But the break did not disturb Athers' or Thorpey's concentration and we won relatively comfortably.

Athers had a new opening partner – Daffy. At one stage I thought we might be chasing 300-plus. The South Africans were 164/1 after 34 overs. But, uncharacteristically, they got careless and extravagant. I didn't mind. It helped my figures when I picked up 3/3 in nine balls towards the close. And how do the locals spend their time when the lights go out? They take off most of their clothes, try to beat the police in a sprint across the cricket square and go home in a police wagon. What fun!

I've swapped Jane for Harvey. He's my new room-mate. The family got home safely and Jane is setting about organising the move into our new house. Illy's given public airing to his views that families were a distraction during the final two Tests and we lost focus. I don't think we did, but I must admit we've resembled a travelling circus at times in the past fortnight. It's a dilemma. If the families didn't come out, we would hardly see them at all this winter. The obvious time for them to appear was Christmas and New Year, when kids are off school, but that turned out to be the crucial time of the tour. The Cape Sun wasn't an ideal hotel, because there wasn't a swimming pool. Winker's wife Sue caught her two kids leaning out of a window they'd opened on the 15th floor. That could have been catastrophic. Unsuitable hotels were apparently a problem during the Ashes tour in Sydney and Melbourne. You know when the families are going to be appearing, so the England team should be in appropriate hotels. The Aussies got it right on their winning tour of the Caribbean last year. At the end of the series, the families travelled out to Bermuda, where the side played a couple of one-day games to pay their way. The pressure was off. Everyone relaxed. By the mere fact of their presence, the families are a distraction. But that presence also gives you a boost. There's no simple solution.

SATURDAY 13 JANUARY WANDERERS

England 198/8 (50 overs) South Africa 199/7 (48.1)
England lost by 3 wickets Man of the Match: Shaun Pollock

SUNDAY 14 JANUARY CENTURION PARK

England 272/8 (50 overs) South Africa 276/3 (48)
England lost by 7 wickets Man of the Match: Shaun Pollock

The lost weekend! Saturday could have gone either way, but we were well beaten today. I was 12th man yesterday with Stewie, as Ramps, Harvey and Craig gave us a fighting chance after the top four had failed. It was the top three really as Daffy went in first again. I think that experiment has been abandoned. I was pleased for Ramps. He knows it's between him and Judgey for the final World Cup batting spot. Daffy and Goughie had SA 114/5, but they held the nerve to ease home. I don't know whether we would have done in a similar position. That's nothing to do with ability, just the side's confidence and performance at the moment. Today was different. Athers took a rest, so Stewie and Judgey opened. They gave England a great start on a fast outfield, but we lost our way again, scoring just 34 runs from the 30th over to the 40th. That was criminal. Our final total of 272 owed much to a cameo knock from Jack, who hit 39 in 19 balls. It never looked enough as Hudson and Kirsten put on 156 for the first wicket in 28 overs. The one bright spark for us was that Goughie is beginning to look his old self. I got a bit of a pasting – 1/65 off ten overs. I wasn't pleased with that. I hate playing badly and I think it's probably the worst I've ever bowled for my country. But it was that sort of wicket. Ask AD – his figures were 3/72 off only nine overs. The word from the media is that Illy wants a word with the bowlers. Wrong target. This was a batsman's paradise and that's where we failed. It wasn't our day. The bus broke down on the way to the ground and the start was delayed for quarter of an hour. Thorpey was summoned to see the match referee Cammie Smith when it appeared he'd signalled for the TV replay. He had just caught Cronje, but umpire Diedricks didn't give him out. Instead, he raised his arms in the air to notify the scorers of a six. In fact Thorpey, who had Stewie and Illy with him at the hearing, explained that he was responding to the jeering crowd, telling *them* to watch the replay. The umpire would have been informed by the third umpire that it was clearly out. Why do we get a match referee for these games, but not even one neutral umpire? It's probably down to money. But it should be consistent. It's symptomatic of the way things are going for us at the moment. We can't afford any more mistakes in this seven-match series.

WEDNESDAY 17 JANUARY   KINGSMEAD, DURBAN

England 184   South Africa 185/5
England lost by 5 wickets   Man of the Match: Allan Donald

Forget the score-line. South Africa did not win this game. We lost it. Threw it away would be a better description. We lost wickets at the wrong times, dropped catches and, generally, fielded poorly.

South Africa have the series 4–1. Pride's all we've got left to play for this weekend. So there's still plenty to play for. We can't head off to the World Cup in this state – on or off the field. We're just not firing. We're practising hard, but it's not translating into performance. We're not thinking. Nobody plays more one-day cricket than us, yet we keep on making elementary mistakes. We look like novices. I'm beginning to wonder whether we can suddenly click out of it or if there's a serious problem. That said, SA look a good outfit. De Villiers is back and with Donald coming on first or even second change, it's a bowling attack to be reckoned with. Stewie and Athers took us past 50, but suddenly we were 78/4. The destroyer was Donald – 4/19 in 26 balls. Thorpey put us back in the game, but we got lost in the run-in again – me included. I removed both openers and we were in with a chance with SA 9/2. But a century stand from Cronje and Kallis took them to safety. It's only the second time I've bowled under lights. The ball seemed to swing a bit more, but these lights weren't great and we had trouble fielding, especially as the white ball got dirtier. Just when Stewie seemed to have settled the opening argument, it's up for grabs again. He split the webbing while fielding and is out for the rest of the series. He's determined not to miss the World Cup, though.

Our stay in Durban was dominated by Devon. He may have flown home a week ago, but he's got under Illy's skin again. Devon's voiced his views in the papers about the way he felt Illy and Plank treated him. I feared he might. He's in breach of his tour contract, too. That may bring a big fine or even a ban. The article originally suggested racial discrimination. I didn't think that will do Devon's case any good and today I read that he has denied that part of it. He also revealed the dressing-room bust-up in Cape Town. Whatever the rights and wrongs of the situation, I don't think it has improved Devon's odds of playing Test cricket again while Illy is around. Went out to the Cattleman's last night with Judgey and Harvey. You can tell we're counting down the days. These tours are hard work when you're losing. The realisation that there's so little time to put our feet up before heading to Pakistan for the World Cup is not helping.

My knees are bothering me. They get sore after a day's play and they seem to be worse when there is so little rest time. I've seen it suggested that maybe I should have gone home with the others and a longer break would have been more beneficial for me. I don't know on that one. I'm not too keen on an England team abroad with me not part of it. Still, a month at home would constitute a proper rest, rather than the ten days we are going to get. Stop whingeing, Cork!

Friday 19 January   Buffalo Park

South Africa 129 (41.4 overs)   England 115 (43.4)
England lost by 14 runs   Man of the Match: Paul Adams

It couldn't get worse? Don't you believe it. Mind you, this wicket was an absolute disgrace for a one-day game. Still, we should have won. We knew precisely what we had to do and at 75/3, should have done it. Only two players got past 20 – McMillan, 45 not out, and Hickie, our top scorer with 39. We bowled well, but they bowled better. I'm not sure our batting order was right. Craig White opened, and Jack came out at No. five before Thorpey and Harvey. A player of Harvey's ability has to be in a more influential spot. I failed again. I might as well go out there with a stick of rhubarb the way I'm batting. I'm actually feeling a little humiliated at the moment. Even the English fans were booing us, and who can blame them? Whatever the problems about the itinerary, the travel, the pitches, the umpires and the end of a long hard tour, there's no excuse for this sort of unprofessional display. This is the lowest I've ever felt as a cricketer. We can't fly home in this state, we've got to pull out all the stops in Sunday's final game.

Sunday 21 January
St George's Park, Port Elizabeth

South Africa 218/9 (50 overs)   England 154 (46.1)
England lost by 64 runs   Man of the Match: Adrian Kuiper
England lost series 6–1   Man of the Series: Shaun Pollock

Monday 22 January
Jan Smuts Airport, Johannesburg

No happy ending. No waking up from the nightmare. Just more of the same. Get me on that plane! The World Cup squad has been announced – no place for Ramps, Winker and Dermot, as expected. We've not only stopped winning. We've stopped competing. Where have I experienced that before? It's probably best to draw a veil over our final game. Goughie's return to form apart, this one-day series has been a disaster for us. For the second time this month, we've had to line up and watch Cronje receive a trophy. I don't like coming second, especially when I don't feel we've put up much of a fight. We should have won the first game and, as Athers told the press, it was all downhill from there. We'd driven from East London to PE, hoping that a change from air travel might break the losing spell. Don't laugh – we're that desperate! It didn't. About the only thing we've achieved in the past weeks is to install SA as one of the firm favourites for the World Cup. Our main hope is that we can't keep playing that badly – can we? Anyway, I'm going to get on the plane that's taking me home, have a final taste of SA wine, drift off to sleep and wake up in England, and forget about cricket for the next week or so, if I'm allowed.

FEBRUARY 1996

World Cup Hopes and South African Hangovers

Packing again. It seems like only last week that I unpacked from the last cricket tour. Correct. It *was* only last week. But, despite the wrench of leaving home again and that tiring three months in South Africa, I'm very excited about taking part in my first World Cup. Much of the build-up has focused on the other group, which is based in India and Sri Lanka. A huge bomb planted by the rebel Tamil Tigers went off in Colombo on Wednesday, killing 73 people (death toll still rising) and injuring over 1,000, and now there is talk of boycotts or switching matches. Shane Warne is one of several Aussies who have already complained about death threats if they return to the sub-continent over bribery allegations during their 1994 tour of Pakistan. Australia, the West Indies, Zimbabwe and Kenya are all scheduled to play in Sri Lanka, and Australia have already hinted that they would rather forfeit the match than put their players in any danger. The papers don't give much for our chances. I'm surprised that so much emphasis has been placed on our disappointing final three weeks in SA, rather than on how well we played in the Test series. I just felt the lads were worn out in those last weeks. Looking back, it was a ridiculous itinerary to put together at the end of a five-Test series. Anyway, I can tell you the spirit in the squad is very positive. Most of us were together at a special World Cup dinner as part of Robin Smith's benefit year. There was a genuine feeling that we can make a real impact, despite the bookies quoting us at 8/1 – well down the list of favourites. I feel the key to our ultimate showing will depend on the first game against New Zealand. A win will put recent poor form behind us and will almost certainly guarantee us a quarter-final spot. Defeat will mean more of the same, but that's not the way we are thinking at the moment. First stop for us is Lahore for almost a week before heading for Calcutta and an opening ceremony that promises to be something very special.

WEDNESDAY 7 FEBRUARY
AITCHESON, LAHORE, PAKISTAN

England 247 Lahore Cricket Association 188
England won by 59 runs

Our first win of the World Cup leg, though not in the tournament. This was a warm-up game after three days of practice. We travelled in style to Lahore, first class on PIA, Pakistan International Airlines. But it was a dry old ship, a foretaste of our time in Pakistan where alcohol is banned. Wayne put us through a training session on Sunday that would have stretched Linford Christie. Afterwards, the North took on the South at soccer. A bad omen and a terrible loss – the South won 5–3. That night we had a full team discussion about how we are going to approach winning this World Cup. Monday was a full day's practice at the Gymkhana Ground, the first time I'd felt happy with my hand since damaging it in the Cape Town Test. Security has been the big issue of this World Cup so far. I've never seen so many police and soldiers. As we fielded and practised, there was a complete ring of them.

Judgey was dismissed twice in three balls by the Pakistan under-19 bowler Ali Asid. So, on Monday night, he shaved off his moustache and had a short back and sides. 'I don't want anyone to recognise me,' was his explanation. They might not have to, since Judgey collapsed after straining a groin muscle while taking a spectacular catch in the deep today. He just got there and had to dive to make it. It was the dive, he reckons, that did the damage. The replacement choice, if necessary, appears to be between Ramps and Nasser Hussain, who captained the A team here a couple of months ago. There seems to be confusion about whether we can go outside the nominated 18 if Judgey is sent home.

The bruised ligaments in my left hand from that Cape Town Test collision with Winker may have healed, but another part of my body is causing trouble. My knee is bothering me again. With my history of knee trouble, I hope that it's just because I haven't bowled for a while. Meanwhile Goughie isn't working flat-out – he's been nursing a hamstring injury picked up in the final game in South Africa.

The South won Monday's fielding match, but the North extracted full revenge for Sunday's defeat in the soccer that followed. Yesterday was more practice, but this time in match situations as we concentrated on how we would bat in the first 15 overs. However much you practise, you need games where there are no second chances. Out total was a good score on this wicket, with Stewie, Jack and Chalky (Craig White) batting well, although Athers, Harvey and Thorpey managed just eight runs between them. My knee was still hurting, but I was reasonably happy with my and the team's bowling performance. We had a spot of local difficulty as the home side tried to bring in batsmen who hadn't taken any part in the game. You've got to keep your wits about you here.

THURSDAY 8 FEBRUARY   AITCHESON

Lahore Cricket Association 166/9   England 167/4
England won by 6 wickets

My worst nightmare. My right knee gave way and I had to limp off after bowling the first ball of my third over. I kept trying to work out how bad it was as I went off. Was this the end of my World Cup? There was certainly no way I was going to risk it any more today. The rest of the day consisted of ice packs and trying to watch the cricket, but not being able to concentrate much beyond my knee. I'm optimistic that I will be able to carry on, but at the back of my mind I'm trying to prepare myself for the prospect of going home early, even before the World Cup begins. If it gets any worse, I might need a cortisone injection and that could sideline me for over a week. Injury seems to be a way of life with England fast bowlers. Devon, Daffy, Gussie, Chalky, Ramble and Goughie have all had more than their fair share. I remember a couple of years ago there was talk of an investigation into the problem and the possible ways of reducing the workload and threat of damage. I don't remember seeing any conclusions.

There still seems total confusion about replacements. Can we have them for 'soft tissue' injuries – whatever that means – and can we bring out who we want? I don't see why not. And I don't see why all this wasn't sorted out weeks ago. Today's game was going to be just amongst ourselves, but when we arrived at the Gymkhana the Lahore CA were there, ready and waiting. Goughie gave his hamstring a good work-out, as the bowlers found a receptive pitch. A typical batting performance – 79/0 to 91/4 – before Harvey and Jack saw us home.

SUNDAY 11 FEBRUARY   CALCUTTA

I've made the World Cup opening ceremony, at least. My knee allowed me to parade in front of 100,000 screaming fans in Eden Gardens. God knows what it's like to play cricket here when it's full. There was a phenomenal atmosphere, despite the fact that much of the laser show and entertainment did not go as planned. Apparently, the Italian director of the show, who was also responsible for the grand openings of the 1990 soccer World Cup and the 1992 Barcelona Olympics, got a fee in excess of a million pounds. Nice money if you can get it. I don't think the wind helped his laser show. The announcements were not always accurate. You might, at a pinch, get Zimbabwe and the United Arab Emirates mixed up, but not South Africa and Pakistan. As a public relations exercise, it wasn't a great start, despite all the emotion of Eden Gardens.

I can tell you that not too many of our party had a good word to say about the trip to Calcutta yesterday morning after a five-hour delay getting here. We eventually got to our beds at three a.m. That's no way to prepare for a World Cup. And we know we've got a couple more nightmare journeys to come. Touring England must be heaven. Finish a game at six, then hop on a coach and you've checked into your new hotel in less than three hours. All done and dusted. Every time we move here, it's a day, and possibly a night, out of your life.

I missed out on practice yesterday, although I feel my knee is improving. Judgey has been given until tomorrow night to prove his fitness. He and I have been under the needle. Wayne's been trying out his acupuncture skills on us. It works, too. Harvey is our latest casualty, after cutting his head while fielding. Is there no end to the ways we can find to hurt ourselves? Last night all the teams were given a briefing about the opening ceremony and the parts we were expected to play. Every time we move outside the hotel, there are about 5,000 fans hanging around to catch a glimpse of us and the other international cricketers. The actual launch dinner was chaotic, not helped by the fact that we have another earlier-than-dawn departure. Player comfort is certainly not a factor when these itineraries are set down.

The famous coloured clothing has turned up, and everyone's trousers are too short. The designs are pretty dull, too. But that's the least of our worries. The Sri Lankan problem has rumbled on all week, with both Australia and the West Indies refusing to go to Colombo and no amount of pleading or reassurances about safety changing their minds. The organisers resisted calls to move the Sri Lankan matches. Australia and the West Indies will forfeit the matches and so the Sri Lankans have four points before the tournament has even started. India and Pakistan have agreed to play a good-will match in Colombo on Tuesday. I'm not sure how England would have reacted if we had been scheduled to visit Colombo.

WEDNESDAY 14 FEBRUARY
GUJARAT STADIUM, AHMEDABAD

World Cup Group B   *New Zealand 239/6 (50 overs)*   *England 228/9 (5?)*
England lost by 11 runs   *Man of the Match: Nathan Astle*

Disaster. Yet another game we should have won. I don't like being outplayed, but at least I can understand that. We're not outplayed, but we still keep coming second. The pressure is on us now. We knew what a losing start would mean in this World Cup. And we've only ourselves to blame.

What a small, small world it is. Nathan Astle and I played cricket together in New Zealand five years ago. Today, he recorded the first century of the 1996 World Cup and provided the platform for our defeat. Nathan batted well, but their score was a very gettable total. Why oh why are we not clicking on the field? The work's going in. We have talented players who want to do well. But there is something missing.

The journey here was another nightmare. I'm not making excuses. We had to get up in the middle of the night for a six-thirty a.m. flight to Delhi on Monday morning. Why were we flying to Delhi? You may well ask. Our Board pressed for charter flights, so that the team could go directly to its destinations. Those pleas fell on deaf ears. You wouldn't mind if the flights were on time, but they never are. Having dragged ourselves out of bed, we had to hang around Calcutta Airport for hours. What was there to do in Delhi? Nothing but kill time. We headed for the British High Commission, where the lads took the rare chance to tuck into sausages, chips and beans. Heaven. Then it was back to the airport and the evening flight to Ahmedabad. Air India once again left us in no doubt that we had landed. In all, hotel to hotel took 17 hours!

It was strange returning to the Ahmedabad ground on Monday morning. I was here just over a year ago with the A team, dreaming of playing for the senior side. I remember being interviewed then and saying that I hoped the trip would give me valuable experience if I was picked for England's World Cup squad. After all my disappointments, I'm not sure I believed it at the time. Judgey was ruled out today, but has been given the all-clear for the rest of the competition. Illy, ever the professional, pointed out that the organisers had ensured that we've had four days, since Thursday, without anyone being able to do any serious work with the bat or ball. My knee felt better after a serious work-out yesterday and I had no doubts about being able to last the New Zealand game.

So what went wrong today? What went right? Athers won the toss and put New Zealand in. Thorpey put down a couple of early chances, one off me when Astle had scored a single. I caught and bowled Spearman, but our successes were few and far between. I thought we might have been chasing a bigger total, but the Kiwis rather lost their way in the closing stages, although we (and I mean we) continued to drop chances. Still, the locals were kind enough to point out that it was the best score ever recorded in a one-day international here. Thanks, lads. But the mood was confident during the break. The ball was in our court. The Kiwis don't have that strong bowling attack. If our batters performed as they can, we would win, simple as that. With one or two exceptions – notably Hickie – we didn't. Hickie became our latest casualty when he tweaked a hamstring and Athers, despite a failure, stayed out as Hickie's runner. Stewie, who'd been hit on the head in a fielding accident the day before, and Hickie put on 99, but then we kept losing wickets, without really reducing the run-rate. We didn't score a boundary for 13 overs in the middle of the innings. The beginning of the end came when Hickie was run out after a sharp call from Harvey. Well, Hickie wasn't. It was Athers who was short of his ground. But the consequence was the same. We were struggling. The final margin might look close, but we were always struggling. Just the start we didn't want. And my knee is sore again. Strange how these injuries hurt a lot more when you've just lost.

SUNDAY 18 FEBRUARY   PESHAWAR

United Arab Emirates 136 (48.3)   England 140/2 (35 overs)
England won by 8 wickets   Man of the Match: Neil Smith

Our first World Cup win. And our first casualty. It's not me, or
Judgey, or Goughie. It's my roomie Chalky White, who suffered the
same fate during England's Ashes trip last winter. The problem is
the same, too – a side strain. That's bad luck on him because he's
put himself back in the England frame with his form here and in
South Africa. Dermot Reeve or Winker Watkinson are favourites for
the call. That should be interesting. Dermot had a few things to say
about being left out of the original 14, complaining that he didn't
get much of a chance to press his claims in South Africa. Neil Smith,
our Man of the Match, was another in trouble today. Whether it
was the pizza he ate last night or something else, no one's sure. He
took ill while batting and was sick on the pitch before retiring. He
looked a bit more perky when he came up for his Man of the Match
award. Stomach problems are an everyday hazard here. However
careful you try to be, the Delhi belly can strike at any time.

Neil took the first three wickets to fall as the UAE struggled with
the pitch and our bowlers, apart from me and Goughie, who bowled
rather too full a length. Our batters went about their business pro-
fessionally. Now, everyone's behaving as if the victory was a formality, but we were only too well aware of the consequences if we
had slipped up today. I'm excused most practice-duties at the moment
after I aggravated the knee problem on Thursday. The doctor's orders
are that I'll need to rest as much as possible between matches if I
want to make it through this World Cup.

We didn't move from Ahmedabad until Thursday evening because
that was the reserve day for our New Zealand match. Everyone was
dreading the journey to Peshawar. It looked horrible on paper, and
it *was* pretty horrendous in the coaches, planes and airport lounges,
I can tell you. We flew to Delhi on Thursday night, where we stayed
until Friday morning. At lunch we took off for Karachi, where we
waited for the connection to Peshawar. Even the sight of the only
bar in Pakistan failed to raise our spirits. We've been far more
interested in getting to our beds than bars in the past week.

Newspapers and the TV are keeping us informed about the rest
of the World Cup. The Sri Lankan boycott rumbles on. The papers
have been full of suggestions that Australia and the West Indies might
be fined two million pounds for forfeiting their matches, while Kapil

Dev has been calling for Australia to be thrown out of the World Cup. The Sri Lankans went through the motions yesterday and turned up for the Aussie match in Colombo. Now there's talk of prosecuting the Indian organiser for bringing the name of his country into disrepute. The favourites in our group, South Africa, made a mess of the UAE, with Gary Kirsten's 188 not out just one run short of Viv Richards' one-day record. One of the craziest things I've ever seen was the UAE skipper coming out to face Donald in a sun hat – not a helmet. I was amazed he was still standing as the very first ball bounced off his head.

THURSDAY 22 FEBRUARY   PESHAWAR

England 279/4   Holland 230/8
England won by 49 runs   Man of the Match: Graeme Hick

Two wins out of three, but that's not as impressive as it sounds. We've beaten the two ICC qualifiers in our group and the senior countries all expected to do that. Our qualifying position will depend on the other results. The batters set a total that Holland were never going to threaten, despite the fact that we did not bowl that well, me included. Hickie and Thorpey's partnership of 143 provided the backbone of our innings. Goughie and I bowled 11 overs between us and they went for 75. Goughie's troubles didn't end there. Fielding near the boundary has always been hazardous here. Bits of fruit and rubbish, ice cubes and plastic bottles (normally empty) whistle past your ear, if you're lucky. Goughie's always been good-natured and likes a bit of fun with the crowd. But his mood changed when a wooden spear landed near him. It was a pointed bit of wood about seven inches long. That could have caused serious damage. He gave it to the umpires, who spoke to the match referee, who contacted the police and I believe an arrest was made.

My knee is still bothering me and I'm beginning to wonder whether it's going to get me through this competition. At least we had no travelling to do after beating the UAE. Monday, the rest day, was given over to a Ryder Cup clash between the North and the South. Harvey and I took on Thorpey and Judgey. The two left-handers had to share a bag that only contained three clubs, No. five and No. seven irons and a putter. The need to improvise became even greater when Thorpey managed to break the five-iron on the first hole. Our match ended in a half, but I'm pleased to say that the honour of the North was maintained. We had two hard mornings of practice on

Above: Goughie with the world's biggest toothpick! In fact, this missile only narrowly missed him during our game against Holland.

Left: my appeals got less energetic as the World Cup campaign went on. This is the one-arm, no-strain-on-the-knees version. But I didn't feel either as comfortable or as convincing with it.

Tuesday and Wednesday. Even then we got into trouble. We were accused in the newspaper *Frontier Post* of bribery. It was suggested that by seeking to practise on the edge of the square England were trying to discover how the wicket would play and were infringing the World Cup rules. Worse than that, money was said to have been offered as an inducement. Bribery and corruption at the very heart of the England team. 'Englishmen at it Again' was the headline. We all thought it was a great hoot. But you don't need a vivid imagination to see how these things can get out of hand very easily.

Our afternoons have been given over to watching World Cup action on the TV. The evenings? This is Pakistan. Nothing happens in the evenings here. South Africa beat the Kiwis comfortably and look favourites to top our group. Yesterday, India beat the West Indies, with Tendulkar in devastating form, although the Windies dropped several chances, while Sri Lanka easily overcame Zimbabwe. We're off again tomorrow, but there'll be no airport lounging about. We're taking a coach to Rawalpindi.

SUNDAY 25 FEBRUARY   RAWALPINDI

South Africa 230 (50 overs)   England 152 (44.3)
England lost by 78 runs   Man of the Match: Jonty Rhodes

This was the contest which was going to show that we had recovered from the traumas of those final weeks in South Africa. On today's evidence, we haven't. It was more of the same. No confidence, no cohesion, no chance. I'm beginning to sound like Scarlett O'Hara in *Gone With the Wind* – tomorrow is another day. But we are running out of excuses – and time. Just as well we're guaranteed a quarter-final place. I dropped an early catch, but I bowled better than recently and the lads were not unhappy with chasing that target. The South African top scorer was Kirsten with 38, but they all chipped in and four other batsmen got beyond 25. Digger Martin was the best of our bowlers. Our problems began when Athers departed fourth ball and we never really recovered. That's ironic because most of the press stories of the last couple of days have centred on Illy ordering Athers to open instead of going in down the order as he did against the UAE and Holland.

By the close we only managed to muster the same number of runs as the UAE did against South Africa. My roomie Thorpey's 46 was the best of the day, but nobody stayed with him. The worst dismissal was Stewie's run-out. I thought he was home and dry, but the replay revealed that he had been rather lax in running his bat in. It was the sort of careless mistake that we desperately didn't need. Daffy, playing his 100th one-day international, and I put on 42 for the eighth wicket, but we were running at nearly ten an over by then. We were never in the frame and won't be in this World Cup unless there is a dramatic improvement.

Athers' bad day continued at the press conference. He's alleged to have called a local journalist a 'buffoon'. I wasn't there, but it seems everything we do at the moment is going wrong. Forget what I said about being relieved about travelling to Rawalpindi by coach. That was a journey I'll never forget. If it had been Friday the 13th – not 23rd – then I would have got off. In three hours, we must have bounced through a thousand potholes and narrowly avoided half a dozen head-on collisions as our driver did a rather good impression of Nigel Mansell. The only good news is that for most of the weekend I've been dining on the High Commission's sausages, beans and chips.

Pakistan entered the competition yesterday, beating the UAE by nine wickets. After today's result, the odds are that England will finish in fourth spot. That will give us a quarter-final tie against the winner of Group A, which is increasingly looking like India or Sri Lanka. No one on the England party is happy with our form, but there is a real feeling that this is the phoney war. The first 30 matches of this World Cup will reject four countries – presumably Zimbabwe and the three ICC qualifiers. Then it's the knock-out stage. Previous World Cups have all gone to semis – that does make every group result very important. If that had been the case this time, we would be out of the competition. Now we have a week off before taking on the team that beat us in the last WC final, Pakistan.

THURSDAY 29 FEBRUARY   KARACHI

The first WC upset, and, amazingly, it does not involve us. The mighty West Indies were defeated by Kenya today. Not just defeated. Absolutely hammered. There was no hint of the sensation to come when Kenya were bowled out for 166 in Pune. But no West Indian batsman reached 20 and only two made double figures as the twice-former WC champions and kings of one-day cricket were rolled over for 93. Now the heat is on. The Windies must beat Australia, who've looked in great form, in their final group match to be certain of making the quarter-finals. For once, the calls for wholesale changes and sackings, the national outcry and the 'send them home early' chant are not directed at us.

The Kenyans haven't looked a bad outfit. They were unlucky earlier in the week – they had Zimbabwe in trouble, but the rain abandoned the match and Kenya lost on the reserve day. The WI defeat has been the shock of the tournament, with most matches so far going as predicted. One of the few real contests saw Australia beat India. Mark Waugh is in devastating form and even the loss of Craig McDermott hasn't affected their status as one of the firm favourites. The South Africans beat Pakistan easily today and they are certain to win Group B.

While England may not be able to make much of an impact on the field, we've atttracted a fair amount of interest off it. The aftermath of the Athers 'buffoon' remark has rumbled on all week. The reaction has reached hysterical proportions with calls for him to be sacked at England captain. What rubbish. Athers has admitted that England's poor performances could cost him his job. That would be unfair. 'Sir Geoffrey' has apparently gone into print in the *Sun* and once again he has suggested that Athers should give up the captaincy. Athers has issued an apology for an off-the-cuff light-hearted remark and that should be an end to it.

He's not the only one under the cosh. Boycott had something to say about me too, of course. 'Dominic Cork had a bad day. He has become the show pony. If you put him in a ring, they'd pin the First Prize rosette to his chest.' Very funny. And my 'bye-bye' to New Zealand Spearman after the caught and bowled did not find favour with some sections of the broadsheet media. Stewie meanwhile is being told that a schoolboy in his first match would not have made the mistake of failing to run his bat in. England professional crickters, it is suggested, can be complacent and arrogant, with very little to be complacent and arrogant about. I think the *Daily Telegraph* described me as a 'bellicose braggart'. I'm not sure what it means, but it sounds pretty good.

Our final day in Peshawar was spent playing table tennis, cards and Balderdash, a sort of *Call My Bluff* with a bit more player participation. Many of us went looking for carpets to take home. One of the shops kept enquiring about a Mr Lamb, who apparently did some business here during the World Cup of 1987. What they want him for I can't imagine! We flew to Karachi on Tuesday. I went up to the cockpit to get a bird's-eye view. These landings aren't so bad when you know that bump is coming! The drive from the airport to the Pearl Continental hotel was amazing. It took us over an hour to travel just over a mile. I've never seen so many people milling about. We've been warned that this place is only marginally safer than Colombo. There have been an enormous number of political deaths in recent weeks, and the hundreds of people milling around the hotel are matched by the number of security guards. Apparently, one of the political parties has warned that something will happen here in Karachi. Just our luck.

The net facilities we had at the Gymkhana Club were the best we've had in this World Cup. It makes it so much better when the batters and bowlers can have a decent work-out. Not that I can, even when the facilities are perfect. I'm still resting my knee at every opportunity. Up to today, I was hopeful of it carrying me through the competition. But then I bowled a little and the worrying process has begun all over again. Worse, actually. My right knee is beginning to ache like the left. I've already spoken to Derbyshire and they have guaranteed me a complete month off, so I don't have to play until mid-April. I would hate to break down now. All the fun of the knock-out stage is about to start.

MARCH 1996
Sri Lanka Conquer the World

FRIDAY 1 MARCH　　　　　GYMKHANA CLUB, KARACHI

England 264/6　Karachi XI 265/5
England lost by 5 wickets

Probably the worst day of both winter trips. The lads looked totally out of sorts as we batted and bowled without conviction against a local Karachi side. I'm sure the press will get stuck into us. On this occasion, I can't really blame them. One thing that does annoy me about the cricket press in general – and yes, there are always exceptions – is how easily they lose faith and begin to belittle everything we do. It seems to be a common occurrence in most sports, golf being just about the one exception. Yet we've no excuses today. Athers and Dermot batted well, but Stewie and the Judge missed the opportunity for a long spell out in the middle Unfortunately, the locals had little difficulty in knocking off the runs. They were helped by two of our party – Jack and Thorpey – but neither was among the three top scorers for Karachi, so we couldn't even claim a moral victory. They were also helped by our bowling, which was wayward to say the least. It's about not giving batsmen width here, but we continue to lack real control.

Even the commentator on the tannoy gave us a hard time today. It's bad enough making mistakes without hearing it broadcast. 'A poor throw there by Hick'; 'Not a good over from Gough'. Eventually, 'Trout' was sent round to tell him to belt up. Athers' problems continued today. Communications, as usual, were vague about the after-match ceremony and our skipper was stuck on the bog when he was due to be presenting an England tie and receiving the losers' cheque. He recovered in time to cut the commemorative cake, but I'm sure the locals will make a big fuss about it. Our blue WC trousers are causing the hotel laundry problems. Half the side are now running around with trousers that stop several inches over their ankles.

Sunday 3 March   Gymkhana Club

England 249/9 (50 overs)   Pakistan 250/3 (47.4)
England lost by 7 wickets

Another bad defeat. The next loss will put England out of the World Cup. Our form going into the WC quarter-finals is less than impressive. Ten straight one-day defeats at the hands of major cricket-playing countries. We couldn't have asked for a better start as Athers and Judgey put on 147 for the first wicket in 28 overs. Once again, we dropped into self-destruct mode – and stayed there. That was a great shame because this would have been a great match to win. I will always remember this day for the amazing atmosphere in the National Stadium. My head is still ringing. The reception and noise when Javed Miandad, the local hero (who is now the only man to play in every World Cup), was incredible. Even he was taken aback. I'm not sure he's ever had a standing ovation before he's even received a ball. Javed saw Pakistan home to victory and received a similar reception at the finish. We saw little evidence to support the rumours that Pakistan were going to throw this match because it would mean they could stay on home territory instead of heading to India and Bangalore. The papers were full of the story and there were one or two rather cruel jibes that it couldn't be true because it would be impossible to lose against us. Sadly, despite a positive and confident team-meeting last night, those slurs on our current playing ability proved not to be too wide of the mark. The only surprise at that meeting was that Stewie was not playing. Dermot came in for his first game of this WC campaign. It's not my job to criticise the selectors and I'm not. Yet it seems to have taken us far too long to find our best line-up and I'm not sure it's settled yet.

We've found an opening pair, at last. Athers and Judgey were magnificent. Athers has been short of runs and his leadership style has been questioned. That's just the environment our captain thrives on and he answered his critics in an emphatic way today. After that start, we should have set our sights – and got – around the 300-mark. But we mustered 102 runs in those final 22 overs, over half coming from Thorpey. It didn't help that Athers and Judgey got out together – one should have aimed to be there after 40 overs – but we can't blame them. Our lack of batting technique on these wickets was exposed yet again. Harvey, Dermot and Jack went in consecutive overs to leggie Mushtaq.

We never looked like bowling them out or even causing them too many uncomfortable moments in their run chase. The Pakistanis went about their business in a professional and methodical way. Nothing we tried interfered with that. The inevitability of it all was rather depressing. And it looks like we're sending for another replacement. Harvey's hamstring has really gone this time. The group matches in this World Cup have gone as badly for us as they possibly could without England getting knocked out. I don't believe we're lucky to make the quarter-finals because with this changed format it would have been a national disaster if we hadn't. I don't think there's any doubt that if this had been like any of the previous World Cups and gone to semi-finals, then England would now be on our way home. Yet, in a way, we must forget the past couple of months. Unfair as it might seem, we're not out of the hunt yet. Now, it's sudden death or glory. I keep looking round the squad. There's so much individual talent there. We can't keep performing this badly – can we?

WEDNESDAY 6 MARCH   KARACHI

All the group matches have been played and the quarter-final draw confirmed. The phoney war is over. Now it's down to the nitty-gritty. That all sounds great, but I fear my own quarter-final place is in real jeopardy. I twisted my knee badly yesterday and was forced to go to Karachi hospital for a scan. I've been so careful with my knee, but it's been touch and go for several weeks whether it would get me through this tournament. My right knee gave way during fielding practice. Blame the press. We had expected to practise at the Gymkhana Club, but it had been booked for a media match between our poison-penned assassins and the locals.

It's just as well I had my mishap in Karachi as it has the only scanner in Pakistan. Initially I feared the worst because it really hurt, but the MRI scan showed soft tissue damage round the tendon which has bothered me since SA. I'll need to have intensive treatment for the next 48 hours if I'm to have any chance of playing on Saturday. That won't cure it – only a six-week rest or an operation similar to the one I had on my left knee two years ago will do that. I can't argue with those journalists who say my breakdown was almost inevitable. I've had hardly any time off over the past year. That would

My own World Cup campaign came to a stuttering stop a few days before England's. Here is a rare action shot of 'Doc Holliday' – Dr Philip Bell – telling me what I knew only too well. *Below:* watching the lads prepare for the quarter-final and desperately hoping I still had a part to play.

be one major advantage of the England players being contracted to the Board. Derbyshire look after me better than most, but you feel a loyalty to the people paying your wages. It's not just the amount of cricket we play, it's the type of cricket – a lot of high-profile, high-pressure international stuff. And let's not forget the travelling, whether at home or abroad. I can't begin to imagine the amount of time I've spent at airports, on planes and stuck on the M1 and M25!

Harvey was definitely ruled out on Monday and has flown home. Ramps is due to arrive tomorrow, although I expect Stewie will be brought back for the Sri Lanka clash. They topped group A with a 100 per cent record. They showed what they are capable of today when they crushed Kenya by 144 runs, setting a WC record total of 398/5 – de Silva 145. Actually, it's a record total in any one-day cricket. They've been great to watch. The openers come out and blast it. Then the rest follow and do the same. They don't seem intimidated by anyone. And that Kenya attack bowled out the great Windies for a total of 93 a few days earlier. Australia, who finished runners-up despite losing to the West Indies yesterday, take on New Zealand in a local derby. There's another interesting one. India against Pakistan in Bangalore. The other quarter is between South Africa and the West Indies. The Windies might be hitting form at the right time. Richie Richardson was Man of the Match against the Aussies with 93 not out. He's been under a lot of pressure and the WI Board held an emergency meeting yesterday following that defeat by Kenya. Richie had already faxed through his resignation. Today, it was announced that the management team of Wes Hall and Andy Roberts had been sacked. Great timing! I always thought our Board had a monopoly on bad timing. Only kidding! Courtney Walsh will take over the captaincy for the home series against New Zealand next month. If England get through, we – and I hope it's we – will play the winner of India and Pakistan in Calcutta. I'd actually thought my knee was going to last, that's the annoying part.

The North beat the South again at golf on Monday, despite some disgraceful barracking off the tees. I was fairly low yesterday after the injury. Lying in my room with my knee packed with ice and eating baked beans and rice, washed down with Pepsi, I thought, 'This is the jet-set lifestyle I've dedicated my sporting life to. Beam me home, Scottie.' I've done a Pepsi TV ad which is a great favourite with the lads. They haven't stopped taking the mickey out of me. The one consolation is that it's not being shown back home.

Our quarter-final total against Sri Lanka was never going to be enough, as Jayasuriya (*above*), among others, proved. It was a disappointing start to 1996 for our skipper, seen here misfielding in the quarter-final. The hero of the Wanderers quickly became the villain of our one-day campaigns, and there was even talk that he should be replaced.

FRIDAY 8 MARCH   FAISALABAD

Tomorrow is the big day. Unfortunately, I'm not going to be able
to make the party. It was always a long shot. Now I've got to pray
that the lads can do the business and the extra time will allow me
to make the semi-finals. Still, it's going to be heartbreaking watching
them take the field without me, I've come so far with Athers and
company over the past year. I've got no worries about them winning
without me. I *need* them to win without me.

The past couple of days have been very frustrating. The doc and
Wayne have been working so hard, trying everything they can, but
we all realised that we needed some sort of miracle improvement. I
suppose that applies to the team as a whole. My injury allows Daffy
a chance to get back in favour. There's even talk of him being asked
to bowl his offies, strange as that might seem. They aren't bad. We
used them a couple of times last summer, most notably when he
turned the ball square at Bristol. Again, I'm surprised that there
seems to be no end to our experimentation.

It's tough not playing. You're part of the squad, not part of the
team. The hotel Serena has some fairly tense cricketers here tonight.
The lads know that one top-class performance could right a lot
of wrongs, while anything less will probably lead to defeat, exit
from the World Cup and confirmation of everything that's been
written and said about us being a second-class cricket nation at
present.

SATURDAY 9 MARCH   FAISALABAD

World Cup Quarter-Final *England 235/8 (50 overs)* *Sri Lanka*
236/5 (40.4)
England lost by 5 wickets

Goodnight England. We're out of this World Cup without causing
so much as a single ripple of excitement or suggesting that we don't
deserve to be ranked number seven or even number eight in the
world. I don't know what's worse. Playing in a side that's struggling
to compete – or watching it. Good luck to Sri Lanka. They fully
deserve to be in the semi-final and, on this form, I wouldn't bet
against them causing a real upset. They brought a freshness of
approach, of ideas, of invention and sheer batting brilliance to this
World Cup. We think we know it all. England, the country that
plays more one-day domestic cricket than just about the rest of the

England weren't the only victims of Sri Lanka's World Cup giant-killing act. They totally outplayed India in the Bombay semi-final, which had to be abandoned after the crowd started rioting. Then it was Australia's turn to suffer in the final (*above*). Aravinda de Silva's magnificent century earned him the Man of the Match award.

cricket world put together, were exposed tactically, technically and totally throughout this tournament.

It's easy to over-react. But if we don't over-react, England are going to get further and further behind. If we give the impression of going backwards, it's because other countries like Australia, South Africa and now Sri Lanka are embracing new ideas and developments in a totally professional set-up. All the public sees is England losing to Sri Lanka. The players are the ones who take most of the stick. I don't think that's very fair, but it's an inescapable fact of cricket life.

But for Daffy's bludgeoning knock, and some support from Dermot and Goughie, we'd have been totally humiliated. As it was, our total was never enough. Once again, we got no luck off the bounce. I certainly do not see how the third umpire could have judged Robin Smith run out. We all watched it from three different angles and not one of them was conclusive. We just haven't been able to handle bad breaks like that. The effect of the last two months was there for all to see in the way our batters played against not the greatest bowling attack in the world. Athers tried the only thing possible to retrieve the situation – a bold approach to match Sri Lanka's batting tactics that have devastated all attack in their group matches. Athers opened up with Illy. The move showed a measure of desperation. But desperate situations call for desperate measures. Illy's first two overs cost 27 runs and included a wicket. It might have been two, but Goughie could not hold on to a hard chance from Gurusinha. That was about as good as it got for England. Jayasuriya, after smashing Illy, laid into Daffy to record the quickest-ever WC 50 – just 29 balls. Digger kept it tight and Goughie's ten overs only cost 36 runs, but the damage had been done with our meagre total and the Sri Lankans' devastating start. They won at a canter with nearly ten overs to spare. I'm sure the obituary notices will start now. Fair enough. We produced nothing in this World Cup. We worked hard, tried hard. But something is missing. I just hope that while the boot is being put into England, that doesn't detract from praise for a fine performance from a talented Sri Lankan side. I'm not sure even a total approaching 335 would have tested this lot today.

We can't even drown our sorrows. Our consignment of Tetley Bitter has been impounded at Karachi docks because it's illegal to drink alcohol publicly here. Apparently, the document stating that the beer would be consumed privately by non-Muslims has gone astray. Also, apparently, it's not the first time this has happened to an England cricket team in Pakistan. So around 2,000 tins of Tetley will never make their final destination. I bet they never get back to England!

It looks like we won't get back home until Tuesday. And this early exit means I'll be in hospital for a nose and tonsils operation on Wednesday, to try to put right the damage from that old rugby accident. That will give me about a month to recover before the start of the next season. We're not the only ones out of the World Cup tonight. The holders, Pakistan, went down to India by 39 runs. Both finalists from last time out have made very little impact in this 1996 event.

TUESDAY 12 MARCH   DERBY

Home at last, after another nightmare journey. We were held up for hours as a couple of passengers got lost. What do airlines do to these people who cost them thousands of pounds? I've got one or two suggestions.

It's great to be back with the family, although I'm leaving them tomorrow to go under the knife. Reading the papers, I'm not the only cricketer for whom that would be a popular punishment after our expedition, although there are odd crumbs of comfort coming out of the sub-continent. I managed a smile for the first time in a month when the West Indies beat the South Africans yesterday. After a whole winter of hearing about their magnificent professionalism and planning, they've gone out of the World Cup at exactly the same stage as us. I'm pleased for the Windies and Richie. The West Indies Board may have just sacked a coach and manager who are going to bring them home the World Cup. The Aussies showed their immense batting power in overtaking the Kiwis. So it's Sri Lanka v India and Australia v West Indies. Not only have the four semi-finalists of the last World Cup all failed to reach that stage this time, but all four qualifiers from Group B have fallen at the first hurdle.

I feel the most depressing factor of England's situation is that it is a deep-rooted problem. We've been papering over the paper that's been papering over the paper that's been papering over the cracks. Sad as it is for us to lose like this, maybe, just maybe, it will wake and shake people up. I'm a competitor. I want to compete with the rest of the cricket world. The word is that Illy won't stay on as supremo, but he might remain as chairman. You can argue about personnel all you like, but everyone knows the structure of our domestic cricket is wrong. Until that problem has been addressed, the rest is incidental. Sorry, if all this sounds maudlin, but that's what a piss-poor World Cup campaign does for you. They even started questioning Athers' captaincy. I can't begin to imagine what this winter would have been like without him as captain and batsman. There's enough wrong with England cricket without mucking about with one of the few things that's right! As far as the World Cup is concerned, too many of us failed to perform to standard. You can't blame the captain for that.

SUNDAY 17 MARCH   DERBY

Maybe England aren't that bad after all. Would you believe it? Sri Lanka are the 1996 World Champions. With a minimum of fuss, they beat the much-fancied Aussies in the final this afternoon. I just about took it all in. I'm still groggy from my operations. My hospital stay lasted two nights rather than the anticipated one. I saw the start of Sri Lanka v. India, but fell asleep and woke to the 9 o'clock news that Sri Lanka were through and the crowd at Calcutta had rioted. I'm glad I was more with it for the next day's semi-final. Those closing overs were something else as the West Indies snatched defeat from the jaws of victory. Australia's winning margin was five runs after the last eight Windies' wickets fell for 37 runs in 51 deliveries. That is cricketing suicide on a major scale, even by our standards. Richie was left stranded on 49 in his final moment as West Indies skipper and as an international cricketer. It was a great fightback by the Aussies, who had been 15/4.

I must admit I wasn't that interested in cricket when I came out of hospital. The nose didn't feel too bad, but my throat was very sore. Maybe the whole winter, even year, caught up with me because I suddenly felt completely out of it. There's nothing I love more than playing cricket, but the thought of a month away sounds heaven at the moment. Still, I enjoyed watching the final today. I thought the Aussies were going to run away with it when they reached 134/1 at the halfway stage of their innings. But then they got bogged down. Even the tactic of introducing Shane Warne – a 'pinch-hitter' – which had worked against the West Indies failed to loosen the Sri Lankans' stranglehold. The Sri Lankans started badly, just as they did against India when they lost both openers after only four balls, but Guru-sinha and de Silva, then Ranatunga saw Sri Lanka home in some style. They were supposed to be the underdogs, but showed no nerves as they neared the winning target. My mind drifted back to Pieter-maritzburg. A strange place to want to return to? Not really, when

I recalled that we were offered odds of 66/1 to back a Sri Lankan World Cup victory. The awards ceremony was something else as Ian Chappell attempted to interview the main players while they received their various trophies and cheques. I gather Chappell has never been one to stand on ceremony. The Pakistani Prime Minister Benazir Bhutto had little option but to concede centre-stage to the former Australian captain. My first World Cup and for the first time ever, England failed to make the semi-finals. I didn't even make the quarters. The next World Cup is in England in three years' time. Will I be around in 1999?

MONDAY 25 MARCH   DERBY

The winter tour is over. The World Cup has been decided. Yet the great England cricket debate continues. It's taking me longer than expected to recuperate from my operation. The nose feels good, but my throat is still aching. I spent much of last week in bed, which gave me a chance to study the papers. I couldn't believe the amount of cricket on the sports pages considering there is no actual action. Illy's future appears to be the main issue. Warwickshire put David Graveney forward as a challenger to Illy's position as Chairman of Selectors, but that contest fizzled out when Graveney withdrew after his employers, the Professional Cricketers' Association, told him he could not remain as their chief executive if he was also chairman. That left Illy unopposed and in charge for the summer. But he's no longer going to be the sole supremo. There is to be a new team manager/coach, whatever you want to call him. John Emburey and David Lloyd are the front-runners for that job. There's been a lot of support for Ian Botham getting involved. My views on that man are well known. There's obviously a lot happening behind the scenes – none of it involving England players, although the outcome of these deliberations will have major implications for the Test team for next summer at least.

I've been down to the club to show my face and pick up my mail. I played golf with Kim today. I think he's really looking forward to a season without the responsibilities of leading Derbyshire. I would think 13 years in that job is a lifetime for anyone. The club have nominated him to be one of the England selectors this year. He wouldn't be a bad choice. I've never understood why current players can't have more of an input like that. Kim has seen all there is to see of the modern domestic game, and the natural schedule of the summer means he's going to see nearly all the candidates.

SUNDAY 31 MARCH   DERBY

The end of my year. The end of my diary. On Friday, I helped with
a raffle whose proceeds are going to the Dunblane Fund. I don't
think you'd need to be the parent of a young child to struggle with
the scale of that atrocity. Next week I'm off to London twice. On
Monday, it's *A Question of Sport* – although as a cricketer, I suppose
I'll be on the opposite team to the great Botham. Ian's joined the
growing list of contenders on this year's selection panel. That battle
is really hotting up. At least this selection is going to be less of a
formality and we might end up with some younger blood on the
panel. England's coach has been chosen, though. It's Lancashire's
David Lloyd. He had the field all to himself when Emburey dropped
out. The new Northants coach didn't feel able to jeopardise a four-
year contract with one that is just for this summer, however pres-
tigious being involved with the England set-up might be. According to
the newspaper reports, the money is nothing special – about £25,000,
which is what an average county performer would get. I do feel such
a high-profile job is worth a lot more than that. On Wednesday
night, I'll be at the East India Club for the 133rd Wisden Dinner.
That's where they launch the publication of the cricketers' bible. The
reason I'm going is that I've been chosen as one of the five 'Cricketers
of the Year'. It's one of the greatest honours in the game. I can't
think of a more fitting end to what has been a remarkable cricket
year for me.

Postscript

That Was the Year That Was. It's over, let it go. So the old song goes. It sounds like sound advice to me. Reading through my diary, I can't believe all the amazing things that have happened to me over the past 12 months. But it's over, finished, history. I've no intention of living on past glories. I feel I have dispelled the doubts that my talent and temperament would not stand up to the rigours of international cricket. But staying there will be even harder than getting there. Cricket and sport is littered with one-day, one-week, one-year wonders. However crazy it might sound, my ambition is to perform even better on the cricket field this summer. That's been my annual plan, although this time my goals have changed. This time last year there was one urge driving me on – I had to play Test cricket for England. That had become an obsession. I can't imagine what life would be like now for me if I had not fulfilled that desire. A year ago, my frustration was almost at breaking point. I've been lucky that my first year of Test cricket has afforded me considerable personal success. Initially, the dream is to play for your country. Step two is to play well for your country. Normally, only after those two objectives are satisfied do players turn their attentions to the most important motivation of all – to help turn your country into the best cricket team in the world. That's what I'm all about from now on. Many may say that I'm starting at the bottom in that respect. That England has never been as low as it is now. That's simply not true. The Cape Town Test defeat was disappointing, the one-day defeats in South Africa were demoralising and the World Cup disaster was devastating. But that entire catalogue of defeats includes only one Test match. Let's take a slightly longer look at England's recent form. In 1995, England played 13 Test matches, won three, lost three and drew seven. That is not the record of a side that is gutless, talent-less and rudderless. England has a captain of substance. The team was not as supportive in performance during the winter as they had been during the summer's series against the West Indies. I'm not sure why. England have performed much better at home than on foreign fields in recent times. There was no denying the mood for change as our results deteriorated towards the end of the tours. England already has a new coach, David Lloyd, and selectors, Graham Gooch and David Graveney. Illy is back as chairman of selectors. By the end of the summer, David Acfield's working party, which includes Mike Gatting, Bob Bennett, David Gower and Micky Stewart, will have reported to Lord's. Their brief is the running, organising and administration of the England team. We will have to wait and see if the counties agree to their proposals. Certainly the World Cup showed that England have been left behind off the field in planning and preparation. I'm not one for excuses, but it partly explains why we were left behind on it. I must confess I found the workload of a county and England cricketer over the past year totally exhausting, with few periods available for recovery and rest. There is no denying that my performances tailed off towards the end of the 12 months. That may have been my fault. The pressure and exposure and schedule were all new to me. Perhaps I will handle those demands better a second time around. Yet I was not the only one to suffer. Those with greater experience than me were also affected. That was no coincidence. A non-stop schedule of 11 Tests against the West Indies and South Africa, followed by 13 one-day internationals in South Africa, India and Pakistan in a period a little over nine months was destined to wipe out the hardiest of competitors. I am convinced that non-stop playing, practising and travelling seriously affected my form and performance by the end of the winter. Injury problems don't help. My knees are not great. That's a well-known fact. I am not being asked to be wrapped in cotton wool. I want no special favours or privileges from anyone. Yet I feel that if England want me to take wickets at the rate at which I've started my Test career for more than a couple more years, that work-load must be substantially reduced. I love playing cricket. I love playing for England. I love playing for Derbyshire. Don't forget to add a full county programme to my England commitments. But I doubt very much if I can go on at this rate. At the very top, it should be about quality, not quantity. I never want playing for England to become a chore. I want to puff out my chest and feel my heart beat every time I walk out for my country. I always want it to be special – because it is. We are not machines. We cannot perform to order. Cricket fans want us to play with pride as well as playing in a professional manner – perform with our heads and hearts. But we must be allowed to. The current set-up hinders that. True, I would not have changed a moment of the past year – even the bad days, at Edgbaston, Cape Town and Faisalabad. They only served to make the good ones, like Lord's, Old Trafford and the Wanderers, all the more memorable. I'm glad I kept this record of what turned out to be my first year as an England Test player. It permits me to relive some great moments and, more importantly, serves to remind me that, however confident I might be now of my place on the international scene, it wasn't so long ago that I doubted whether I might ever get the chance to make the grade. Being reminded of that fact alone should stop me ever getting too big for my boots!

Dominic Cork, Derby, April 1996

Index

Acfield, David 206
Adams, Bryan 112
Adams, Chris 10, 12, 16, 30, 64, 81, 92, 103, 106,
Adams, Jimmy 25, 26, 44, 48, 60, 73, 83
Adams, Paul 120, *121*, 123, 132, 134, 153, 157, 165, 166, 170
Adelaide 1
Afford, Andy 15
Agassi, Andre 44
Agnew, Jonathan 33, 140
Ahmedabad 173, 183, 184, 185
Air India 183
Aldred, Paul 33, 34, 36, 92
Alexandra 112
Alfred, Paul 30
Ali Asid 180
All Blacks 150
Alleyne, Mark 91
Allsop, Ron 83
Aqib Javed 20
Ambrose, Curtly 2, 42, 43, 46, 50, 57, 58, 60, 70, 79, 83, 87, 93, 94, 95, 96, 98, 143
Andrew, Rob 36
Antigua 96
Argentina 28
Arthurton, Keith 24, 44, 45, 48, 60, 68, 69, 73
Ashes 1, 5, 16, 20, 46, 174, 185
Ashton, Malcolm 160
Astle, Nathan 183, 184
Atherton, Michael 8,
  v. West Indies 26, 27, 28, 41, 42, 43, 44, 47, 48, 50, 52, 53, 56, 58, 60, 62, 67, 70, 73, 74, 75, 78, 83, 84, 85, 86, 87, 94, 96, 97, 98, 100

playing for Lancashire 107, 108,
touring South Africa 110, 114, 118, 120, 122, 126, 127, 130, 131, 133, 136, 138, 139, 141, 142, 143, 144, 145, 146, *147*, 148, 150, 154, 157, 158, 160, 161, 164, 165, 166, 168, 173, 175, 176, 177
World Cup 181, 184, 188, 189, 190, 192, 193, *197*, 200
Athey, Bill 12
Atkinson, Andy 164
Austin, Ian 107
Australia 1, 2, 4, 9, 36, 141, 145, 160, 162, 174, 179, 183, 185, 186, 189, 196, 200, 201, 202,
AXA Equity & Law 15, 18–19, 22, 32, 39, 56, 62, 65, 92–3, 105–6
Azharuddin, Mohammad 7

Bacher, Dr Ali 112, 131, 133
Bailey, Rob 10
Bairstow, Andrew 17
Bairstow, David 17
Balderstone, Chris 72, 73, 75
ball-tampering 65, 151
Bangladesh 7
Bangalore 196
Bannister, Jack 125
Barbados 10, 143
Barcelona Olympics 182
Barclay, John 146, 192
Barnett, Kim 4, 6, 7, 10, 11,12, 13, 15, 16, 19, 21, 30, 31, 34, 38, 39, 40, 52, 53, 56, 62, 66, 83, 90, 91, 92, 101, 103, 106, 107, 116, 117, 128, 203
Base, Simon 7
Beatles, The 112

Bell, Philip 'Doc', 111, 123, 129, 196
Benjamin, Kenny 28, 68, 71, 86, 87, 96
Benjaman, Winston 57
Bennett, Bob 206
Bennett, D. R. 161
Benson & Hedges Trophy 4, 10, 16, 18, 24, 28, 65
Bermuda 174
Betley CC, 2, 54, 82
Bevan, Michael 17
Bhutto, Benazir 203
Bicknell, Martin 86
Big Breakfast, The 51
Bird, Dickie 68, 71, 72
Birmingham 56, 164
Bishop, Ian 7, 11, 42, 45, 49, 57, 60, 68, 71, 72, 79
Blackpool 150
Blakey, Richard 17
Bloemfontein 132, 136
'Bodyline' 9, 65, 158, 160
Boland 144, 146–8
Bombay 4
Border 117–19
Botham, Ian 4, 24, 53, 73, 111, 127, 140, 141, 142, 143, 150, 160–1, 203, 204, Pl.11
Boycott, Geoff 16, 82, 96, 97, 109, 110, 140, 190
Bowler, Peter 6, 36, 37, 38, 39
Bradman, Donald 9, 28
Bragg, Billy 112
Brazil 36
Bremner, Rory 87
Briers, Nigel 20
Bristol 90–3
Britannic Championship 11–12, 13–14, 17–18, 19–21, 30, 33–4, 36–7, 53, 100–5
BBC 72, 135
British High Commission 112, 163, 183, 189
Bucknor, Steve 151
Buffalo Park 117–9, 177
Byas, David 83

Cafe Royal 108
Calcutta 5, 180–1, 183, 196, 202
Capel, David 10,
Cairns, Chris 13, 14
Cambridge 37
Cambridgeshire 47–51
Campbell, Sherwin 25, 48, 60, 73, 87, 90, 93, 96

Canterbury 105, 107
Cape Sun Hotel 174
Cape Town 144, 152, 161, 164–72, 176, 180, 207
Carling, Will 15, 52, 84, 128
Carr, John 30
Centurion Park 115, 124–32, 166, 174
Chanderpaul 97
Chandigarh, Shivnarine 5
Chappell, Ian 203
Chapple, Glen 8
Chesterfield 66
Childs, John 102
Christchurch 133
Colombo 179, 183, 186, 191
Colvile, Charles 93
Cork, Dominic
education 2, 4
family 2, 3, 4
injury 4, 39, 110, 180, 181, 182, 184, 186, 191, 194, 196, 198, 201, 202, 206
playing for Derbyshire 10–12, 13–23, 30–40, 35, 47–51, 49, 62–6, 80–2, 90–3, 100–4, 106–8
playing for England
v. West Indies 24–9, 42–7, 58–62, 67–79, 76, 77, 82–90, 89, 93–100, 99 Pls. 1, 2, 3, 4, 5, 6, 7, 8, 9, 10
touring South Africa 109–178, 121, 159, 167, Pls. 14, 15, 16, 17, 18, 19
World Cup 179–201, 195
Cork, Gerald (father) 2, 3, 45, 71, 154, 155
Cork, Gregory (son) 5, 34, 45, 50, 55, 56, 58, 65, 71, 79, 82, 110, 119, 152, 153–4, 155, 162, 173, Pl. 12
Cork, Jane (wife) 5, 34, 39, 45, 47, 51, 52, 54, 55, 56, 58, 65, 71, 75, 79, 82, 100, 110, 116, 152, 153–4, 155, 162, 165, 173, 174, Pl. 12
Cork, Jonathan (brother) 2, 3, 83
Cork, Mary (mother) 2, 3, 45, 54, 71, 154, 155
Cork, Simon (brother) 2, 3, 82, 158
Cornhill,
Second Test 42–7
Third Test 58–62
Fourth Test 67–79
Fifth Test 82–90
Sixth Test 93–100

Cottam, Andrew 13, 16
Cowdrey, Graham 54
Crawley, John 20,
  v. West Indies 67, 68, 69, 79, 86, 94,
    98, 104
  playing for Lancashire 107, 108
  touring South Africa 117, 118, 123,
    124, 125, 134, 135, 145, 148, 150,
    151, 153, 154, 155, 163
Crewe Alexandra 82
Cricketers' Association Dinner 108
Cronje, Hansie 21, 23, 126, 134, 140,
    149, 161, 164, 165, 167, 168,
    170, 175, 176, 177
Cullinan, Darryl 7, 8, 10,
  playing for Derbyshire 12, 13, 14, 15,
    17, 18, 31–2, 33, 37, 38, 65, 105,
  playing for South Africa 119, 125,
    137, 140, 142, 156, 167, 168
Curran, Kevin 10

Daily Telegraph 38, 133, 134, 190
Day, Bill 53, 54, 56
DeFreitas, Alexandra 102, 107
DeFreitas, Philip
  playing for Derbyshire 2, 6, 12, 16,
    17, 32, 35, 38, 41, 42, 51, 52, 65,
    81, 91, 101, 102, 107
  playing for England 153, 174,
    175
  playing for South Africa 144, 145
  World Cup 181, 189, 198, 200
Delhi 183, 185
Derbyshire 2, 4, 5, 7, 10–12, 13–23,
    47–51, 62–66, 80–2, 90–3,
    100–4, 106–8, 116, 119, 140,
    145, 156, 160, 172, 191, 196,
    203, 206
de Silva, Aravinda 196, 199, 202
Dessaur, Wayne, 33
Dev, Kapil 186
de Villiers, Fanie 109, 176
Dexter, Ted 109
Dhanraj, Rajindra 86
Dilley, Graham 45
Dippenaar, Hendrik 134
Donald, Allan 8, 9, 81, 105 106, 108,
    109, 126, 127, 133, 136, 138,
    139, 140, 141, 144, 150, 162, 164,
    165, 166, 167, 168, 175, 176,
    186
Dougie (liaison man) 126, 146
Durban 150, 151, 166, 176

Ealham, Mark 64
Eastern Transvaal 112–14
East India Club 204
East London 115, 116, 178
East Midlands Sports Personality of the
    Year 155
East Shirley 133
Eden Gardens 182
Edgbaston 2, 8–9, 58–62, 65, 104–6,
    143, 164, 207
Edrich, John 16, 118, 130
Edwards, Jonathan 56
Eksteen, Clive 132, 138, 139, 141
Emburey, John 30, 33, 51, 67, 83, 106,
    203, 204
England 1, 2, 5, 206
  Team selection 4, 39, 104, 110, 177
  Under-19s 2, 46, 69
  v. South Africa 125–32
  v. West Indies 24–29, 36, 42–46,
    58–62, 67–79, 82–90, 93–100
Essex 33, 100–4
Evans, Chris 58
Excelsior Hotel 109

Fairbrother, Neil 'Harvey' 26, 156,
    174, 177, 181, 182, 184, 186,
    194, 196
Faisalabad 198–200, 207
Fletcher, Keith 24
Fraser, Angus 26, 181
  playing or Middlesex 31, 33, 51
  v. West Indies 44, 45, 60, 67, 68, 78,
    84, 85, 87, 90, 97, 100
  touring South Africa 116, 122,
    127, 128, 132, 133, 135, 145, 149,
    154, 163, 164, 168, 170,
    181
Frontier Post 188

Gallian, Jason 57, 59, 61, 62, 94, 97,
    98, 104, 107, 151, 154, 155, 157,
    161, 163, 164
Gatting, Mike 30, 51, 120, 163, 206
Gibson, Ottis 48
Giddins, Ed 65
Gloucestershire 90–3
Gooch, Graham 20, 28, 100, 101, 102,
    104, 206
Gough, Darren 1,
  playing for Yorkshire 17, 18
  v. West Indies 25, 29, 42, 43, 45, 46,
    47, 54, 62, 67,
  touring South Africa 104, 111, 116,

Gough, Darren *cont.*
118, 119, *121*, 122, 124, 128, 130, 132, 133, 137, 140, 145, 148, 149, 153, 163, *165*, 175, 177, Pl. 13
World Cup 180, 181, 185, 186, *187*, 192, 200
Gough, Anna 54
Gower, David 43, 52, 127, 131, 206
Grace Road, Leicester 19–24
Graveney, David 20, 133, 203, 206
Greig, Tony 98
Gunn & Moore 109
Gurusinha 200, 202
Guyana 152

Hall, Jamie 64
Hall, Wes 2,196
Hampshire 12, 53, 108
Hancock, Tim 92
Harare 109
Harden, Richard 38
Harrison, Tom 13, 16
Hartley, Peter 18
Hayden, Matthew 66
Haynes, Desmond 10, 11
Haynes, Gavin 16
Hayter, Peter 123, 151
Hayter, Reg 108
Hayhurst, Andy 38
Headingley 33, 36, 43, 75, 141, 160
Hick, Graeme 16, 26,
    v. West Indies 43, 45, 48, 60, 67, 83, 84, *88*, 94, 95, 97, 100
    touring South Africa 116, 118, 119, 122, 126, 127, 128, 132, 135, 137, 142 150, 151, 157, 165, 166, 170, 172, 177
World Cup 184, 186, 192
Hill, Alan 2
Hindson, Jimmy 15, 16
Hobbs, W. G. 28
Holland 186, 188
Holmes, Jon 52, 53, 54, 58, 80, 84
Hooper, Carl 24, 26, 29, 42, 44, 47, 59, 67, 74, 75, 83, 94, 97
Horton, Mike 53, 55, 83
Hudson, Andrew 149, 156, 166, 170, 172, 175
Hughes, Simon
Hunt, Conrad 32
Hussain, Nasser 104, 180

Illingworth, Ray 8, 9, 17, 24, 41, 57, 60, 61, 79, 84, 87, 109–10, 112, 115, 118, 124, 125, 128, *129*, 130, 132, 133, 134, 135, 136, 144, 145, 146, 149, 153, 157, 158, 164, 166, 168, 170, 174, 175, 176, 184, 188, 200, 201, 203, 206
Illingworth, Richard 62, 83, 86, *89*, 114, 135, 164
Ilott, Mark 8, 9, 83, 111–12, 119, 122, 124, 126, 127, 130, 149, 156, 158, 163, 165, 181
Imran Khan 156
Ince, Paul 4
India 1, 2, 7, 8, 179, 183, 188, 189, 193, 196, 201, 202, 206
ICC 151, 152, 170, 189
Islandhlwana 149

Jack, Steve 124
Jayasuriya 197, 200
Jardine, Douglas 9
Javed Miandad 193
Jones, Dean 109
Johannesburg 110, 116, 177
Johnson, Paul 13
Johnson, Richard 30. 104

Kallis, Jack 149, 176
Karachi 185, 189–91, 200, 200
Karachi XI 192
Kent 62, 105, 107
Kenya 179, 189, 196
Kimberley 124, 136
Kingsmead, Durban 148–53, 175
Kirsten, Gary 137, 149, 158, 160, 161, 175, 186, 188
Knight, Nick 68, 69, 78, 83, 86, 87, 94, 104, 105, 106
Knott, Alan 109, 166
Krikken, Karl 14, 16, 17, 31, 32, 64, 119
Kuiper, Adrian 177
Kumble, Anil 108

Ladbrokes 59
Lahore 180
Lahore Cricket Assocaition 180, 181
Lamb, Allan 10, 190
Lancashire 4, 6, 11, 57, 106–8, 204
    Second XI 17
Lara, Brian 8, 24, 26, 27, 29, 47, 48, 59, 60, 67, 68, 73, 74, 75, 78, 82, 85, 87, *88*, 90, 93, 96, 97, 98, 100, 108, 118, 145
Larwood, Harold 9, 160

Law, Stuart 66
Leicestershire 6, 19–24, 36, 104, 106
Lever, John 52, 109
Lever, Peter 16, 78, 115, 117, 120, *121*, 128, 130, 176
Lewis, Chris 1–2
Lewis, Tony 83
Liebenberg, Karl 138, 141
Lineker, Gary 52, 84
Lloyd, Clive 140, 151, 152, 161
Lloyd, David 33, 34, 203, 204, 206
Loader, Peter 75
Long Walk to Freedom 130
Lord's 9, 27–33, 37, 39, 40, 42–7, 206, 207
Love, Jimmy 10, 66

Madonna 133
Mail on Sunday 53, 151
Malcolm, Devon 2, 6, 65, 181
  playing for Derbyshire 10, 11, 13, 14, 17, 18, 20, 32, *35*, 37, 38, 39, 80, 91, 92
  v. West Indies 94, 97
  touring South Africa 109, 112, 114, 115, 116, 117, 119, *121*, 123, 124, 125, 127, 128, *129*, 134, 135, 138, 140, 149, 154, 163, 164, 166, 176
  World Cup 181, 186
Mandela, Nelson 109, 112, *113*, 125, 130, 164
March, Cambs 47–51
Marshall, Malcolm 10, 17, 96
Martin, Peter 20, 25, 26, 28, 32, 43, 44, 48, 62, 67, 107, 125, 148, 149, 157, 158, 166, 168, 188
Martin-Jenkins, Christopher 134
Matthews, Craig 126, 128, 150, 151, 152, 157
May, Tim 164
McDermott, Craig 190
McGague, Martin 64
McMillan, Brian 130 126, 128, 137, 140, 141, 149, 158, 164, 168, 173, 177
Middlesex 30–3, 48, 57, 104, 105, 106, 108
Midlands Today 83
Mitchley, Cyril 71, 87, 127, 157, *159*, 160
Morris, John 37
Morton, Wayne 112, 123, 130, 136, 148, 155, 182, 197
Mossop, James 123

Moxon, Martyn 17, 18
Mulally, Alan 20, 106
Munton, Tim 81, 152
Murray, Junior 27, 43, 48, 71, 74, 75
Mushtaq, Ahmed 37, 38, 194

Nantwich Town 83
Natal 153
NatWest Trophy 47–51, 64–5, 80–2, 90, 103, 160
Newlands 161, 164–72
News of the World 165
New Zealand 2, 69, 144, 179, 183, 184, 188, 196, 201
Nicholas, Mark 125
Noon, Wayne 13
Northamptonshire 10, 11, 33–6, 104, 108, 204
North Staffordshire League 2
Nottingham Forest 155
Nottinghamshire 13–16

Oakman, Alan 2
O'Gorman, Tim 16, 22
Old Trafford 4, 65, 67–79, 90, 95, 207
Oppenheimer, Nicky 111, 114
Oppenheimer's XI 112
Orange Free State 132–4
Orchard, David 151, 170, 172
Ostler, Dominic 81
Oval 9, 25–27, 93–100, 109
Owen, Johnny 13, 66
Owen, Nick 52

Paarl, 142–6
Palmer, Ken 30
Palmer, Roy 20, 30
Pakistan 1, 2, 4, 104, 160, 176, 179, 182, 183, 185, 188, 189, 190, 193–4, 196, 201, 206
Pakistan International Airlines 180
Parkinson Show, The 135
Parsons, Keith 38
Patel, Min 9
Penney, Trevor 105
Pepsi-cola 109, 196
Peshawar 185–8, 190
Pienaar, François 164
Pierson, Adrian 22, 106
Pietermaritzburg 153, 202
Piper, Keith 9
Plews, Nigel 38
Pointing, Ricky 66
Pollock, Graeme 156

Pollock, Peter 125
Pollock, Shaun 125, 126, 139, 144,
    150, 158, 160, 162, 165, *171*, 172,
    173, 174, 177
Pooley, Jason 31
Port Elizabeth 116, 152, 154, 156–62,
    166, 170
Pretoria 115, 130
Princess of Wales 84
Pringle, Merryck 132
Professional Cricketers' Association
    203

Queen's Park, Chesterfield 17–19
Question of Sport, A 150, 204

Radio Derby 80
Radio Five 39
Ramadhin, Sonny 2
Ramiz Raja 160
Ramprakash, Mark 1, 4, 8, 104, 105,
    106
    playing for Middlesex 31, 33
    v. West Indies 24, 46
    touring South Africa 117, 118, 134,
        136, 138, 139, 141, 144, 149, 173,
        174, 175, 177
    World Cup 180, 196
Ranatunga, Arjuna 202, Pl. 21
Randell, Steve, 170, 172
Randjesfontein 112
Rawalpindi 188–9
Red Stripe Trophy 10
Reid, John 72, 96
Reeve, Dermot 80, 81, 104, 105, 106,
    108, 156, *167*, 173, 177, 185, 192,
    193, 194, 200
Rhodes, Jonty 139, 149, 156, 158, 188
Rhodes, Steven 20. 39, 42
Richards, 28, 98, 186, 186
Richardson, Dave 139, 140
Richardson, Richie 24, 25, 26, 28, 44,
    48, 60, 71, 73, 74, 75, 83, 85, 94,
    96, 97, 137, 157, 158, 196, 201,
    202
Rice, Tm 133
Roberts, Andy 46, 72, 196
Roebuck, Peter 22
Rollins, Adrian 13, 14, 17, 31, 33, 65,
    90, 91, 102, 106
Romaines, Paul 92
Rorke's Drift 149
Rory (bodyguard) 130, 136
Roslin, Gaby 44, 52

Rouse, Steve 57, 60
Russell, Ailee 146
Russell, Jack 4,
    v. West Indies 68, 83, 85, 87, 90, 91,
        92, 93, 94, *95*
    touring South Africa 110, 111, 124,
        127, 128, 130, 134, 137, 139, 141,
        143, 145, 146, *147*, 148, 152, 155,
        157, 163, 165, 175, 177
    World Cup 181, 182, 192, 194
Russell, Phil 148
Russell, Robert Charles 79

Sainsbury's 54
St Georges Park 156–61, 166, 177
St Joseph's College 4
Schultz, Brett 109, 116, 125, 126, 132
Shepherd, David 48
Shropshire 160
Sky TV 53, 72, 93, 103, 127, 151,
    152
Sledging 4
Smith, Denis 90
Smith, Neil 80, 156, 185
Smith, Robin
    v. West Indies 42, 45, 46, 51, 53, 59,
        61, 62, *63*, 70, 75, 79, 83, 86, 95
    touring South Africa 118, 122, 124,
        128, 135, 139, 144, 145, 148, 150,
        152, 157, 163, 165, 170, 172, 175,
        176
    World Cup 179, 180, 184, 186, 192,
        193, 200
Sobers, Gary 2
Somerset 6, 36–40, 108, 160
South Africa 1, 4, 54, 104, 206
    1st Test 125–32
    2nd Test 137–42
    3rd Test 149–52
    4th Test 156–62
    5th Test 164–72
    World Cup 182, 186, 188–9, 190,
        200, 201
South African Invitation XI 114
SA Universities 153–4
Soweto 114, 115, 132
Spearman, Craig 190
Springbok Park, Bloemfontein 132–4,
    173
Sri Lanka 1, 179, 183, 185, 186, 188,
    189, 196, 198, 200, 201, 202
Srinath, Javagai 91, 92
Stransky, Joel 150
Staffordshire 2

Under-19s 66
Steele, David 122
Stemp, Richard 9
Stewart, Alec 8, 24, 39,
　v. West Indies 43, 47, 48, 51, 61, 62
　touring South Africa 114, 118, 119,
　　122, 131, 133, 136, 141, 148, 150,
　　152 154, 157, 161, 162, 165, 170.
　　173, 174, 175, 176
　World Cup 181, 184, 188, 190, 192,
　　193, 196
Stewart, Cammie 175
Stewart, Micky 206
Stoke City FC 5
Stoke-on-Trent 4, 6, 71, 79, 130
Stone, Steve 155
stump-tampering 71
Such, Peter 102
Sunday League 15, 22, 33, 39, 62, 92,
　103
Sun 96, 110
Sunday Times 22
Surrey 108
Sussex 11–2, 57, 64
Swanton, E. W. 135
Swarbrook, Fred 122
Symonds, Andrew 91, 93

Tamil Tigers 179
Tasmania 4
Taylor, Bob 50, 83–4, 138–9, 141
Taylor, Paul 34, 36
Taylor, Mark 199
Test Match Special 135, 140
Tendulkar, Sachin 118
Tetley Bitter Challenge 8
Tetley's 137
Texaco 1,
　1992 4
　1993 4
　1994 4, 7
　1995 1st 13, 14, 20, 22, 24–29, 44
Thorpe, Graham 26,
　v. West Indies 42, 43, 45, 46, 48, 58,
　　60, 68, 69, 71, 94, 98
　touring South Africa 111, 117, 118,
　　122, 133, 138, 139, 140, 142, 150,
　　157 165, 168, 169, 170, 172, 173,
　　175, 177
　World Cup 181, 184, 186, 192, 193
Thorpe, Nicky 117
Transvaal 156
Trent Bridge, Nottingham 7, 13–16,
　24–5, 82–90, 95

Trinidad 60, 78
Trueman, Fred 137
Tufnell, Philip 30, 94, 106
Turner, Rob 38, 39
TV-am 51, 52
Tweats, Tim 66, 103
Twickenham 128
Twose, Roger 8, 81
Tyson, Frank 2

Ubogu, Victor 28
United Arab Emirates 182, 185, 186,
　188, 189
Uxbridge 105, 106

Valentine, Alf 2
Vaughan, Mike 17
Victoria 1

Walsh, Courtney 20, 42, 43, 45, 57, 59,
　62, 70, 78, 96, 196
Wanderers, The 115, 132, 135,
　137–42, 145, 154, 156, 161, 164,
　166, 172, 174, 207
Warwickshire 2, 8–9, 16, 57, 80–2,
　104–6, 107, 108, 152, 203
Warne, Shane 120, 164, 179, 202
Warner, Allan 'Jack' 18, 30, 37, 91, 92,
　108
Warren, Russell 34
Watkinson, Mike
　playing for Lancashire 107
　v. West Indies 57, 67, 68, 73, 79, 85
　　87, 89, 96, 97
　touring South Africa 124, 125, 136,
　　164, 165, 170, 177
Watkinson, Sue 174
Waugh, Mark 100, 101, 190
Webb, Jonathan 40
Weekes, Paul 48
Wells, Alan 8, 9, 11, 20, 28, 83, 93, 94
Wells, Colin 21, 30, 34, 37, 40, 104,
　107
Western Province 168, 172, 173
West Indies 10–11, 24–9, 42–7,
　67–79, 82–90, 93–100, 157,
　162, 179, 183, 185, 189, 196, 201,
　202, 206
West Indies Board 11, 196, 201
Whitaker, James 21
White, Craig 1, 17, 20, 67, 93, 163,
　173, 174, 177, 181, 185
Whittingdale Young Cricketer of the
　Month 109